Round in Circles

The Story of Rodgers & Hammerstein's Carousel

Barry Kester

ISBN: 978-1-914933-28-8

Published By: -

i2i
PUBLISHING

i2i Publishing. Manchester.
www.i2i.publishing.co.uk

This book is dedicated
to my grandchildren, Matilda, Jake, Milo, Amelie,
Kaydon, Rafi and Kyra.

If I loved you,
Time and again I would try to say
All I'd want you to know.
If I loved you,
Words wouldn't come in an easy way –
Round in circles I'd go!

Contents

Preface and Acknowledgements

Time Magazine described Rodgers and Hammerstein's 1945 show *Carousel* as the greatest musical of the twentieth century. Composer Richard Rodgers made the same choice when asked to name the favourite of all his shows. Yet it was not their most popular work, and it had the shortest Broadway run of their five standout hits; the film version was the least successful big-screen adaptation, and by 1979 when Rodgers died, new productions were comparatively few and far between.

Then in 1992, in the unlikely setting of London's Royal National Theatre, Nicholas Hytner produced a stunning revival and audiences on both sides of the Atlantic discovered the show anew. The effect was instantaneous. Over the past thirty years, numerous new productions of *Carousel* have been seen on theatre and opera stages around the world, and audiences have come to realise that *Time Magazine* might just have been right.

Despite this upsurge in the show's popularity, which coincided with the publication of a profusion of books on musical theatre in general and of individual show biographies in particular, there was, at that time, no history of *Carousel,* which had long been my own favourite musical.

So it was that when I retired in 2010, I decided to try and rectify that omission. Of necessity, it has been rather a stop-start project as life has a habit of getting in the way of the best of intentions.

One of the joys of my research was getting to discover some of the behind-the-scenes people who worked so hard alongside Rodgers and Hammerstein to put *Carousel* on the stage. Producers Laurence Langner and his partner Theresa Helburn, the pint-sized driving force behind the entire production: The highly talented but temperamental director, Rouben Mamoulian: The ambitious and equally temperamental choreographer, Agnes de Mille. Her dance arranger, the almost unknown, yet supremely talented Trude Rittman whose life story is surely worth a book in its own right; and orchestrator Don Walker, a quiet man who was brought in at the last minute, and yet gave us what is undoubtedly one of the best arranged scores in Broadway history.

These are some of the extraordinary people I became acquainted with over the years: I was fortunate enough to meet Richard Rodgers in person at a preview of *The Boys From Syracuse,* at the Theatre Royal, Drury Lane. I was nineteen at the time and whilst the meeting was all too brief, it remains one of my most treasured memories. The programme he autographed for me still sits in pride of place on my piano. How I wish I could have met Oscar Hammerstein too, and all these other extraordinary people I encountered only in print. A disparate group who came together at the height of their creative powers, and when the going got tough, as it did on opening night in New Haven, worked as one, egos cast aside, to ensure that the show would not fail.

My aim with this book is to tell not only the story of one of the classics of Broadway's 'Golden Age' but also to pay tribute to those who contributed to its creation, acknowledging that all theatrical productions, especially that of a major musical, are truly collaborative efforts. It is intended, therefore, not only for those who share my love of *Carousel,* but also for students of musical theatre who want to learn about the trials and tribulations encountered in producing a musical at that time when Rodgers and Hammerstein were transforming such shows into the unique American art form that we still enjoy today.

***

Writing might be thought of as a solitary occupation and to a large extent it is.

Nonetheless, during the dozen or so years that it has taken me to complete this book, I needed and received considerable help from several people, all of which was willingly given, and I wish to record my gratitude to them here.

Ted Chapin, who last year stood down as president and chief creative officer at the Rodgers and Hammerstein Organisation after forty years with the company, has been totally supportive from the moment I first approached him. He did not know me from Adam, but his immediate response was "always happy to hear from people dedicated to the cause," and so it proved to be. When I visited New York in the cause of my research, immediately, he agreed to meet with me and proceeded to provide me with a great deal of information; he showed me the R&H

archives and introduced me to Bruce Pomahac, the former director of music at the Rodgers and Hammerstein Organisation who was also only too happy to offer advice on the history of the score and to help me, a non-musicologist to better understand Richard Rodgers' composing techniques. They both read early drafts of the book, corrected errors and shared their unrivalled knowledge of Richard Rodgers, Oscar Hammerstein and some of the other incredible people who made *Carousel* possible. I hope I did not take too great an advantage of their generosity in responding to my endless questioning.

My thanks also to Bill Gaden and his team at Concord Theatricals, who eased my way through the maze of rights and permissions, without which this book would not have been possible.

Mark Eden Horowitz of the Music Division at the Library of Congress was most helpful as were his colleagues, Walter Zvonchenko and the rest of the team. Similarly, the staff at the Beineke Library at Yale University and at the Performance Arts Division of the New York Public Library all helped to make my limited time in the US more valuable than it might otherwise have been.

Professor Dr. Dominic McHugh who is perhaps the UK's leading authority on the 'Golden Age' American musicals, met with me early on and offered useful advice.

Amy Asch, the editor of *The Complete Lyrics of Oscar Hammerstein* was another generous authority who did not hesitate to answer my questions coming at her from out of the blue.

Stephen Done, the curator of the museum at Liverpool Football Club was also very happy to assist me regarding that club's association with *You'll Never Walk Alone,* notwithstanding my lifelong devotion to Premier League rivals, Tottenham Hotspur.

Karl French of the Literary Consultancy read an early draft and offered invaluable suggestions which undoubtedly have helped improve the final product.

Tim Sheader, the artistic director of the Regents Park Open Air Theatre agreed to an interview and gave me a valuable insight into how a new generation of directors stage so called problematic shows in these progressive times.

Alexandra Silber, who I saw give a wonderfully sensitive performance as Julie at the Savoy Theatre in 2008, met with me via Zoom to give me her perspective on the difficulties of playing that role, and of the challenges facing the entire company in preparing for a show now considered problematic.

I am grateful to the trustees of the estates of Richard Rodgers and Oscar Hammerstein II for their permission to reproduce material in this book and to Ann Liebgold, daughter of Don Walker and to Dr. Jonathan Prude, the son of Agnes de Mille who similarly allowed me to quote from their parents' memoirs; also, to Professor Joseph P. Swain who readily gave me permission to quote from his seminal book, *The Broadway Musical.*

Round in Circles began life as a labour of love. That you, dear reader, are now holding it in your hands is due to the imagination and dedication of my publisher Lionel Ross. Thank you, Lionel, not only for your faith and your vision, but also for your patience over the many months it took to acquire all the rights and permissions I needed before we could go to print. Many thanks also to my editor Mark Cripps for his unflagging zeal and determination in ensuring that my book has been completed in as good a condition as it possibly could be. He achieved this with tact and humour and if any imperfections remain, they are mine and mine alone.

***

This book would not have happened without the love and support of my late wife Greta. For forty-two wonderful years, she tolerated my obsession for all things Rodgers and Hammerstein. Any production of one of their shows, she knew, had to be seen, whether it was a major revival in one of London's grandest theatres, or a fringe production in a tiny space above a pub in one of the less salubrious parts of town, with a battered old upright piano serving as the orchestra. She looked on with a wry smile as an ever-growing library of books about Broadway and musical theatre gradually took over my study.

When I started this project, Greta gave me every encouragement, and continued to do so right up to the end. She will always be in my heart as she is in the hearts of my children, Gaby, Richie and Ross. I thank them too, from the bottom of my own heart for their continued love and support. I am sure I don't say it often enough, but I am enormously proud of them and all that they have achieved and continue to achieve, and I can say with one hundred percent certainty, Greta would be too. Their lives have been filled with the sound of Rodgers and Hammerstein's music from birth. Whilst some might have been put off by such indoctrination, instead, they have all developed their own love of musical theatre and that in turn, I am delighted to see, is being passed on to my seven grandchildren, the *Hamilton* generation.

Finally, special thanks and love are reserved for my partner Carol, who like me, was widowed far too soon. How fortunate we are that mutual friends kept nudging us together until we finally took the hint. Because of them, neither of us must walk alone and that is a gift beyond price. Carol has shown tremendous belief in me and in this book during our time together. Now in our golden years when we could, indeed should have been, exploring with our friends and families all the cultural and natural delights that surround us, she has been content to stay at home and let me get on with my research and writing. Such devotion is above and beyond the call, and I promise that I will make it up to her.

Julie Jordan (Jan Clayton) and Billy Bigelow (John Raitt)
ride the original 1945 Broadway carousel.
Courtesy of The Rodgers & Hammerstein Organization:
A Concord Company, www.rnh.com

Introduction

It is February 2020, and I am sitting in the spacious boardroom of the Open-Air Theatre in London's Regents Park. The centrepiece of the theatre's forthcoming summer season, the anticipated big money spinner, is to be the Rodgers and Hammerstein classic musical, *Carousel* celebrating its seventy-fifth anniversary this year.

I am here to meet Timothy Sheader, the young artistic director of the company, to talk about his plans for the production which he himself is to direct. I am keen to know how he intends to tackle a show which whilst it is much loved by many, is also now considered by some to be 'problematic'. *Carousel* is not alone in being so described in this #Me Too age. *My Fair Lady, The King and I* and *Kiss Me Kate* are three more 'Golden Age' musicals whose appropriateness have been similarly questioned.

Carousel is based on a 1909 play *Liliom* by Hungarian playwright, Ferenc Molnár. Although the location of the play has been transferred from its original setting in Budapest to a coastal town in Maine, the story remains very much the same, telling of the ill-fated love of a strong, young woman for a troubled and sometimes violent carousel barker. In the musical, as in the play, the barker, Billy Bigelow hits his wife, Julie. You do not see him do so on stage, but it is referred to in the dialogue and the audience knows he has done so. Worse still, from the current perspective, is that with the song *What's the Use of Wond'rin',* Julie seems to shrug off Billy's violence as she does with her line to her daughter Louise, "It is possible, dear - fer someone to hit you - hit you hard - and not hurt at all." Billy is given the opportunity to atone for his actions and earn a place in Heaven by helping Julie and his daughter Louise move forward with their lives, but does that penance make sufficient amends for his abuse to satisfy a twenty-first century audience, even if it did so in 1945?

Ironically, in the 1940s, it was the eponymous anti-hero of a Rodgers and Hart show, *Pal Joey* who created more controversy than Billy Bigelow. So much so, that when Richard Rodgers and Oscar Hammerstein were first asked to consider writing a musical version of *Liliom,* Rodgers worried that the title character might be considered too similar to Joey Evans.

He may well have been remembering how *New York Times* critic Brooks Atkinson concluded his 1940 review of that show, 'Although it is expertly done, can you draw sweet water from a foul well?'

Yet, just five years later, Atkinson referred to *Carousel* as a "Masterpiece", and when the show was revived in 1954, he wrote, '*Carousel* has no comment to make on anything of topical importance. The theme is timeless and universal: the devotion of two people who love each other through thick and thin, complicated in this case by the wayward personality of the man who cannot fulfil the responsibilities he has assumed ... Billy is a bum, but *Carousel* recognizes the decency of his motives and admires his independence'.

It seems incredible today that Atkinson could query the morality of *Pal Joey,* and yet so soon thereafter, be apparently oblivious to the domestic abuse taking place in *Carousel.* The answer to that conundrum can be found in the care Rodgers and Hammerstein took to ensure that Billy Bigelow came across as a more sympathetic character than both Molnár's Liliom and Rodgers and John O'Hara's Joey Evans. They did not whitewash his actions, nor did they downplay the consequences of his actions, but with subtle tweaks of dialogue and with songs such as *If I Loved You* and *Soliloquy,* they enabled us to see him through Julie's eyes, and if she could love and forgive him, so could we; and in 1945, audiences did. What Rodgers and Hammerstein could not have foreseen is that by working so hard to make Billy more forgivable in 1945, they were creating problems for the future of their favourite show, even though those problems would not materialize until years after their deaths.

It is not just in the world of musical theatre that producers and directors are having to consider potentially problematic material. Public perceptions have undergone so material a change that today the entire arts world is under scrutiny. There is much in Shakespeare, *Taming of the Shrew, The Merchant of Venice* and *Othello* spring immediately to mind, that trouble modern sensibilities, as there is in a number of the world's favourite operas; think *Tosca, Rigoletto, Madama Butterfly* and *La Traviata,* where women are often treated appallingly and die horrible deaths. Books by Charles Dickens, T.S. Elliot and Roald Dahl; art by Gaugin, Degas and Renoir; music by Tchaikovsky, Chopin and

Wagner; classic films by Woody Allen. All of these icons of Western civilisation are now considered questionable because of either their subject matter or the prejudicial behaviour of their creators. Should these great works be consigned to history? Or should they continue to be available to a twenty-first century audience, better educated and more culturally aware than any that has gone before, but presented in a way that excites an audience's imagination, prompting it to ask the questions and form its own conclusions as to how society should conduct itself now and in the future?

These are the issues that young directors like Timothy Sheader must consider when they are invited to take on the challenge of presenting a work such as *Carousel* and he had no doubts about taking on that challenge.

He and I reminisce for a while about the magnificent 1992 National Theatre production on which he spent time shadowing director, Nicholas Hytner during a technical rehearsal, and how he has loved the show ever since. Even though that production was greeted by rave reviews and won a host of awards on both sides of the Atlantic, the term problematic was being used about it for the first time, and Hytner later expressed major regret at not cutting Julie's "Not hurt at all" line. If those words jarred in 1992, they do so even more today, and it is no surprise to hear that the decision has already been taken to cut that line from the script. He reminds me that lines are cut from Shakespeare every day.

What comes across very clearly though, is that Sheader is truly excited about staging this show for the first time, and that while he has not formulated all his plans, he has been giving it a great deal of thought. Nor is he unaware of the size of the task before him.

Cutting those offending lines is just one step he will be taking to put his own stamp on the production, and it will be a 2020 stamp, not one harking back to 1945; it is clear also that it will be driven by the text. One of the reasons that *Carousel* resonates so strongly with Sheader is his own background. He is from a Scarborough fishing family, resolutely working class and one that was faced with many of the life choices faced by the characters in the show.

As a director, he has no interest in romanticising that background, or the historical social context in which the characters are living. Sheader emphasises that he is interested in the characters' present circumstances and the life cycles that they may have been through with their families. That is the carousel - not the one in the fairground - that keeps going round and round in circles.

Sheader was amazed at the courage of Rodgers and Hammerstein in tackling Molnár in 1945 and portraying "real life more than a decade before John Osborne put an ironing board on stage in *Look Back in Anger.*" He made this point more than once emphasising how wise Hammerstein was to leave so much of Molnár's original text unchanged. He was also greatly impressed with Hammerstein's original 'HE and SHE' scene, the version of Heaven that was in the show when it opened on its New Haven try-out run, but which was replaced in Boston with the 'Clothesline' scene. He has permission to use the original dialogue in this production and my impression is that he just might do so.

Nor does he have an issue with the song *What's the Use of Wond'rin'* because he knows it addresses a problem that is still relevant today; the forgiving attitude shown by many women to an abusive partner. Sheader does wonder though about the confluence of the music and the words, suggesting that at times, Rodgers' music is almost "too beautiful" and at odds with the subject matter. Dealing with that is a challenge he is relishing.

Aware that in 1945, *Carousel* was radical and ground-breaking both in form and content, Sheader is working on how to deliver it so that there can be a real conversation between today's audience and the now seventy-five-year-old material, not just sentiment for lovingly remembered past productions.

As with Hytner's production, the new *Carousel* will feature actor-singers rather than singing actors. He wishes he could have both, but "... there is so much text, so much text. Layered, complicated to deliver, and I feel so much responsibility to deliver this subject matter with the correct amount of sensitivity and interrogation, and you need actors for that."

Again, there is that emphasis on the strength and quality of the text, and this, even though in *Carousel,* there is half again as much music as there is in most other shows of its time.

In conclusion, Timothy Sheader wants his production to be totally new; he wants the conversation to be live and for the audience to "absolutely connect" with this material. His production will come from a deep respect for the material. He will not make excuses for it. His wish is to allow it to live as fully as it can today and, although he did not say so, it is obvious he means well into the future too.

***

When Rodgers and Hammerstein began writing *Carousel* in 1944, the world was engulfed in the flames of the Second World War. That fact undoubtedly influenced their work, helping them create not only a beautiful, albeit tragic love story, but one of hope and redemption too.

Just a month after my meeting with Timothy Sheader, the world was hit by the greatest catastrophe it has had to face since that war - the global Covid pandemic. During the war, places of entertainment were able to remain open and indeed, proved vital in maintaining morale. Now, as the pandemic spread and country after country went into lockdown, one of the first casualties was the entertainment industry, with theatres forced to close their doors for an indeterminate period. It would be some eighteen months before, little by little, they began to reopen for audiences hungry for live entertainment.

As an open-air theatre, Regents Park was one of the first to be able to re-open, so Sheader's interpretation of *Carousel* finally arrived on the stage in the summer of 2021. It proved to be quite in keeping with the thoughts he shared during our meeting. Whilst always respectful of its source, as he promised it would be, his *Carousel* was very different. For a start, it had been transplanted to a northern fishing town in England, similar to Scarborough where he grew up. Furthermore, he moved the story forward in time to the 1960s. These changes, of course, created certain anomalies - the English do not have clambakes, nor do they hope their children will become President of the United States, but these are minor quibbles, compensated for by the fact that the characters, as Sheader portrayed them, are possibly closer to those in Molnár's *Liliom,* than the New Englanders we are used to seeing.

The change of setting and time to something far removed from what Rodgers and Hammerstein envisaged, required a new orchestration to create a completely different sound, not just a reduction, as is almost mandatory today when thirty-nine--piece orchestras are unheard of. This was achieved by filling the pit with brass and guitars, thereby reproducing both the sound of a traditional northern brass band - that sometimes appeared on stage - and that of the sixties. It is a device which worked remarkably well, thanks to the skill of the orchestrator, Tom Deering. Whilst Rodgers' music cannot help but remain beautiful, it could no longer be thought of as at odds with the story, one of the issues Sheader had raised at our meeting.

At that meeting, we spent some time talking about the cut 'Mr. & Mrs. God' scene, and I had a sense that somehow or other, he was going to find a way to use it; which indeed he did; for among many alterations to the show's second act, he found a way of replacing Hammerstein's re-written dialogue with that from the deleted scene.

All these changes, combined with a dramatically revised Second Act ballet, put Billy's abuse of Julie and its terrible consequences at the heart of the show, and did so at a time when some eighteen months into the pandemic, reports of domestic violence had risen sharply. Seventy-five years ago, Rodgers and Hammerstein sought to soften Billy from the character that Molnár created and offered hope of redemption for his soul, as well as a brighter future for Louise. They made these changes not to try and justify Billy's actions, nor to excuse them, but because of sincerely held beliefs that some good can be found even in the worst of us, and in the power of hope. Timothy Sheader, for equally sincerely held beliefs, reversed those changes, and in his production at least, there can be no redemption for Billy, nor is Louise's future at all certain.

Sheader's radical re-interpretation of *Carousel* was one for our times. He correctly concluded that no play, irrespective of how beloved it may be, can be preserved in aspic and expect to survive from generation to generation. The Rodgers and Hammerstein Estates deserve praise too for recognising this truism and allowing such radical alterations to the original material. It may not have pleased the purists who had hoped to see yet another traditional production, but it certainly pleased the critics who understood the reasons for and welcomed the changes.

The summer of 2021 was a good one for British Rodgers and Hammerstein fans, for in addition to *Carousel,* there has been a new production of *South Pacific* at Chichester. *South Pacific,* like

Carousel, is of its time and viewed through a modern lens, might upset some sensibilities, but Daniel Evans' thoughtful re-interpretation, although not so radical as Sheader's *Carousel,* also delivered a sparkling, sensitive production that earned critical acclaim.

It gives one hope that as long as there are directors like Sheader and Evans, visionaries who have the skill and the imagination to critically examine and question what is now ageing material, there is every reason to believe that *Carousel* and all the 'Golden Age' musicals will continue to be revived and enjoyed for many generations to come.

Prologue

It all began on a Thursday afternoon in November 1943 in Sardi's on West 44th Street, a favourite restaurant for those who earned their living in the Broadway theatres that surround it. Three middle-aged men and a diminutive, silver-haired woman, all of them earning a very good living indeed from their show running at the St. James Theatre next door, were meeting for their regular weekly lunch.

Sardi's was at the height of its fame, renowned for its homely Italian cooking and for its walls decorated with caricatures of Broadway's great and good, as they still are today. It was the go-to place for either a pre - or post - theatre meal, and it was a popular venue too, for opening night parties where stars, writers and producers waited nervously for the first editions of the morning papers, and the reviews that most likely would decide the fate of their show.

A few months earlier, these same four people had hosted their own opening night party at the restaurant. That show was a new musical called *Oklahoma!* The expectation amongst the Broadway know-it-alls was that it would fail disastrously, but to almost everyone's surprise, when the reviews arrived, they were unanimous raves and the queues at the box office began to grow and grow. Even now, six months later, tickets could not be had for love nor money.

Two of the four people responsible for this theatrical sensation were well-known far beyond the confines of the Broadway bubble. One was composer Richard Rodgers; the other was his *Oklahoma!* lyricist partner, Oscar Hammerstein II. Their companions were the producers, Lawrence Langner and Theresa Helburn who together, ran the Theatre Guild, one of New York's most prestigious production companies.

Prestigious it may have been, but prestige alone does not pay the bills, and by 1942, a series of box office failures had left the Guild teetering on the brink of bankruptcy. Desperate for a substantial hit, they decided that a moderately successful play they had produced in 1931 called *Green Grow the Lilacs* might form the basis of a good musical, the only kind of show that could generate sufficient revenue to save them. Rodgers and Hammerstein were brought together to write it and the result was *Oklahoma!* They had taken a colossal gamble, but it was one that had come off and was now paying handsome dividends.[1]

Since that exciting opening night, the four of them arranged to meet at Sardi's for lunch every Thursday. They referred to these lunchtime gatherings as meetings of the Gloat Club, as well they might. Their new creation was breaking every record in Broadway history.

The Gloat Club lunches were not just about the gloating, however. They had a serious purpose too. It was obvious that *Oklahoma!* was going to be around for a long time, so as well as poring over the financial returns, they had to discuss how to keep the production fresh, always an issue with a long running show; casting was another one, both for the continuing Broadway run and also for the first touring production that had just opened in New Haven. One day too, when the war was over, there would be overseas productions to supervise; also, no doubt, Hollywood would soon be calling. All these issues required their regular attention.

On this November Thursday, Langner and Helburn had an additional item on their agenda and that was to discuss Rodgers and Hammerstein's future. Having dealt with *Oklahoma!* they moved on to this next item. Tentatively, Langner asked the pair if they would consider doing another show for the Guild. Rodgers set his mind at rest on that issue by confirming they would work for anyone who brought them a good idea

Encouraged by that response, Helburn looked from left to right to make sure that no one was listening, put her finger to her lip and whispered, "How would you like to do a musical play based on Ferenc Molnár's *Liliom*?"

Richard Rodgers and Oscar Hammerstein both also looked from left to right, put their fingers to their lips, and then whispered back in unison, "No."

How that "no" eventually became a "yes", and then became *Carousel* is what I shall be exploring in the following pages.

---

[1] During its first fifty years, *Oklahoma!* earned $2.5million for each $1,000 invested in the original production.

Chapter 1

An End and a Beginning

In the spring of 1942, when Lawrence Langner and Theresa Helburn realised that producing a successful musical was probably the only way to stave off bankruptcy, they turned to the one song-writing team in town that could all but guarantee them a hit; that team was Rodgers and Hart.

Having returned to New York in 1935 after a frustrating spell in Hollywood, the pair had proceeded to dazzle Broadway with a succession of smash hit shows: *Jumbo, I'd Rather be Right, I Married an Angel, Babes in Arms, On Your Toes, The Boys from Syracuse, Pal Joey* and their latest hit, *By Jupiter*. Not only were these shows the outstanding hits of their time, but they contained a significant number of the songs that make up 'The Great American Songbook.' Among the numerous standards they wrote during this extraordinarily rich creative period were *My Romance, Bewitched Bothered and Bewildered, Falling in Love With Love, There's a Small Hotel, Where or When, The Lady is A Tramp, My Funny Valentine, Spring is Here, I Could Write a Book* and *Wait Till You See Her.*

Both Lawrence Langner and Theresa Helburn were long term admirers of Richard Rodgers' music and constantly urged him to write something "for posterity." Rodgers told them he would like to but reminded them that he had a family to support. Now, Helburn called the composer and told him of her plan to turn Lynn Riggs' play *Green Grow the Lilacs* into a musical and that she would love Rodgers and Hart to write the score. Rodgers knew the play and was immediately enthusiastic. Here was a chance to compose a score, if not for posterity, then at least for the kind of musical he had been wanting to write for a long time. He told Helburn he would speak to Larry Hart and get back to her.

Even as he was talking to Helburn though, Rodgers knew that his partner was in no condition to work on anything. Larry Hart was by now a non-functioning alcoholic and an unreliable partner. During the writing of what would be their last original show, *By Jupiter,* he was so badly drunk, he had to be admitted to Doctors Hospital; under pressure to get the score completed in time for opening night, Rodgers checked himself into a room adjoining Hart's and borrowed a piano[2] so that they might work while Hart sobered up. Not even this extreme measure was enough and according to orchestrator Don Walker, many of the lyrics for the show were in fact, written by Rodgers during the Boston try-outs.

Rodgers did all he could to try and persuade Hart to work with him on *Green Grow the Lilacs,* but Hart turned him down flat. In the first place, he did not share his partner's views about the play's potential as a musical and second, he pleaded tiredness after their last show and was planning a long vacation in Mexico.

Rodgers even suggested that Hart book himself into a sanatorium, that being the only way he might ever dry out. Rodgers would check himself in at the same time and together, they would complete the score. This suggestion too, fell on deaf ears.

In a final desperate attempt, Rodgers invited Hart to a meeting at the offices of their friend and publisher, Max Dreyfus of Chappells. Hart arrived looking pale and haggard. It was obvious to Rodgers that Hart had not slept properly in weeks. Rodgers laid it on the line; he really wanted to do the show and if Hart would not agree, then he would approach someone else. When Hart asked him if he had anyone in mind, Rodgers told him, yes, he did: Oscar Hammerstein. Even the realisation that Rodgers was not bluffing had no effect on Hart, "You couldn't pick a better man," was his response. "You know Dick, I've never understood why you've put up with me all these years ... The best thing you could do is forget about me."[3]

When Hart left the room, Rodgers went to convey to Dreyfus the outcome of the meeting but broke down in tears. Hart set off for Mexico, and on his return a month later, he had to be carried off the train on a stretcher. Meanwhile, his hand having been forced, Rodgers did indeed turn to Oscar Hammerstein who was equally enthusiastic about the project - he had once discussed it briefly with Jerome Kern who turned it down on the basis that it was hard enough turning a hit play into a musical, let alone a

---

[2] Bought for the hospital by Cole Porter whilst he was having treatment following a riding accident.

[3] Richard Rodgers, *Musical Stages,* p217.

relative failure. Contracts were drawn up with the Theatre Guild and the new team set to work on the show that eventually, would become *Oklahoma!*

In fact, a year earlier, in a state of some despair at his then situation, Rodgers had already sought out Hammerstein's advice. He had known for some time that the day would come when he would have to seek out a new partner. As he described in his autobiography, 'much as I loved Larry and much as I took pride in what we had accomplished together, in the summer of 1941, I realised that the situation was becoming critical. I was thirty-nine years old, in good health and supremely grateful to be able to do the kind of work I loved, but I was linked professionally to a man, forty-six years old who was compulsively bent on self-destruction and who no longer cared about his work. I had to think the unthinkable: I had to think about life without Larry Hart'.[4]

Once he reached that conclusion, Rodgers began thinking about the many gifted lyric writers with whom he might work. But it wasn't just a lyricist that he was looking for. He needed a collaborator, someone who shared his vision and with whom he could exchange suggestions and discuss ideas about the kind of musical theatre he wished to create. Many famous names came to mind, Ira Gershwin was one, but he was busy with his late brother's archive.

Time and again, Rodgers found that he was always returning to just one man: Oscar Hammerstein. He also knew there were several reasons why Hammerstein might not be the sensible choice as a new partner. Hammerstein's career path had been very different from his own, part of a more romantic theatre; operetta rather than the bright, witty musical comedies of Rodgers and Hart and their contemporaries. His composers too, with the notable exception of Jerome Kern, had often been of a classical European background and training and, most significantly, Rodgers could not ignore the fact that Hammerstein had suffered a long, lean spell of almost ten years without a hit show.

Against that, however, Rodgers had absolute faith in Oscar's talent. 'I was convinced that any man who could write *Show Boat, Sweet Adeline* and the lyrics to Jerome Kern's *All the Things You Are* (from the 1939 flop *Very Warm for May*) was far from being

---

[4] Richard Rodgers, Ibid, p206.

through'.[5] The fact that Hammerstein had worked so frequently with Rodgers' idol, Jerome Kern, may also have been a factor.

During this troubling period in 1941, Rodgers was acting as an uncredited producer (he did not want to be the cause of any rumours of a rift between Hart and himself) on a new show by Hugh Martin and Ralph Blane called *Best Foot Forward*. Whilst that show was trying out in Philadelphia, Rodgers put in a call to Hammerstein, inviting himself to lunch at Oscar's Doylestown farmhouse. Once there, he found himself pouring out his problems. Hammerstein's response was typical. He did not want to be responsible for the break-up of the Rodgers and Hart partnership. Furthermore, if Dick walked away while Larry could still function, even partially, it might well kill him. If, however, things got so bad that it truly was impossible for them to continue, he would love to work with Dick. On a practical note, Hammerstein added that if Larry was unable to complete their current show, he would happily work as a silent collaborator to get the show finished.

Rodgers acknowledged the wisdom and humanity of Hammerstein's words and as he headed back to New York, he felt enough of the weight had been removed from his shoulders to make him feel more optimistic than he had for months. He laboured with Hart on *By Jupiter*, ironically their most successful show, but that was it. When Hart set off on his trip to Mexico, Rodgers knew he had no option but to get back in touch with Oscar Hammerstein. On 22 July 1942, the first official announcement of their partnership was released to the press.

Eight months later, *Oklahoma!* opened on Broadway on 31 March 1943. It may have been by Rodgers and Hammerstein and not Rodgers and Hart, as the Theatre Guild originally had envisaged, but in every other respect, it was all that they hoped for and more, restoring both its reputation and its fortune.

Nonetheless, Rodgers and Hammerstein had only signed a contract for that one show, and whatever they and others might have assumed, their long-term future together was far from assured. Richard Rodgers the man, does not enjoy the great reputation that Richard Rodgers the composer does. His was a complex personality to say the least, of which more later. But at

---

[5] Richard Rodgers, Ibid, p207.

this moment in time, notwithstanding all the problems he had endured because of Hart's drinking, he wanted to try and assure him they still had a future together and, "to help postpone a dear friend's drinking himself to death."

When Richard Rodgers telephoned Oscar Hammerstein about *Green Grow the Lilacs,* the lyricist was working on a pet project of his own. For some time, he had been nurturing the idea of updating Georges Bizet's *Carmen,* giving it a twentieth century, American setting with an all-black cast. He was some way into the task when Rodgers called. He put it to one side whilst writing *Oklahoma!* but with that show now safely launched, he could pick it up again.

Knowing that Hammerstein was otherwise engaged, Rodgers sought a way to help his former partner. Hart had been gracious in congratulating Rodgers on the success of *Oklahoma!,* telling him it would run for ever. But Rodgers knew that his success with his new partner would be eating Hart up inside, as indeed it was.[6] He was aware too, that Hart's beloved mother had died just a month after the show had opened, causing yet more pain to an already tortured soul.

Rodgers decided the best way to boost Hart's spirits was to get him working again. Perceptively recognising that Hart was still quite frail, both mentally and physically, Rodgers proposed that rather than work on a brand-new show, they should instead stage a revival of one of their earliest hits, *A Connecticut Yankee* for which they would write just six new songs. Rodgers would produce the show with a budget of $100,000, part of which, he would put up himself. To make the experience even better for Hart, the project would reunite the pair with their old friend, Herb Fields who wrote the original book and who was similarly concerned with Hart's wellbeing. Additionally, actress Vivienne Segal, who Hart loved more than any woman in the world apart from his mother,

---

[6] There is a moving account by Alan Jay Lerner in his autobiography, *The Street Where I Live* which describes an evening he spent with Hart and Frederick Lowe just after *Oklahoma!* opened. He describes how Hart, puffing on a giant cigar, became increasingly agitated, the tip of the cigar glowing ever brighter, when no matter what radio station they tuned into, was found to be playing music from that show. Only when the radio was switched off, did Hart finally calm down.

and to whom he had proposed marriage on more than one occasion, was signed to play Morgan le Fay.

Dick and Dorothy Rodgers invited Larry to use their country home in Connecticut in which to work, and were delighted that he stayed there and remained on the wagon whilst he wrote the new songs. At first, Hart seemed invigorated by the task, glad to be back working with Rodgers again. He produced some scintillating lyrics, particularly his wickedly funny *To Keep my Love Alive.*

It would not, perhaps could not last, for as soon as his work was completed, Hart found himself with too much time on his hands. When the show hit the road, he began hitting the bars again. Once more, Rodgers found himself in Philadelphia, keeping a watchful eye both on the try-out and on his partner.

Opening night on Broadway was 17 November 1943. New York was icy cold and wet; Hart was drinking as much as ever. Fearing that he might create a disturbance, friends and family had been delegated to prevent him getting into the Martin Beck Theatre, but he managed to give them the slip and saw the first act quietly from the back of the stalls. During the interval, again he evaded those charged with watching over him and left the theatre, without a coat, to visit a nearby bar. He resumed his place for the second act, now wet through and thoroughly drunk. When the curtain rose, he started humming along with the singers; before long, he was creating such a disturbance that he had to be removed. He was taken home by his sister-in-law, Dorothy Hart who settled him down and left him asleep. By morning, he had vanished. He was eventually found by composer Frederick Lowe, sitting soaking wet on a kerbside. He was rushed to hospital but this time, it was too late. Not even the intervention of Eleanor Roosevelt who arranged for him to receive some of the new wonder drug penicillin, at that time, only available to the armed forces, could save him. On 22 November, Hart died of double pneumonia. He was just forty-eight years old. His last words were, "What have I lived for?"

A seemingly unbreakable partnership, one of the most successful in Broadway history, was over. Perhaps it had been since that decisive meeting in the boardroom at Chappells, eighteen months earlier.

In the early days, as they took Broadway by storm, they were inseparable. The trouble was, Rodgers grew up, married, and had a family. Hart never really grew up. In the end, each of them had somewhat ambivalent feelings toward the other; Rodgers frustrated by Hart's unreliability, Hart frustrated by Rodgers' necessary bossiness, as evidenced by his description of the composer as the 'high school principal'.[7]

***

Richard Rodgers was the youngest son of a successful physician, growing up in an elegant brownstone house on West 120th Street in Manhattan and enjoying a conventional, middle-class upbringing. His parents loved the theatre and with his mother at the piano, they would sing the songs from the popular shows of the day. Consequently, the young, future composer was exposed to music almost from birth and by the time he was five years old, not only was he picking out the melodies he heard his parents sing but was also making up his own tunes on the piano. Recognising his talent from the start, Rodgers' parents encouraged his musical education with a series of private tutors. After attending Columbia University where he fulfilled a lifelong ambition by writing the music for the annual varsity show, the final formal stop in his musical education was the Institute of Musical Art (now the Juilliard School of Music). There, he studied theory, harmony and ear-training and of course, contributed to the annual review.

His musical training may have been strictly classical, but Rodgers knew from an early age the type of music he wanted to write. By the time he reached his early teens, he was accompanying his parents to the theatre, and once he saw his first Princess Theatre Show,[8] he had a new idol in the form of composer Jerome Kern, and a heart set on a career as a Broadway composer. 'It pointed the way I wanted to be led', Rodgers wrote of Kern's music.[9]

It may not have been the career his parents had in mind for him when he was born, (his older brother followed his father into

---

[7] Joshua Logan, *Josh*, p188.

[8] The Princess Theatre Shows were a series of seven, story-driven musicals by Jerome Kern, Guy Bolton and P.G. Wodehouse, written specifically for the 299-seater theatre between 1915 and 1918. The most famous were *Very Good Eddie* and *Oh Boy!*

[9] Richard Rodgers, *Musical Stages*, p20.

medicine), but as soon as his extraordinary musical gift became apparent, as evidenced above, he received nothing less than their full support. He frequently paid tribute to his parents' attitude. 'I don't suppose anybody ever went into music with less opposition or more encouragement than I', he wrote in his autobiography. Again, in answer to a query from *Young Homemakers* magazine, he said that the wisest thing his parents did for him was "to not interfere with my wish to go into a ridiculous career like writing music."[10]

Rodgers was introduced to Lorenz Hart by his older brother Morty who was at Columbia with the future lyricist. Dick was sixteen at the time and Hart twenty-three. With the benefit of hindsight, Rodgers was able later to recall of that meeting at Hart's house, that he had acquired that afternoon, 'a lyricist, a partner, a best friend and a source of permanent irritation'. [11]

The pair set to work writing songs together, mostly for amateur productions, but nonetheless, gaining valuable experience all the time. During Rodgers' time at Columbia, they wrote the score for *Fly With Me,* the 1920 production of the annual varsity show which was always staged in the ballroom of the Astor Hotel. They hoped that experience might open some important doors for them, but it didn't, and they laboured for a further five years trying to get the break that would allow them to write a score for a Broadway show. Finally, in 1925, after years of writing for amateur productions and benefits, thanks to the recommendation of a family friend, they were approached by the Theatre Guild to write the music and lyrics for a review that the Guild was staging for just two performances to raise money for tapestries that would adorn their new theatre. The review would be an opportunity for young, unknown singers and actors to perform before a live audience. At first, they were inclined to turn it down - "not another benefit" - but because it was for the Guild, by then already a major power on Broadway, they said yes. The score they wrote for the review, called *The Garrick Gaieties,* included their first hit song *Manhattan* and instead of just the scheduled two, the show ran for two-hundred and eleven performances.

---

[10] Richard Rodgers Collection, New York Public Library, Performing Arts Division.

[11] Richard Rodgers, Ibid, p28.

A Young Richard Rodgers.
Courtesy of The Rodgers & Hammerstein Organization:
A Concord Company, www.rnh.com

A string of hit shows followed that first success; a second edition of the *Gaieties*, *A Connecticut Yankee*, *The Girl Friend*, *Dearest Enemy* and *Evergreen* to name but some. There then followed that frustrating time in Hollywood before their return to New York and still greater triumphs; and still greater problems.

The problems were nothing new. Hart grew up in a household where normal rules did not apply. His wheeler-dealer father craving respectability was always hosting lavish parties for New York's literary and theatrical crowds, parties that often lasted all night. From an early age, therefore, Hart became used to days which did not begin until noon and frequently ended in a drunken stupor at dawn. It was a lifestyle which enabled him to forget his other troubles. He was always sensitive about his height - he was barely five feet tall and tried to disguise it with lifts in his shoes and by smoking extra-long cigars. He also was a gay man at a time when there was no choice but to hide that inconvenient truth in the closet. He struggled with his homosexuality his entire life, attempting to disguise it by pursuing - always unsuccessfully - one leading lady after another. Distressed by his appearance, bitter about his sexuality, careless of his genius and above all, desperately lonely, alcohol for Hart, was a means of escape from the sad reality of his daily life, a sadness that was so often revealed in the pathos of some of his finest lyrics.

***

In contrast to his own somewhat turbulent state at the time, when Richard Rodgers called Oscar Hammerstein to discuss a musical version of *Green Grow the Lilacs,* he found the lyricist strangely at peace. Rather than sit around and mope at his run of failures, Hammerstein had decided to return to his farm in Doylestown, Pennsylvania, there to begin work on a project that he had long been nurturing. This was to write his updated version of Bizet's opera *Carmen*. It was a project that he began in January 1942 and one he thoroughly enjoyed. He was under no pressure and faced no deadline. No composer was chasing him for a missing lyric. It was simply a labour of love and at that stage he neither knew nor cared if it would even be produced.

If he had searched for a hundred years, Rodgers could not have found anyone more different from Larry Hart. Hammerstein was a big, burly, craggy-faced man who preferred the peace and quiet of his Pennsylvania farm to the bright lights of the city. Whereas Hart was like quicksilver with a hundred and one things at a time on in his mind, Hammerstein was calm and collected, organising his thoughts carefully before committing them to paper. And whereas Hart had to be tied down with Rodgers' finished melody in his hand before he would even think about a lyric, Hammerstein was totally disciplined. When working on a show, he could be found every day, either writing at the tall lectern-style desk in his study, or walking around the farm, deep in thought as he tried to get inside the heads of the characters he was creating.

Oscar Hammerstein II
Courtesy of The Rodgers & Hammerstein Organization: A Concord Company, www.rnh.com

He had been born into a theatrical family. His grandfather, Oscar Hammerstein I was one of the most influential impresarios of the late nineteenth and early twentieth centuries. It was he who was largely responsible for turning Times Square into a centre of theatrical activity, building four theatres there, including the Victoria. In 1906, he built the Manhattan Opera House on 34th Street which with stars such as Nellie Melba, Luisa Tetrazzini and Mary Garden, for a while successfully challenged the hegemony of the longer-established Metropolitan Opera.

Oscar's grandfather, Oscar Hammerstein I, died penniless in 1919, after a lifetime of spectacular successes and equally spectacular failures, but his legacy would live on, not least in the success of his grandson, Oscar II.

Oscar II's father William managed the Victoria Theatre for his father and was an extremely successful vaudeville producer in his own right until his untimely death at the age of thirty-eight. Like both Richard Rodgers and Larry Hart, the younger Oscar Hammerstein went to Columbia University, where he was a contemporary of Hart's. Although there ostensibly to study law, again like Dick and Larry, Columbia's principal attraction was its annual varsity show, staged each spring in the Grand Ballroom of the Hotel Astor.

Hart and Hammerstein both wrote and appeared in the shows. It was after a matinee performance in 1916 that one of his fraternity colleagues, Morty Rodgers, introduced Oscar to his then fourteen-year-old brother Dick who had admired his performance in the show. According to Rodgers, Hammerstein made his approval seem the greatest compliment he could receive, and that moment only added to Dick's resolve to go to Columbia and to write the varsity show.

Through Morty, Rodgers and Hammerstein's paths crossed frequently over the next three years and in 1919, they wrote their first two songs together, this time for a review staged by the Akron Club.

By now, Oscar knew he was not destined to be a lawyer – he never wanted to be one anyway and begged his producer uncle Arthur to give him a job in the theatre. Bowing to the inevitable, his uncle took him on as an assistant stage manager. It was not long before he was helping with the occasional lyric and by 1923, after a few not very successful shows he had his first hit, *Wildflower*, book and lyrics co-written with Otto Harbach and with music by Vincent Youmans and Herbert Stothart. The following year came *Rose-Marie* by the same team, except for Rudolf Friml replacing Vincent Youmans, and in 1925, came his first show with Jerome

Kern, *Sunny* again with Harbach collaborating on the book and lyrics.

Other hits followed, including *The Desert Song* with music by Sigmund Romberg in 1926. Although still suffering the occasional failure, in 1927, Hammerstein provided the book and lyrics, and Jerome Kern the music for arguably the most important show to arrive on Broadway prior to *Oklahoma!* That, of course, was the ground-breaking *Show Boat,* which opened on 27 December 1927. It was also the first, but by no means the last show, in which Oscar Hammerstein showed that he was not afraid to tackle controversial issues. Significantly too, it was the musical where integration of the book, music and lyrics was taken to a much higher level than had been seen before. More success followed with *The New Moon* (Romberg), *Sweet Adeline* (Kern) and then *Music in The Air* (Kern), but these would be his last hits for a decade, until out of the blue, there came the call from Richard Rodgers.

We will never know what might have happened had Hart said yes to a musical based on *Green Grow the Lilacs*. It would, of course, have turned out to be a very different show, and Hart was probably quite right to say that it was not for him, even if he had been sober. It is possible, probably more likely, that the partnership was doomed anyway, Rodgers' patience at Hart's increasing unreliability finally having run out. "There has to be a statute of limitations on gratitude," he once said. Throughout his career, Rodgers had been working towards what would become known as the integrated musical, and in *Green Grow the Lilacs,* he knew he had the ideal subject to work on. He was determined to do it, and in Oscar Hammerstein, who had similar ambitions and had taken a giant step in that direction with *Show Boat,* he knew he had the perfect partner.

For Rodgers, the change in working relationship must have been extraordinary. From the very beginning, he and Hammerstein established a method of working that would serve them throughout the years of their partnership. At a series of meetings, (sometimes held at Hammerstein's farm in Bucks County, Pennsylvania, otherwise sitting under a massive old oak tree at Rodgers' country home in Fairfield County, Connecticut), they would discuss the structure of the show, where the songs might arise, what type of songs they might be, and which characters would sing them. Hammerstein would then begin to write the book and lyrics. Once completed, he would either mail or telephone the lyrics to Rodgers who would set them to music. No more would the latter have to wonder where his partner might be, or in what state he might find him; no more would he have to chase a missing lyric that was holding up an entire production. If something needed doing, Hammerstein was on hand to do it.

For both, this was a significant change in the way they worked. With Larry Hart, Rodgers always provided the music first. Similarly, all of Hammerstein's composers had given him a completed melody. Why change now? Hammerstein believed that by writing the lyrics as he wrote the book, he would better be able to achieve the seamless transition from dialogue to song that was so important to the new style of musical they were trying to create. Rodgers was quite happy to work this way, and not at all concerned that by doing so, his own creativity would be hindered.

Meanwhile, on 2 December 1943, Broadway welcomed Oscar Hammerstein's revamping of Georges Bizet's *Carmen*, now called *Carmen Jones*. It settled in at the Broadway Theatre for a run of five hundred and two performances. Perhaps not quite believing how his fortunes had changed after ten years in the wilderness, and in typically modest fashion, Hammerstein placed an advertisement in the Christmas edition of *Variety* in which he listed his seven flops from the thirties with their pathetically short runs and then at the bottom the words, 'I've done it before, and I can do it again'.

That there was a tragic inevitability about Larry Hart's death did not make it any easier for Richard Rodgers to deal with. He acknowledged as much in a letter to a friend a couple of weeks later. 'It's been a nasty wrench and there's very little we can have in the way of philosophy. We knew what he was doing to himself and there was just no way to stop him'.[12]

However distraught he might have been, Rodgers knew he had to carry on. Years later, just after Oscar Hammerstein's death, he wrote to Edna Ferber saying, '… that the compulsion to live and

---

[12] Letter to Col. Hans Christian Adamson, 22 December 1943, Richard Rogers Collection, New York Public Library, Performing Arts Division.

to work is beyond my control'.[13] It is not unreasonable to assume that this compulsion drove him on after Hart's death too. He was only forty-one and in the prime of life. His priority was to secure his professional future, and he had no doubt that the best way to do that was to make his partnership with Hammerstein permanent. That turned out to be not quite as straightforward as he might have hoped.

Whilst many composers were happy to work with several different collaborators, Rodgers was not. He had spent twenty successful years with Larry Hart and now having created such a resounding hit with Oscar Hammerstein, it seemed obvious to him that they should stay together. Not only did it make commercial sense, but they were on the same wavelength regarding the future direction of musical theatre, and most importantly, he found inspiration in Oscar's lyrics. Rodgers recalled his reaction when he read the first lyric that Hammerstein wrote for *Oklahoma!* It was *Oh, What a Beautiful Mornin'.* "When you're given words like that you get something to say musically. You'd have to be made of cement not to spark to that." His assumption was that for the same reasons Oscar would see things in the same way. He was more than a little alarmed, therefore, when his lawyer, Howard Reinheimer, who also happened to be Oscar's lawyer, told him that he was trying to put together a show to be written by Hammerstein and Jerome Kern.

Rodgers immediately informed Reinheimer about his own plans and then arranged to have lunch with Hammerstein who at once, told him about the talks with Kern. Hammerstein and Kern were good friends and corresponded regularly. The composer had been living in California for a number of years but was anxious to return to Broadway. For several years now, they had been kicking around an idea for a musical based on an old film script about Marco Polo and independently, both had picked it up again. Rodgers listened to what Hammerstein had to say, but then proceeded to explain why he thought that the two of them should become a permanent partnership. To his immense relief,

---

[13] Letter to Edna Ferber, 6 September 1960, Richard Rogers Collection, New York Public Library, Performing Arts Division.

Hammerstein agreed.[14] The new team would spend the next sixteen years together, the partnership cemented by nothing more than a handshake and ended only by Hammerstein's death in August 1960.[15]

Even before they had sealed their writing partnership, the two had decided to publish their own music and had set up a company, Williamson Music, for this purpose. The name reflected the fact that both their fathers were called William.

In addition, they set up a production company to produce not only their own future works but those of other writers too. Rodgers loved producing and Hammerstein, after his recent barren spell, was anxious about his financial security should he ever become unable to write. Their first production was John Van Druten's play *I Remember Mama*. It opened at the Music Box Theatre in October 1944 and gave Marlon Brando his first Broadway role. The play was both a critical and popular success running for nearly two years. In 1979, a musical version, also called *I Remember Mama* would be Richard Rodgers' final show, opening just a few months before the composer's death.

Inevitably, the success of *Oklahoma!* generated interest from Hollywood, so their first writing project as permanent partners was not a new show for the stage, but a film. No movie version of *Oklahoma!* would be made for many years, so 20th Century Fox asked the pair to turn one of its old hits, *State Fair* into a musical. Neither of them had happy memories of Hollywood and neither wanted to work there. Only when the studio accepted that they could stay in New York to write the screenplay and the score, and offered them $50,000 each to do so, did they agree.

The film which starred Dick Haymes and Jeanne Crain became a big hit and Rodgers and Hammerstein produced a lovely

---

[14] Exactly when Rodgers and Hammerstein agreed to work exclusively together is not known but Oscar Hammerstein and Jerome Kern were in touch regarding the *Marco Polo* project as late as April 1944. Kern said, 'I'm knocking together some tunes'. Letter, 24 April 1944. Oscar Hammerstein Collection, Library of Congress.

[15] Jerome Kern did return to New York in the autumn of 1945 to supervise a revival of *Show Boat* and to write the music for a new show Rodgers and Hammerstein were producing based on the life of Annie Oakley. He died following a massive stroke before he could start on the new show which became *Annie Get Your Gun* with a score by Irving Berlin.

score, the only one they wrote specifically for the big screen. The score included the Oscar winning *It Might as Well be Spring* and a typically lilting Rodgers' waltz, *It's a Grand Night for Singing.*

***

So intertwined are their names, and so successful was their collaboration, that it would be easy to assume that Rodgers and Hammerstein were close friends. They had known each other for years and were certainly close enough for Rodgers to invite himself over in 1941, to discuss the deterioration in his relationship with Larry Hart, but they were not intimate. Rather than a close personal friendship, their collaboration was based on mutual need.

Whilst their respect for each other was total, they kept their emotions at arm's length. They did not confide in each other, nor did they share their views on philosophical issues. Their loyalty was total as was their discipline. Most importantly, they were sure to exercise restraint whenever they disagreed, something which in the febrile atmosphere of the theatre, could not always have been easy.

Richard Rodgers and Oscar Hammerstein II
Courtesy of The Rodgers & Hammerstein Organization:
A Concord Company, www.rnh.com

Furthermore, following *Oklahoma!'s* triumphant opening, the pair were permanently in the public eye, a fact which could only increase the pressure on the partnership. Under intense scrutiny they had to reach agreement on all matters concerning the show, sharing all responsibilities and all rewards, sometimes having to set aside damaged egos in the process. "We will try it your way, and if that does not work, we will try it mine," was how Rodgers described it to a television audience in 1961.

As much as they admired each other professionally, so different were their outlooks and personalities, each must have had certain qualities the other did not particularly admire. For the sake of their partnership, they were able to put those negatives aside and find sufficient qualities they did like and concentrate on those instead.

Agnes de Mille refers to their singularity in her autobiography, *And Promenade Home.* She devotes an entire chapter to Rodgers and Hammerstein and given her unrivalled viewpoint, working with them on three shows, it is perhaps the definitive description as to how the pair operated.[16]

'R. & H. appear publicly together; they refer to one another in all interviews. They make decisions jointly, their joint word is pledged on all deals, and they receive joint and equal honours. One might think that a double opinion on all questions would cause delay; it does not. They act with dispatch.

'They always hold their first conferences privately and come to staff meetings united and in perfect agreement. They decide quickly, and they stand by their decisions ... R. & H. examine all newcomers personally, even the totally unknown. They can see, no one better, talent or lack of it in a face, they can hear it in a voice. For years, anyone could appear for an audition and be heard and everyone, even the well-known, had to - a precaution, although seemingly arrogant, designed to guarantee a high calibre of production ...'[17]

In appearance, Richard Rodgers is most frequently described as resembling a banker. Of average height and always

---

[16] Agnes de Mille worked on three shows with Rodgers and Hammerstein. *Oklahoma! Carousel* as choreographer, and *Allegro,* as director.

[17] Agnes de Mille, *And Promenade Home,* p229.

immaculately dressed, he had, as de Mille noted the developed hands and forearms of a pianist. Hammerstein was very tall, burly and with a pock marked face, which in later years was topped by a close, crew cut hairstyle; he was the epitome of a gentle giant. Rather than a banker like her father, Rodgers' daughter Mary remembers Hammerstein looking like "a rumpled paper bag."

They were very different in temperament also. Hammerstein was universally beloved. Read through all the biographies and musical theatre books and you will find it hard to find anyone with something bad to say about him.

Rodgers' reputation on the other hand is the opposite. Stephen Sondheim who practically grew up in Oscar Hammerstein's house, said in a 1973 interview that his mentor "Oscar Hammerstein was a man of infinite soul but limited talent, while Richard Rodgers was a man of infinite talent but limited soul,"[18] a remark that some might suggest says more about Sondheim than either Rodgers or Hammerstein. Was Rodgers concerned by such negative comments? It would appear not, judging by this self-deprecating story he was fond of telling. Walking along the street with Larry Hart he heard someone say, "There goes Larry Hart with that big son-of-a-bitch, Dick Rodgers." Years later, when walking along the same street with Oscar Hammerstein he heard someone else say, "There goes Oscar Hammerstein with that little son-of-a-bitch, Dick Rodgers."

Of course, the truth lies somewhere in the middle. Hammerstein was not quite the saint he was painted; he did have a dark side, was aggressively competitive and could occasionally be sulky or insensitive; he avoided confrontation like the plague.

Likewise, Rodgers was not all bad. Agnes de Mille said of him: '... at moments of direct personal approach, he can be gentle. I suspect he feels in some ways cut off, even yearning; the banter is too constant, the quips too quick and sharp to betoken anything but vulnerability ... But just as the greatest quality in his music is a lilting delicious scherzo with overtones of hovering sweetness, so in his manner and in his eyes (when he is off guard), there is a brooding quiet, a kind of unappeased hunger, a woe'.[19]

---

[18] William Hyland, *Richard Rodgers,* p285.

[19] Agnes de Mille, *And Promenade Home,* p231.

Those traits may well date back to his childhood which, notwithstanding his parents' encouragement for his music, was not a happy one. The source of his unhappiness was the fact that his mother and father shared a house with his mother's parents, an arrangement which seems to have benefitted no-one. As he explained in his autobiography, 'There was hostility between my father and his mother-in-law, between my grandmother and my grandfather, and between my brother and me'. Often, these hostilities led to long silences, which could last for weeks. For the young Richard, 'the piano was the one means through which I could escape from the generally unpleasant atmosphere of my family life'.[20]

As part of my research for this book, I spent some time perusing Rodgers' correspondence in the Performing Arts Division of the New York Public Library. I wanted to see if that correspondence might reveal something of the man himself. Was he really as cold-hearted and humourless as his reputation suggested? From what I saw in the limited time available, maybe not. For example, after his battle with cancer of the jaw in 1955, Rodgers received several letters from fans similarly afflicted. He replied personally to them all, offering hope and encouragement.

Another apparent Rodgers' contradiction exists regarding his attitude to performances of his music. The orthodox view is that he disapproved of any version that deviated from the way a song was originally written. A famous case in point is Peggy Lee's supercharged version of *Lover* which Rodgers allegedly hated. Yet, in a letter to Dave Brubeck who had recorded an album of his songs, Rodgers emphasised that he did not object to his jazz treatment. 'Most songs would die of attrition were it not for the fact that good artists played varied arrangements'.[21] And therein probably lies the truth regarding Rodgers' attitude to the treatment of his music. If it is done well, and with respect, it was fine. If it wasn't, well then, he might complain, but what composer wouldn't?

He gave encouragement to young writers such as Burt Bacharach, '... what you are doing is to open a window and let

---

[20] Richard Rodgers, *Musical Stages,* p5.

[21] Letter to Dave Brubeck, Richard Rogers Collection, New York Public Library, Performing Arts Division.

fresh air into a room that has become too noisy in one way and stuffy in another'.[22] A generous tribute from an older composer to a younger one who was leading popular music in a direction that he would be unable to follow.

Another example of the apparent contradiction between perception and reality was a telegram Rodgers sent to P.G. Wodehouse on the latter's eightieth birthday in 1961:

> On this happy day, I wish to thank you on behalf of Larry Hart, Oscar Hammerstein and myself for all you taught us through the years. Please stay well and Happy. Affectionately.

Wodehouse wrote to Ira Gershwin telling him how much receiving Rodgers' telegram meant to him. 'I nearly cried when I read it. I had only met him once for a minute when he and Oscar passed the table where I was dining with Max Dreyfus, and it never occurred to me that he would remember my existence. He must be an awfully nice chap'.[23] Rodgers never forgot the influence Wodehouse's Princess Theatre shows had on him all those years before, and where they led him.

This warmth of tone and openness appeared in most of the correspondence I examined. Perhaps it confirms that it was only when sitting at a piano or at a writing desk that this rather complex personality was best able to communicate his true feelings.

Both men were generous with their time and their money where charity and good causes were concerned. They were both liberal in their political outlook, though, Rodgers was somewhat more circumspect in the causes and candidates he supported. He was, however, vocal in his condemnation of the House Unamerican Activities Committee, earning himself an F.B.I. file in the process. Hammerstein found it harder to say no when asked to support a cause in which he believed. Among the bodies he joined were the United World Federalists, the NAACP, the Anti-Nazi league, the Writers War Board and many others. It was perhaps

---

[22] Letter to Burt Bacharach, 14 April 1970. Richard Rogers Collection, New York Public Library, Performing Arts Division.

[23] Letter, 10 November 1961. P.G. Wodehouse, Richard Rogers Collection, New York Public Library, Performing Arts Division.

not surprising that he too found himself the subject of a F.B.I. file, one that remained open until his death. Of all their causes and beliefs, nothing was more important to both Rodgers and Hammerstein than their abhorrence of racial intolerance of any kind. It was a constant in their lives; they wrote about it; they spoke about it, and as they would later demonstrate in *South Pacific,* they were not afraid, going against many people's advice, to address the issue directly with the song *Carefully Taught.*

Rodgers is the one who has the reputation for being a tough businessman, but Hammerstein was equally tough when he needed to be. They both were keenly aware that the extraordinary success of *Oklahoma!* gave them enormous power which they were not afraid to use. The organization that now bears their names and licences all their works, together with those of other composers and lyricists, is testimony to both their foresight and acumen.

That Rodgers was a perfectionist demanding the best of everyone, is no doubt true. His reputation for a fondness of chorus girls was also no doubt fully deserved, but I searched in vain for the 'Godzilla' that Stephen Sondheim called him. True, there may have been legendary arguments between the composer and strong willed (is there any other kind?) directors over the staging of his songs. Rodgers was always concerned that they should be performed in a way that showed them off to their best advantage, notwithstanding the demands of the *verismo* musicals that he and Hammerstein were themselves creating. According to Agnes de Mille '... he kids and jokes companionably at all rehearsals, but he is a figure of some terror, through sheer nervous tension, high voltage, and the unforgettable overtones of his world power'.[24]

Writing about Hammerstein, Agnes de Mille said, 'Oscar seems solider, more the country gentleman, the paterfamilias, the benevolent, genial, eighteenth-century man of letters. He looks too neighbourly, too understanding, too philosophic for our gipsy and disreputable trade. He is a tall ... gentle-faced man with a soft voice, a Yankee twang when excited and a chuckle that is one of the most auspicious sounds our theatre has ever housed'.[25] Even at his busiest, he would take time out to read scripts from aspiring playwrights and offer advice. He was someone you could talk to

---

[24] Agnes de Mille, *And Promenade Home,* p231.

[25] Ibid, p232.

about anything at all, and if you were ever in need, he was there to help or to write out a cheque. De Mille once sought him out on behalf of the Ballet Theatre, and sensing her purpose, Hammerstein just said, "All right, yes, a $1,000. Do you want scotch or bourbon?"

As hinted at by Hugh Fordin in his biography of Oscar Hammerstein, *Getting to Know Him,* such was their relationship that after Hammerstein's death, Rodgers remarked that he had no idea whether Oscar liked him or not. Hammerstein had once said something very similar about him. But whatever personal differences there may have been, those differences remained private, and to a large extent still do. Their professional need for each other would ensure that there would be plenty of give and take on both sides. In years to come, the strength of the partnership would be tested almost, but fortunately never quite to breaking point. In the autumn of 1943, the only concern Rodgers and Hammerstein had, was to find their next project. And, as they were about to find out, the Theatre Guild was convinced it had done just that.

Chapter 2

Liliom - And Helburn's Obsession

Although not so well known to the public at large, Rodgers and Hammerstein's 'Gloat Club' companions at Sardi's were highly respected figures on Broadway.

The Theatre Guild was established in 1918 by Lawrence Langner and his wife Armina Marshall as a successor to the Washington Square Players, an amateur theatrical company they had founded four years earlier. It was to be a professional company whose aim was to produce high quality plays by both American and foreign playwrights and at the same time, provide the opportunity for previously undiscovered talent to perform in those works. Over the years, it became the producer of plays by writers including George Bernard Shaw, Eugene O'Neill, Maxwell Anderson, Sidney Howard, William Saroyan and Ferenc Molnár. To perform in those works, it introduced actors such as Helen Hayes, Alla Nazimova, Alfred Lunt and Lynne Fontanne to the Broadway stage.

Lawrence Langner was of Welsh origin, having been born in Swansea in 1890. After his father's early death, the family moved to London where he studied law and developed his love for the arts before emigrating to America at the age of twenty. Theresa Helburn noted in her autobiography that for Langner, the American dream certainly turned into reality. He was not a man ever to be put off by obstacles in his way. Where there did not appear to be an outlet for his ideas, he created one. After settling in New York, he went on to become a highly successful patent lawyer while at the same time, indulging his love of the theatre by establishing the Theatre Guild, the American Shakespeare Festival and the Westport Country Playhouse, all with his wife.

Theresa Helburn was born in New York in 1887. Educated at Bryn Mawr where she produced all her class plays, she went on to spend a year in Paris furthering her education at the Sorbonne and attending soirees where she met many of the artists and intellectuals who flocked to the French capital following the end of the First World War. Gertrude Stein, Igor Stravinsky, Pablo

Picasso, Isadora Duncan and Pablo Casals were amongst those with whom she mingled on a regular basis.

Her original intention was to pursue a career as a playwright, but on returning to New York, she was persuaded by Langner whom she had first met before she went to Paris, to join his newly formed Theatre Guild. Her first job was as unpaid literary manager and then as casting director. When two board members resigned a year later, she was invited to act as a temporary executive secretary. It would just be for two weeks or so they told her, until they could find a permanent replacement. It was a job nobody wanted, herself included. She still thought of herself as a writer. She had nothing to give them, she believed, other than her inexperience, but she proved to be so invaluable, she was soon promoted to executive director and with Lawrence Langner splitting his time between his law practice and running the Guild's finances, she immediately assumed responsibility for the Guild's day-to-day operations.

It turned out to be a task for which she was ideally suited; she had all the qualities necessary to be an outstanding theatrical producer. Oscar Hammerstein reminded those attending her funeral in 1959 of those attributes. He described her as, "A hopeful innocent in fair weather, a stern pilot in stormy weather, a mathematician who prefers to ignore the laws of mathematics and trust intuition, an idealist, a realist, a practical dreamer, a sophisticated gambler, a stage-struck child. That's a producer. That was Theresa Helburn ... She seemed never to be still, never to be letting you or anyone else alone. Always prodding like a very small shepherd dog, pushing you relentlessly to some pasture, which she had decided to be good for you."

Now, some twenty years later, considering herself instrumental in bringing Rodgers and Hammerstein together in the first place by offering Rodgers the chance to turn *Green Grow the Lilacs* into a musical, Helburn thought it her duty to come up with their next project. It was all a remarkable change of mind from someone who used to think of musicals as inferior theatre; "intellectual slumming" was how she put it when she was very young and opinionated. Over the years though, she warmed to the genre, sometimes writing to Larry Hart with suggestions for plays to be turned into musicals. Nothing came of those suggestions – indeed Hart often did not respond at all as his drinking took hold, but after the Guild produced the Gershwins' *Porgy and Bess* in 1936, staging a quality musical play became her number one priority.

She knew what she wanted: A musical play, definitely not a musical comedy, nor an old-fashioned operetta, but a form of theatre where the drama, the music and ballet, would meld into one theatrical experience, each element contributing to the telling of the story. How fortunate it was that her vision matched so precisely that of both Richard Rodgers and Oscar Hammerstein. From being 'Helburn's Folly' (the name Lawrence Langner teasingly gave it) whilst they were desperately trying to raise the $83,000 cost of the production, *Oklahoma!* had become a massive triumph for the Guild, and now Helburn wanted to repeat the feat.

She and Langner made a list of plays to which they owned the rights and which they thought might benefit from the *Green Grow the Lilacs* musical treatment. One was Robert Sherwood's *Reunion in Vienna.* Another was *Liliom* by Hungarian playwright, Ferenc Molnár. First produced by the Guild in English in 1921, it became one of her favourite plays. Furthermore, it is no exaggeration to say that in recent years, she had become obsessed with the idea of turning this modern classic into a musical.

***

Molnár was born Ferenc Neumann in Budapest on 12 January 1878, to well-to-do Jewish parents. It was only after he started writing that he changed his name to the more Hungarian, Molnár. His literary career began at the age of eighteen as a journalist. Soon, he was writing sketches and short stories as well. Such was the charm of his stories that even at that young age, he became a national success. His popularity grew still further in 1906 when he published his great novel for young people, *The Paul Street Boys,* still a hugely popular book in Hungary today.

Liliom was Molnár's fourth play. It began life as a feuilleton [26] entitled *Bedtime Tale* in 1907 and was published the next year in his short story collection, *Music.* In early 1909, he expanded the story into a play, writing almost round-the-clock for weeks, mostly on the balcony of Budapest's world-renowned New York Café.

---

[26] A part of a European newspaper or magazine devoted to fiction, light literature and criticism.

The finished play was premiered in Budapest's Comedy Theatre on 7 December 1909. It was originally entitled *Liliom: The Life and Death of a Scoundrel – A Suburban Legend in Seven Tableaux* and set in Budapest in the early years of the twentieth century.

Both critics and audiences were left bewildered by this new work, and unlike his previous plays, all of which had been successful, it failed, closing after only twenty-six performances. Why did he kill his hero in the fifth scene? Why take him to Heaven in scene six and then bring him back to earth in the next? Was Liliom a saint or a sinner and what was meant by his abortive redemption? These were the issues that left his audience bemused.

Three years later, it was produced more successfully in Berlin. It now had a new title, *Liliom: A Legend in Seven Acts and a Prologue.* It was for this production that the play was translated into German by Molnár's close friend, Austrian born writer, Alfred Polgar,[27] who not only translated the play, but also, (presumably with Molnár's agreement) added the Prologue and made Mrs. Hollunder Julie's aunt rather than as she was in the original script, a relative of Liliom. This change was made to emphasise the pressure mounting on the title character. It was Polgar too, who added the now infamous line for Julie at the end of the play, about how it is possible to be hit really hard and for it to not hurt at all.

In its finalised form, Liliom is a barker for a carousel in a fairground in the outskirts of the city. He is introduced to us during the play's Prologue, and we see that his demeanour can change instantly from being charming with the young ladies, to ugly and menacing to any man who objects to his flirting with their girl. In Molnár's Prologue, Julie and her friend Marie come to the carousel and whilst Liliom makes a point of noticing them, the first encounter between him and Julie is not developed in the way it is in the musical. Nor is there any reaction from Mrs. Muskat, the carousel owner.

However, anyone familiar with *Carousel* will immediately recognise *Liliom* as the source material for the musical: The first act in particular is identical in almost every significant way but

[27] Born in Vienna in 1873, Polgar soon established himself as a leading writer of German prose with a series of essays, reviews and articles.

throughout the play, one can see how close Oscar Hammerstein stayed to the Molnár original.

The young couple move in together, staying with Julie's aunt, Mother Hollunder. She runs a photographic studio in what Molnár describes as a 'dilapidated hovel'. Liliom misses his job, can't find anything else to do, and vents his frustration by beating Julie. Mother Hollunder is desperately trying to persuade Julie to leave Liliom and marry a widowed carpenter. When Liliom learns that Julie is pregnant, in order to get money for the baby, he allows himself to be persuaded by his no-good friend, Ficsur, to take part in a robbery. The robbery goes wrong, and rather than go to jail, Liliom kills himself.

Joseph Schildkraut (Liliom), Evelyn Chard (Louise) and Eva Le Gallienne (Julie) in the Theatre Guild production of *Liliom* (1921).

The play now moves to a heavenly court where Liliom is sentenced to sixteen years of purification by fire. He is told that after that sixteen-year period, he can return to earth for one day, and if he can do something good for the child he left behind, then he may gain entry to Heaven itself. Sixteen years later, Liliom returns to earth, stealing a star on the way. He is disguised as a beggar and approaches Julie and Louise, his daughter, telling them that he knew Louise's father. When he is left alone with Louise, he tries to give her the star, but she refuses to take it, and once again, he lashes out, slapping her. Louise cannot understand why the slap - real loud and hard - did not hurt her. Liliom is taken away, by heavenly policemen, presumably to spend eternity in the crimson fire.

Molnár's biographer, Clara Györgyey said that the author 'claimed that with *Liliom,* he meant only to "dramatize a primitive legend of Budapest's lower depths" relating it is as naively as "old woman tell-tales." Nonetheless, his friends and many critics viewed it as his most subjective work, a naked self- analysis'.[28] At the time he was writing the play, his marriage to Margi Veszi was disintegrating and the couple quarrelled bitterly. Budapest's cafes and salons bubbled with gossip about his allegedly cruel treatment of his family. There even were rumours that he beat not only his wife but also his little daughter.

Molnár, Györgyey suggests, wrote *Liliom* to justify himself against these charges and to appease his angry spouse by showing how even the rudest exterior might conceal a gentle nature and how often people hurt those they love most. The play can, therefore, be viewed as a public statement and a partial explanation of the author's occasional violent behaviour.

Is the play autobiographical? Both Molnár and Liliom were cursed with a constitutional inability to avow love. Both were capable of extreme cruelty, and both were also capable of genuine tenderness. Perhaps the clearest indication that it can be considered autobiographical are the words that Molnár's widow, Lily Darvas chose to have inscribed on his tombstone. They are the final words of the moving speech that Julie gives over Liliom's body, "Liliom. Sleep my boy, sleep."[29]

It took ten years and the horrors of the First World War for audiences in Hungary and elsewhere to take to the play, but when it was revived in Budapest in 1919, it became an immediate triumph. That success was repeated throughout Europe and then in America, in an English translation about which there is something of a mystery.

---

[28] Clara Györgyey, *Ferenc Molnár,* p148.

[29] Ibid.

As mentioned earlier, initially, *Liliom* was translated from Molnár's original Hungarian into German for a 1912 production in Berlin. It was this German version that was subsequently translated into English for the 1921 New York production by the Theatre Guild. This English translation has always been credited to a Broadway actor and writer called Benjamin F. Glazer.

To this day, his is the name you will see on all English language versions of *Liliom.* Similarly, on all material relating to *Carousel* you will find the credit, 'Based on the play "Liliom" by Ferenc Molnár as adapted by Benjamin F. Glazer'. Whether he is entitled to that credit, however, is in some doubt, as rumours soon began to spread that the bulk of the work was undertaken by a young, German-speaking lyricist who was paid fifty dollars a week for the four weeks allowed for the task. The work was commissioned by one Gustave Amberg, an associate of the Shubert brothers who frequently needed translations of the European plays they were thinking of producing in New York.

What then appears to have happened is that whilst the Shuberts were contemplating producing *Liliom,* simultaneously, the same German version fell into the hands of an actor called Joseph Schildkraut who just happened to be friendly with Glazer. Schildkraut was so enamoured with the play that he persuaded the Theatre Guild to produce it with himself in the title role. He also persuaded them to allow his friend Glazer to translate it into English. Glazer, so the story goes, heard on the grapevine that *Liliom* had already been translated into English for the Shuberts who by then had turned it down, and so, rather than do the work again, acquired that existing version from Amberg and presented it to Schildkraut. It is this English translation that the Theatre Guild successfully produced and is still in use today. Whether or not Glazer paid any more for the translation is not known.

What we do know is the name of the young lyricist who was very likely responsible for the English version of *Liliom*. It is Lorenz Hart. His sister-in-law, Dorothy Hart was certain that Larry did indeed do the translation that was used. Her insistence is because Joseph Schildkraut himself told her categorically that he knew this to be the case.

According to Rodgers and Hart's biographers, Jan Clayton (*Carousel's* original Julie) and Samuel Marx, the fact that *Liliom* was Larry's work, was known by only a few select friends who were sworn to secrecy. Unusually for him, Larry was clearly deeply upset at the time, giving way to self-pity. "They won't let a new man in," he complained to a friend.[30]

***

In 1925, Molnár moved to Vienna where he enjoyed further success until the 1938 *Anschluss* forced him to flee to the U.S. to escape the Nazis. He took up residence at the Plaza Hotel in New York where he held court until his death in 1952. Notwithstanding his many other successes, *Liliom* remained his greatest triumph and was always his favourite play.

Although occasionally produced now in Europe, *Liliom* is seldom to be seen on the English-speaking stage, so it is easy to forget how well thought of it was before *Carousel.* Following the 1940 revival, the *New York Post* critic Richard Watts Jr. wrote, 'It is strange how touching the story of this violent young scapegrace and his loyal wife can be, and it is a great tribute to Molnár, who has combined fantasy with realism amid so much romantic effectiveness'. In similar vein, John Mason Brown of the *New York Evening Post* wrote, '… no dramatic statement of the second chance seems to me to have been more moving than was the final scene in *Liliom* in which a Budapest barker returned to earth to strike his daughter even as, when he was living, he had struck her mother. In fact, few plays to have come out of the modern theatre have equalled Molnár's fantasy in imagination or pathos, in charm or universality, in tenderness or timelessness'.

It is easy to understand why Theresa Helburn, particularly in the midst of wartime, thought that such a highly regarded play which casts doubt on the seeming finality of death, was such a good prospect for Rodgers and Hammerstein. They, however, were not going to commit until they were absolutely certain it was right for them, and at first glance, there seemed to be many reasons why it might not be. Much later, when *Carousel* was in rehearsal, Richard Rodgers explained to Ferenc Molnár over lunch at Sardi's, just how careful one had to be to avoid making a wrong choice.

---

30 Jan Clayton and Samuel Marx, *Rodgers and Hart, Bewitched, Bothered and Bedevilled*, p35.

Molnár recalled the conversation in his memoirs. Rodgers told him that there were many mistakes one could make when putting on a play, and most of them could be rectified. It might cost time and money, but it could be done. If an actor turned out to be not right for a part, he could be replaced. So could a director. If a set wasn't right, it could be repainted. If the ending was unsatisfactory, a new ending could be written. The one mistake you must not make though, the big one that cannot be undone, is the one that happens at the very beginning when you ask yourself the question, "shall I write this play?" Get that wrong, and the damage is irreparable. It was that potential disaster that Rodgers and Hammerstein were desperate to avoid.

***

Theresa Helburn's infatuation with the idea of turning *Liliom* into a musical began in 1936 after her conversion to the idea that musicals could be serious works of art. In January 1937, she met composer, Kurt Weill at a party. Weill was a recent arrival in New York and to Helburn, his central European background, similar to Molnár's, made him an ideal choice to write the score. In fact, Weill knew the play well and had tried to obtain the musical rights to it himself in 1930, but Molnár consistently had refused. Weill's hope now was that because of the good relationship Helburn had with Molnár as producer of his plays, obtaining the musical rights might become a real possibility and he agreed at once to Helburn's proposal.

In a series of letters to Helburn, Weill set out his vision for the musical. At one point, he even thought that Larry Hart might be the ideal person to adapt the play and write the lyrics, although he was unsure if Hart would be available. (Was that thought prompted by the rumours about the original translation?) James Cagney was one of his suggestions to play Liliom. Weill's letters[31] show that he had spent some considerable time thinking about a musical *Liliom*. 'I have now very definite ideas about it. I know what to do with the book, how to introduce songs, in what style I would write and what form I would give it'. He had sent Helburn a recording of the short opera *Mahagonny* which he had written

---

[31] Theatre Guild Collection at Beinecke Library, Yale University.

with Berthold Brecht in 1927 and said that the *Liliom* music would be in a similar vein. He suggested too, that he would use an orchestra of no more than sixteen pieces, no chorus, but, as Rodgers and Hammerstein would eventually demand, good singing actors, or good acting singers.

However, it was not to be, because much to Weill's disappointment and notwithstanding some intense lobbying on his behalf, Molnár once again turned him down. In fact, his refusal, written in a letter to his agent dated 4 May 1937 and forwarded to Weill, shows the strength of his feeling on the matter at that time. 'Please note that under no circumstances will I consent to a musical production of *Liliom* no matter in what form it will be proposed. This is my definite decision and I will not deviate from it'. [32]

That he was in good company would have been scant comfort to Weill. Molnár previously had turned down an approach from the composer Giacomo Puccini to turn *Liliom* into an opera. "*Liliom*, is my best play: it is my masterpiece. I want it to be remembered as a Molnár play and, not simply as the libretto of a Puccini opera," the playwright is reputed to have said. George Gershwin, Emmerich Kalman and Franz Lehar are all rumoured to have expressed an interest in adapting *Liliom*, but they too, had been rebuffed. Molnár might have been predisposed anyway to say no to Puccini because the composer had been rather rude about some Hungarian folk music played at a party given in his honour to celebrate the Budapest premiere of *Madama Butterfly*. The evening ended in an icy chill, Molnár later recalled.

Helburn, however, never gave up on her belief that the play would make a great musical. After that last categorical refusal in 1937, there had been a successful revival of the play on Broadway in 1940, with Burgess Meredith and Ingrid Bergman in the lead roles. Now Rodgers and Hammerstein had written their ground-breaking new musical *Oklahoma!* and she knew that Molnár was familiar with the Lynn Riggs' play from which it been adapted.

Helburn and Langner decided that there would never be a better time to have one last try to persuade him to change his mind. They guessed it would not be easy and they were right. From the outset, he doggedly refused their approaches to turn his theatrical classic into a musical play. Finally, after several rejections, they

---

[32] Theatre Guild Collection at Beinecke Library, Yale University.

had a brainwave. They proposed to Molnár that he, at least, see *Oklahoma!* Then, he could judge for himself how sensitively they would adapt his play into a musical.

They put this suggestion to him via his agent, Edmond Pauker and to their delight, on 15 October, received a positive response. 'Molnár thanks you for the invitation for next Thursday and will be glad to attend. Where should he meet you?'[33]

That fixes the date for Molnár's visit to see *Oklahoma!* as Thursday 21 October 1943. On the very next day, he met with Theresa Helburn and Lawrence Langner, and finally, after all those years of saying no to any form of musical adaptation, he was ready to give his consent. There was one proviso: Rodgers and Hammerstein would have to treat his beloved *Liliom* as tastefully and charmingly as they had treated *Green Grow the Lilacs.*

Exactly why Molnár changed his mind has never been established. Was it because he realised how sensitively Rodgers and Hammerstein would treat the play? Was it to repay the Theatre Guild who had been so supportive of him over the years? Might it have been the money? His eventual percentage in the show was eight-tenths of one percent, the smallest of anyone, though he did also receive a consultant's fee of $2,500. Even with that small percentage, he would have known that with the box office records that *Oklahoma!* was breaking, he could anticipate a considerable income. Nobody can say for sure, but whatever the reason, change his mind he did.

Both Lawrence Langner and Theresa Helburn must have had an extra spring in their step as they set off for that significant Gloat Club lunch a couple of weeks later, the most likely date of which was Thursday 4 November 1943. Against the odds, they had secured Molnár's agreement and now, armed with that consent, they were about to present the idea of a musical *Liliom* to the architects of their newly restored fortune: Richard Rodgers and Oscar Hammerstein.

What could possibly go wrong?

---

[33] Theatre Guild Collection, Beineke Library, Yale University.

Chapter 3

Changing their Minds

Rodgers and Hammerstein's devastating "no"; that's what could go wrong, and Langner and Helburn clearly were taken by surprise. Langner's somewhat theatrical account of that response gives the impression that Rodgers and Hammerstein's rejection was absolute. The truth is, that after their initial, instant dismissal of the idea, they went on to list a host of reasons why they thought *Liliom* would not make a good musical. Theresa Helburn listened politely, but relentless sheepdog that she was, would not take a single no for an answer, and using all her persuasive powers, she managed to convince the pair to agree to another, more formal meeting on 7 December, to discuss the matter further.

Meanwhile, on 21 November, Langner felt either sufficiently confident or had sufficient chutzpah to write to Edmond Pauker, 'I am glad to be able to tell you confidentially that Rodgers and Hammerstein are both very much interested. They are now studying the script'.[34]

The evidence suggests it was more a case of chutzpah than anything else. Hammerstein was in Boston supervising his *Carmen Jones* try-out, while Rodgers was at the hospital bedside of Larry Hart who would die the following day. A musical *Liliom* was probably the last thing on either of their minds.

Two days earlier, Langner had sent a memo to Helburn setting out the financial terms of the proposed deals agreed on behalf of the Guild, both with Molnár as author of the original play, and with 20th Century Fox who owned the motion picture rights to *Liliom*. The agreements specified that Rodgers and Hammerstein would have an entirely free hand with no interference by Mr. Molnár. It also gave Fox the opportunity to invest up to a maximum of thirty per cent of the production cost of the musical. In a handwritten postscript, Langner asked Helburn to 'Keep this in your file and we can modify to suit H&R when they agree'.[35]

---

[34] Theatre Guild Collection, Beineke Library, Yale University.

[35] Ibid.

Fox had earlier sent Pauker confirmation that '... the engagement of Oscar Hammerstein and Richard Rodgers for writing the book, lyrics and music for the musical version of 'LILIOM' is satisfactory to us ...'[36]

There is no doubt that both Richard Rodgers and Oscar Hammerstein did have very real reservations about doing *Carousel;* they were not merely playing hard to get. Rodgers gave a eulogy at Lawrence Langner's funeral in 1962 in which he said, "we were afraid to do *Liliom* as a musical, but the Guild refused, for six or seven months to take no for an answer. If they had listened to Oscar and I, we all would have been cheated out of *Carousel.*"[37]

There were many reasons for their initial dismissal of the idea. Hammerstein knew the play well and loved it, admitting that he had read and studied it many times. He had never considered it a subject for a musical because of the serious tone of the play. Furthermore, neither Rodgers nor Hammerstein liked forlorn endings, and *Liliom's* ending is certainly that; also, they both thought that the element of fantasy was a problem for musical treatment.

Above all, they both rejected the idea of a musical with a Hungarian background. They could not envisage how to dress the production, either in traditional peasant costume or in drab modern Hungarian dress, and given the uncertain political situation at the time, it was not inconceivable that they might have to re-write the play at a moment's notice. According to an article by Elinor Hughes in the *Boston Herald,* Hammerstein said that a Hungarian location suggested "gypsies playing violins, untamed passions, uncertain politics and old-fashioned operetta," he added that there had "been too many musicals and romantic novels set against such a background for him to add still another to the collection." In conclusion, "It struck me that I myself wouldn't enjoy seeing a show about Central Europe - and that's a big test for me." [38]

---

[36] Ibid.

[37] Eulogy for Lawrence Langner, Richard Rodgers Collection, New York Public Library, Performing Arts Division.

[38] Elinor Hughes, *Boston Herald,* 27 March 1945.

Yes, they admitted, elements of the story were beautiful and full of possibilities and the characters were interesting, but there just seemed to be too many problems. They did not want to make the 'Big Mistake' that Rodgers would later discuss with Molnár.

The further meeting that Rodgers and Hammerstein agreed to, the first production meeting, took place on Tuesday 7 December 1943 at Oscar's New York House at 157 East 61st Street. Despite all the other distractions that had occupied them since 4 November, and whatever their doubts, they both not only had studied the original play, but also given the whole project a great deal of thought.

They began the meeting by addressing the thorny issue of the play's setting. They talked about moving it away from Hungary, maybe to America or perhaps to Western Europe. Unable to suggest anywhere thought to be a significant improvement, for the time being they decided to leave the play in Hungary or maybe, Czechoslovakia.

Other items discussed at that first meeting proved to be less contentious, and suggest that both writers, professional as ever, had looked for the positives as well as the negatives. Hammerstein, for example, envisioned that the opening scene of the play, the Prologue, might be expanded to introduce the principal characters and that it might include dancing and a chorus number.

He loved the first act scene with Julie and Liliom and thought that Molnár's writing was too tight and beautiful to change in any significant way and that it would lend itself to a beautiful musical number. He thought it would make a wonderful curtain closer with the acacia blossoms falling as the curtain came down - and of course, that first scene, including its falling blossoms, did remain much as Molnár had written it.

They saw a possible musical number for Mrs. Muskat, the carousel owner. The song was suggested by lines in the play:

> As for you, you're an artist and you belong among artists. All the beer you want, cigars, a krone a day and a gulden on Sunday - and the girls, Liliom, the girls ...

The major problem with the play for musical purposes was what Hammerstein referred to as 'the tunnel': the number of gloomy scenes set in the Hollunder house, the culvert (where the attempted robbery takes place) and Liliom's suicide. It was felt that they probably did not need to make the house as drab as it was described in the original and it could be made more attractive scenically.

Then it was Richard Rodgers' turn to offer his thoughts, and in doing so, he provided the first real glimmer of hope that the project might actually happen. How did he do so? He outlined his ideas for what would eventually become the *Soliloquy.* According to the minutes taken of the meeting, 'Mr. Rodgers suggested a fine musical number for the end of the scene where Liliom discovers he is to be a father, in which he sings with pride of the growth of a boy and then suddenly realises it might be a girl, and changes completely with that thought. It was felt that number would provide the perfect end to Act 1'.[39] This was the moment that brought the idea of doing *Liliom* to life for both Richard Rodgers and Oscar Hammerstein. It gave them the motivation for Liliom's robbery, which had seemed the most impossible thing to do musically. Now, with that obstacle overcome, they felt that all the other challenges could be solved.

The importance of that moment cannot be overstated. In an interview with Arnold Michaelis recorded a few months before his death, Hammerstein said, "without it, I don't think you have a play. If you didn't show Billy Bigelow, the inside of Billy Bigelow, the soft side, the human side, he would just be a lout for whom you'd have no sympathy whatever."

Also, at that meeting Rodgers said that he "felt that the time was ripe for a new and brilliant use of modern orchestration and instrumentation" which could be "more closely integrated with the play." [40]

Another idea discussed was Julie's speech over Liliom's body, which everyone imagined could be turned into a beautiful song. [41]

As noted previously, a major concern was whether a musical theatre audience would accept as the play's hero, an

---

[39] Minutes of meeting, 7 December 1943. Theatre Guild Collection, Beineke Library, Yale University.

[40] Ibid.

[41] In the end, Hammerstein thought the speech as Molnár wrote it was too perfect to change.

unsympathetic character such as Liliom. Shortly after that first production meeting, Helburn wrote to them to report on what she described as an 'inquiring reporter stunt' that she had carried out.

'I've asked a number of people about Liliom himself and they all say they liked him enormously. When I say, "Why? He was such a bastard," their replies vary, but it's usually, "Yes, but he was so human" or, "Such a cute bastard" or, "Such an insolent and charming devil" or, "I agree after you were married to him, he wouldn't supply milk for the baby, but you couldn't help loving him."'[42]

Helburn concluded her stunt by saying, 'I'm sure he gets over much closer to Clark Gable than to Pal Joey'. Presumably referring to Gable's famous role as Rhett Butler in *Gone With The Wind*. In that same report to Dick and Oscar, Helburn added, 'By the way, two Liliom fans told me they remembered the end of the love scene, where Liliom and Julie sit on the bench and smell the acacia blossoms, and it has remained in their minds as high spots in the theatre - so I guess Oscar put his finger on something really lyric [sic]'.

Although much remained to be resolved, sufficient progress had been made for everyone to agree to a second production conference on 20 January 1944. No location is recorded for this meeting.

The minutes of that second meeting began by recording that 'Mr. Rodgers and Mr. Hammerstein said they didn't have time to do much work on it'.[43]

'There was discussion about the character of Julie who Langner wanted to show a lot of spirit and maybe get a job. There was much talk about Liliom and Julie moving to America and Dickie felt there was a good song in what she expected to find there'.

Interestingly, at that early stage, Hammerstein seemed to be looking for light relief to offset the natural darkness of the original, as the minute refers to him saying that Mrs. Hollunder could be

---

[42] Letter to Oscar Hammerstein and Richard Rogers, 17 December 1943. Oscar Hammerstein Collection, Library of Congress.

[43] Minutes of Conference, 20 January. Theatre Guild Collection, Beineke Library, Yale University.

developed amusingly, as could the conflict between her and Mrs. Muskat and that the carpenter could be written comedically.

There was talk of some casting possibilities, including Walter Slezak as the Sparrow. Richard Rodgers suggested that Liliom's dream of heaven could be identified with his dream of America. He saw excellent potential in this for comedic, pictorial and musical treatment.

However, perhaps the most prescient comments at that meeting came from Theresa Helburn, 'Miss Helburn reiterated that upon re-reading the book, she felt the play halfway between CARMEN JONES and OKLAHOMA! in tone - more serious than the latter and not as serious as the former - that the underlying emotional theme had great audience appeal. It seemed to her clearer than ever that a strong love motif underlay everything that Liliom did, and that the heavenly judge understood this completely, even to understanding that his striking of his child, which left no feeling except that of a caress, was again nothing but a thwarted gesture of love'.[44]

If those minutes accurately reflect the comments made by Theresa Helburn at that meeting, and there is no reason to suspect that they do not, then together with the responses she received to her mini opinion poll regarding Billy, we can see just how little concern there seemed to be in the early 1940s regarding what is now seen universally as his completely unacceptable behaviour. Billy hit his wife, he hit his daughter and yet it is him with whom women at the time apparently sympathised, not his victims. It is perhaps a testament to Molnár's writing that this perception of his hero (himself?) remained unchallenged for so long.

The general feeling at the end of the conference was that while the play remained a challenge, it would be an inspiring one to meet. Certainly, there seemed to be sufficient optimism around for Lawrence Langner to write to Joseph Moscowitz at 20th Century Fox on 25 February 1944:

---

[44] Oscar Hammerstein Collection, Library of Congress.

Gentlemen:

Re: LILIOM

Further with respect to our letter to you of 7th January. This letter approved, as you will notice by Messrs. Oscar Hammerstein II and Richard Rodgers, is a declaration of their willingness to write and compose a musical version of LILIOM.

We are, therefore, notifying you that we are proceeding in accordance with our understanding as expressed to you in our letter of 7th January 1944.

Very truly yours,
THE THEATRE GUILD, INC.
Lawrence Langner

Approved:

Oscar Hammerstein II
Richard Rodgers[45]

Even though Rodgers and Hammerstein had yet to sign contracts with the Guild, a musical production based on *Liliom* was announced on 29 February 1944 and first stories appeared in the press the next day. One (unidentified) press cutting reported, 'The Guild having just become imbued over the potentialities of the ballet as an art form, there undoubtedly will be a couple of ballet numbers in the offering, especially one for the scene depicting the court room of the next world'.

In an attempt to solve the location problem, Helburn suggested moving the setting to America, specifically Louisiana. "Move it from Hungary to Louisiana. You boys say you want to write about America. Louisiana is America - but it also has a European flavour. Liliom can be a Creole." Dick and Oscar promised to think about that, and Oscar spent some time researching the Creole locale.

---

[45] Theatre Guild Collection, Beineke Library, Yale University.

In Box 6 of his papers in the Library of Congress are a number of index cards with his various ideas for possible occupations for the Hollunders in New Orleans. One was an antiques shop selling relics of old New Orleans. This would be in the French Quarter, (Vieux Carré). Another possibility was a store selling religious artefacts whilst another idea was for a masker's costume shop; he saw comic potential if Liliom and Ficsur were to plan the robbery here. Liliom could approach a figure and say, "excuse me sir, do you have the time?" At that moment, a skull could fall down, making an eerie atmosphere. Hammerstein even went so far as to sketch out a map of the Quarter showing the location of his possible scenes.

He also drafted suggestions for an opening scene set in New Orleans.

> Crowd gathers round LILIOM as he sings epithets about various people in the amusement park, or as they go into the merry-go-round. Caliope music, banjos, maybe tambourines. Children letting air out of their balloons. Pralines being sold. Baskets of flowers to be sold, carried on Negroes' heads. Noisemakers. People carrying picnic baskets to spread later on the Fair Grounds (This is a racetrack, but think it is also used for picknicking [sic] and frolicking) or in Audubon Park. Color predominates the scene.[46]

A musical's journey from initial concept to opening night is a long one, with many deviations and wrong turnings along the way!

In the end, he decided that he was getting too far away from Molnár, and that the dialect, full of 'zis' and 'zat' and 'zose' would be both horribly corny and difficult to incorporate into lyrics. His decision may have been further influenced by the painful memory of his one of his recent flops, *Sunny River,* a show that had been set in New Orleans and had survived for only six weeks on Broadway. Another New Orleans musical was just not for him.

This is what Hammerstein reported at their next 'Gloat Club' lunch at Sardi's, sometime in February 1944. Mulling over what

[46] Oscar Hammerstein Collection, Library of Congress.

Hammerstein had said, Richard Rodgers suddenly suggested that if he was not at home with the Southern vernacular, why not set it in New England? According to Rodgers' biographer William Hyland, this idea came to Rodgers simply because he had a house in Connecticut and could imagine a New England setting. At first, Oscar considered the idea "downright silly." But, as he went on to say, "it sounded silly only for a few seconds." [47]

Once they settled on New England, it did not take too long to establish a more precise location, which would be a small town on the Maine coast. They also decided to move the time of the play back some thirty years to the 1870s. This solved several problems for Hammerstein. 'I began to see an attractive ensemble—sailors, whalers, girls who worked in the mills up the river, clambakes on near-by islands, an amusement park on the seaboard, things people could do in crowds, people who were strong and alive and lusty, people who had always been depicted on the stage as thin-lipped puritans—a libel I was anxious to refute. The poignancy of the story, I was certain, would not suffer from gaiety of background. It would enhance it. As for the two leading characters, Julie with her courage and inner strength and outward simplicity seemed more indigenous to Maine than to Budapest. Liliom is, of course, an international character, indigenous to nowhere. So now, Dick and I felt that irrational enthusiasm that lures men into the harrowing project of writing a musical play. And away we went'.[48]

Still the writers must have had some doubts because contracts remained unsigned.

Theresa Helburn wrote to Rodgers on 19 May, reminding him 'about putting a little dynamite under the *Liliom* contract. We want to tie up Agnes and discuss others as soon as possible'.[49]

Ultimately, contracts with the Theatre Guild would not be signed until October, and when they were, they were very different to the one that Molnár signed.

They stipulated that, Rodgers and Hammerstein would act as co-producers although the billing would remain 'The Theatre

---

[47] William Hyland, *Richard Rodgers*, p157.

[48] Oscar Hammerstein II. *Turns on a Carousel*. Article for *New York Times*. 15 April 1945.

[49] Theatre Guild Collection, Beineke Library, Yale University.

Guild Presents.' Dick and Oscar would jointly receive a straight 7.5% of the weekly gross, (compared with the norm at that time of 2% each for the composer and lyricist and 1% for the book writer) plus 50% of the Guild's share of profits, after repayment to investors, of which there was no shortage this time. The generous terms of the contract, indicative as to how much the Guild wanted Rodgers and Hammerstein to do the show, were the Guild's own unprompted proposals from the very start. A little later, on the advice of the Guild's lawyers, Theresa Helburn realized that perhaps they had been too generous and tried to get the deal changed.[50] She suggested that as it stood, the Guild would not earn an adequate return on its investment.

Oscar Hammerstein's response was withering. He began by stating, 'The "breakdown" of figures on *Liliom* which depresses you are about as cock-eyed a set of fallacious statistics as anyone was ever depressed by'. He went on, 'In your anxiety to be depressed, you even cast some doubt on whether you can get the play financed on a basis of not more than 50% to the investors. Are you really worried about this? ...' He concluded his response with, 'Beyond all these misconceptions of your plight, there is the very important fact that this was not a deal we extracted from you by any grim bargaining. It was your own proposition made to us by people experienced in producing and familiar with the mathematical contingencies of all kinds of shows. It may be that at the time you were over-anxious to persuade us to write *Liliom* (We were lukewarm at first, you will remember) and that you over-rated the importance of signing us before some other manager wooed us away. Even understanding this, and forgiving it, we are

---

[50] The letter from H. William Fitelson is in the Theatre Guild Collection at Yale University. In it, he says, '*In my opinion, your proposed arrangements with Messrs. Rodgers and Hammerstein with respect to "LILIOM" insofar as The Theatre Guild Inc. is concerned, are entirely inequitable, if not improvident. Originally, I was under the impression that Messrs. Rodgers and Hammerstein would assume the considerable obligation and burden, as well as responsibility of a co- producer with you. I think it is important for you to bear in mind that your success with "OKLAHOMA" [SIC] is in the nature of a "freak" – I need not direct your attention to the substantial risks involved in the production and presentation of musicals, as well as the great amount of time and attention necessary, not only in connection with the production and presentation, but the entire operation*'.

disturbed that after we have worked on the play for four months, and rejected all other offers, the subject of terms is now reopened'.[51]

If Rodgers and Hammerstein's reputation as hard-headed businessmen had not been established before, it certainly was now. It is interesting that this letter came from Oscar Hammerstein rather than Richard Rodgers, the partner with the harder-than-nails reputation. Perhaps they thought their message would carry more weight coming from Mr. Nice Guy. One possible reason for the strength of their feeling on this matter is that when they wrote *Oklahoma!* knowing the parlous state of the Theatre Guild's finances, they did so without receiving any advance.[52] As it turned out, Rodgers and Hammerstein later gave up a part of their share in *Carousel* to Rouben Mamoulian to persuade him to direct the show.

On 23 October 1944, the *New York Post* reported as follows. 'After 15 months, all the legal technicalities involved in the production of the musical version of *Liliom* were settled last week. The smallest percentage: eight-tenths of one percent go to Ferenc Molnár, who merely wrote the play.

At this point, Benjamin Glazer, who as the credited translator of the English version was entitled to a royalty from the musical's receipts, threatened to bring the entire project to a halt. He had heard that Ferenc Molnár was negotiating with the Guild a fee for directorial services which he erroneously thought was a hidden part of the 'rights agreement' in which he was entitled to share. Through his lawyers, he threatened to 'to take action necessary to prevent the consummation of the production of LILIOM ...'[53]

A firm rebuttal, dictated by his lawyer but signed by Lawrence Langner, resolved the issue but the incident must have set a few heartbeats racing.

A month later, Langner circulated a 'Production Set Up' for *Liliom*. Dated 24 November 1944, it gives a fascinating insight as to

---

[51] Theatre Guild Collection, Beineke Library, Yale University.

[52] Contrary to the old joke when in response to the question as to what comes first, the music or the lyrics, the answer is the cheque!

[53] Letter, 22 November 1944, Theatre Guild Collection, Beineke Library, Yale University.

how a show was produced on Broadway at the dawn of its 'Golden Age':

1. Director will direct production including dialogue and songs, confer with scenic artist and costumer in suggesting the work to be done, and getting it satisfactory. Songs with dances to be directed jointly with dance director. Dances by dance director, subject to suggestions by director and producer.
2. Selection of Dance Director, Scenic Artist, Costume Designer, and Cast to be by Producer and Director, with usual author's veto.
3. Rodgers to control orchestra and singing.
4. Producer will be consulted by Director regarding the work being done; Producer will settle all disputes; Rehearsal schedules to be set by Producer in consultation with Director.
5. Scenic artist to consult with Director regarding lighting. Scenic artist will make first set up of lights. Same to be modified if not satisfactory to Director and Producer.
6. Hammerstein, Rodgers, Helburn and Langner together will act as Producer.[54]

Unfortunately, there is no written record of who suggested the name 'Carousel' for the new show. Whoever it was, made an inspired choice given the name evokes not only the fairground ride, but also the cycle of life on which we all go 'round in circles'. What is known is that Bill Fitelson, the Guild's lawyer was asked to check out that the name had not been used for any other vehicle, including any film, and on 26 December 1944, he sent around a memo confirming that since 1915, 19,628 motion pictures had been released, none of them with that name. In those circumstances, he said, they were safe in announcing 'Carousel' as the name for the new musical.

---

[54] Richard Rogers Collection, New York Public Library, Performing Arts Division.

Chapter 4

Opera or Musical - What's in a Name?

Not long after *Oklahoma!* opened on Broadway, Richard Rodgers received a call from Sam Goldwyn, the flamboyant, Hollywood producer. He was coming to New York and obviously wanted to see the show that all America was talking about. Tickets were duly provided and Rodgers together with Oscar Hammerstein arranged to meet him after the performance.

Goldwyn was famous for his one-liners, "A contract isn't worth the paper it's written on" and "Go see it and see for yourself why you shouldn't see it," are just a couple of examples.

He had another one ready for Rodgers and Hammerstein when he came out of the theatre, "You know what you boys should do now?" he asked before answering his own question, "Shoot yourselves!"

The 'boys' did not need Sam Goldwyn's humour to remind them that no matter how good their second show might be, negative comparisons with their first were almost inevitable. They were fully aware that whilst the success of that first show gave them unprecedented power, at the same time, it made them rather vulnerable, with everyone on Broadway wondering what they would do next, including some, no doubt, who would be only too happy to see them reverting to the status of mere mortals.

Hammerstein admitted as much in November 1944 when he took time out from writing the new show to comment on the unique position in which he and his partner found themselves. "We're all fools," he said. "No matter what we do, everyone is bound to say, 'This is not another *Oklahoma!*' It isn't trying to be, but that will make no difference. As a matter of fact, every musical play that everyone else writes meets the same irrelevant comment, so that every time a new musical opens, *Oklahoma!* gets another string of good notices."

Similarly, on that weight of expectation after *Oklahoma!* Rodgers recalled in a 1974 interview for the BBC, "Always after your first big success, people wonder if you are going to be able to do another one."

So, they were not going to shoot themselves. Nor were they going to retire. What they would do is meet the challenge of creating a worthy successor to *Oklahoma!* head on. But choosing the subject on which to base it was not easy.

Notwithstanding all their initial reservations, they decided to continue with Molnár's dark, fantastical play, because it required so much more, musically, dramatically and choreographically, than its predecessor. Their hope was that for all its many problems, it was so far removed from their first show that the inevitable comparisons might be considered invidious.

The differences are considerable. Just compare the two sets of principal characters. Molnár's Liliom and Julie are much deeper and far more complex than Lynn Riggs' Curly and Laurey in *Green Grow the Lilacs.* Clara Györgyey described them succinctly in her biography of Molnár, 'The dualistic hero, Andreas Zavoczky (Liliom), is not a villain, only a maladjusted creature who ends up doing the wrong things in spite of all the possible good intentions. This braggart dreamer is an obstinate nonconformist, a primitive person with a vicious temper, yet a noble man full of compassion. When he cries, "I am going to be a father," it is the cry both of a child receiving a much-coveted toy, and of an archetypal man's joy over his virility and the promise of progeny. Julie … emerges as the eternal female ideal. She loves unselfishly, with undemanding devotion and endurance. With almost supernatural insight and common sense, she grasps the realities of life and the true nature of her man ... She is taciturn and inarticulate but her farewell speech to her husband is genuinely moving and poetic'.[55]

With characters as richly drawn as these, it is no wonder Puccini travelled to Budapest to try and persuade Molnár to grant him the musical rights to his play. Their bittersweet story together with its element of fantasy, was one that was ideally suited to the opera stage. But would it work as a Broadway musical and how do you write such a show?

By its very nature, are you not forced to create a piece of musical theatre unlike any other? Oscar Hammerstein certainly thought so. In an article he wrote for the *New York Times* on setting *Liliom* to music he reflected that 'the very difficulties of the job we knew would lead us into unusual devices. We knew we wouldn't

---

[55] Clara Györgyey. *Ferenc Molnár.* p154.

wind up with a conventional musical comedy. It was obvious that we would have to mix in values from the dramatic stage and opera'. [56]

Rodgers too, seems to have sensed that it would present his greatest musical challenge to date. Unlike his friend George Gershwin, Rodgers had no desire to swap Broadway for Carnegie Hall. His ambitions were firmly rooted in musical theatre. Nonetheless, he had been tremendously impressed by *Porgy and Bess.* Gershwin played the score for Dick and his wife Dorothy at their house one evening before its premiere and they were at the first night of the opera at the Alvin Theatre on 10 October 1935. The very next day, Rodgers felt compelled to write to Gershwin, 'I've loved the tunes ever since you played them for us here one night but I never thought I'd sit in a theatre and feel my throat stopped up time after time. Let them never say that Mr. Gershwin can't be tender; you kicked hell out of me, for one'.[57]

Rodgers was not renowned for handing out lavish praise to all and sundry; if he said something was "adequate," you knew it was actually pretty good. So, for him to admit that Gershwin "kicked hell" out of him must be seen as a sign of his very real admiration for his friend's masterpiece. But did it signify something more? We know Rodgers was striving towards creating a more mature musical theatre. Did seeing *Porgy and Bess* trigger an awareness of how much further he still had to go? Furthermore, two years later, in what must have been a huge shock to an arch hypochondriac like Rodgers, George Gershwin was dead from a brain tumour at the age of thirty-eight, a dreadful reminder that time might not be on his side if he was to fulfil all his ambitions.

Shortly thereafter, he began to take further piano lessons with Gershwin's former teacher Herman Wasserman. Under his tuition, Rodgers not only honed his piano skills but also studied anew the harmonies and melodies of the great romantics, such as Brahms and Schumann. Precisely why he started studying again at this time, cannot be stated with certainty. Was it merely to improve his skill as a pianist? Did he suddenly feel his musical education was lacking? Or were the lessons merely to provide a

---

[56] Oscar Hammerstein Collection, Library of Congress.

[57] Letter, 11 October 1935, Richard Rogers Collection, New York Public Library, Performing Arts Division.

distraction from the deterioration of his relationship with Larry Hart?

Following these sessions with Wasserman, Mary Rodgers thought that her father's music whilst it did not lose the sparkle and vitality of his earlier work, deepened and darkened, becoming richer and more serious. One might also add dramatic to that list of adjectives, the very quality he would need when he teamed up with Oscar Hammerstein.

Certainly, his approach to composing the score for *Carousel* was unlike that for any other he had written, and he said as much in some of the many interviews he gave with various opera critics in the run up to the show's opening.

The most in depth interview he gave was with Olin Downes, whose usual beat as music critic of the *New York Times* was writing about composers such as Prokofiev, Shostakovich, Ives, Stravinsky and above all, Sibelius. For years, Downes had been chairman of the Metropolitan Opera Quiz, broadcast on Saturday afternoons during the intervals of live radio relays from the Met. Clearly though, he had a fascination for what Rodgers and Hammerstein were doing with musical theatre for he had previously written a lengthy article about *Oklahoma!* which he called *Broadway's Gift To Opera – 'Oklahoma' [sic] Shows One of the Ways to an Integrated and Indigenous Form of American Lyric Theatre.* He wrote that he found *Oklahoma!* to be a delightful show, paying tribute to the 'especially good tunes by Richard Rodgers and excellent lyrics of Oscar Hammerstein II ...' and concluded with the opinion that he considered it to be heading in 'a direction that American opera of native cast might take in the period before us. For look you: real national opera has always begun somewhere in the vicinity of the position now occupied by *Oklahoma [sic].*'

Now, on 24 December 1944, following a lengthy interview he conducted with Richard Rodgers, Downes advised his readers that the 'opera' Rodgers and Hammerstein were currently preparing, based on Ferenc Molnár's *Liliom* was due to premier that coming March.

He began this new article by again referring to the quality and the success of *Oklahoma!* and continued by reporting the challenges of turning such a serious play as *Liliom* into a musical. From Rodgers' description of his and Hammerstein's ideas for the book and score, Downes understood that this new show was going to be very different in tone from its predecessor. Once again, Rodgers voiced their concerns about audience expectations, not only because their *Liliom* was not intended to be another *Oklahoma!,* but also because of what they were attempting to do to a much-loved classic. Downes however, had the foresight to advise his readers, that if Rodgers and Hammerstein succeeded, they might create a piece of far greater significance than anything that America's native musical theatre had so far produced.

Much of the article of course, focussed on the music. Rodgers discussed at length his plans for an orchestra far larger than usual, describing it as being of 'nearly symphonic calibre'. He explained that with full brass and woodwind sections one could create a *fortissimo* quite different from that produced by a handful of instruments simply lacerating the air. In this show, the quality of sound produced by the orchestra was going to be crucial.

Rodgers also explained his decision not to have an overture. No one listened to them he believed, so what was the point? (American audiences were notorious for arriving late to the theatre, always rushing in, banging seats, and falling over each other). He did promise however, that he would set the tone for the second act, by having an *entr'acte* which would summarise the main musical and dramatic ideas.

Instead of the overture, he told Downes of his plans for the music for the Prologue; a series of waltzes arranged for brass and woodwind, which would be dictated by the structure of the play and replicate the steady grind of a carousel. Olin Downes likened Rodgers' decision not to have an overture to similar decisions taken by some of the great opera composers, Richard Strauss, Verdi and Puccini.

Finally, Rodgers set out for Downes his overall ambition for the score. Although the songs would be separated by dialogue rather than traditional operatic recitative, his intention was that the score should be looked upon as one organic piece, with the songs, themselves organic, developing naturally from the dialogue and in complete harmony with the dramatic needs of the play. In closing his article, Downes noted that notwithstanding the challenges confronting him, writing this musical version of *Liliom* was a task in which Rodgers was 'intensely and happily engaged'.

Another interview with Richard Rodgers was conducted by Warren Smith of the *Boston Post* and appeared on 8 April 1945. It was entitled, 'Including the Opera and Mr. Rodgers's remarkable Music for *Carousel*'. Smith asked Rodgers if *Carousel* was not, by degree, more operatic than *Oklahoma!* Rodgers agreed that it was but cautioned, "we don't wish to scare people off by telling them so." This may have been a touch of tongue-in-cheek humour from the composer, or it may have reflected the doubt he had about the project that persisted from the very beginning, perhaps reinforced by the uncertain reception the show received in New Haven.

Rodgers gave a further insight to his thinking in yet another interview whilst the show was trying out in Boston, this time with Elinor Hughes of the *Boston Herald* and entitled, 'Rodgers and Hammerstein Discuss Their New Musical'.

'Songs for musical shows have come to mean, more and more, a tenor or a baritone coming out and singing "I Love You" partly at a blushing soprano, but mostly at the audience. The words convey nothing, there is no emotion involved; it is, in short, just a convention song, having nothing to do with the story and nothing whatever in relation to character or situation. Music must not only spring from character and situation, but it must also advance them. In the case of this production, which is definitely more of a musical play, almost a music drama, than it is a musical comedy, we have no recitative, but music is used to develop and forward the action whether through actual song numbers or ballets or by itself. The first act, for example, is two-thirds music to one-third dialogue." He also commented on the reason he insisted on a larger than usual orchestra. "There are more strings as well as more brass and the whole effect will, I hope, be not so much an increase in noise but in quality and richness of tone."[58]

Rodgers emphasised this point regarding the quality of the sound in a conversation with John Fearnley who, on looking into the packed orchestra pit asked, "Dick, why sixteen violins?" (Fearnley had mistakenly included the violas as part of the violin section). Rodgers replied, "Because sixteen can play softer than four."

Once, when asked if he had ever considered writing an opera, Rodgers admitted that he and Hammerstein were sorely tempted a couple of times. He imagined *Carousel* in those terms

---

[58] Elinor Hughes, *Boston Herald,* 27 March 1945, Theatre Guild Collection at Beineke Library, Yale University.

and believed they "came very close to opera in the Majestic Theatre" (where the musical opened). "I had a brass section in there the size of the Met. Only I didn't let them play as loud. I had forty men in the pit ... There's much that is operatic in the music ... but I have found more flexibility in the theatre and I like this freedom."

Although Rodgers was a lover of classical music and opera, (he spent every Saturday night as a teenager at the Met, taking advantage of special student prices[59]), he was not comfortable with the idea of having his music sung in the formal, somewhat self-conscious style used by professional opera singers. In his mind, such a singing style destroyed the intimacy, naturalness and realism that he required to tell the story of the show. Certainly, he wanted trained voices, but ones that could seem natural and untrained; and if the owner of such a voice looked good and could act as well, then Rodgers was a very happy man indeed.

So, it seems certain that they did not seriously consider turning *Liliom* into what might be considered a European-style grand opera, even though, just as Puccini had twenty-five years earlier, they realised that it was a story that lent itself to the medium.

What they did seek to do, however, was to advance considerably, as Theresa Helburn foresaw, American musical theatre as a new indigenous art form that began with *Show Boat,* continued with *Porgy and Bess* and *Oklahoma!* and would develop further through the 1940s and 1950s.

Interestingly, when orchestrator Don Walker first saw Rodgers' score, he was so impressed with it that he decided that he would treat *Carousel* as though it were a Puccini opera.[60] He said, "I always felt it was an opera. It should sound different from other shows. This show has its own character and sound, and you don't want to mess it up."[61]

---

59 Richard Rodgers. *Musical Stages,* p21.

60 Ted Chapin. Rogers & Hammerstein Organisation inter-office memo of conversation with Don Walker. 10 March 1986.

61 Letter from Jon Alan Conrad to Ted Chapin summarising interview with Don Walker, 7 October 1987.

As we shall see later, Walker was not wrong, for today, *Carousel* is performed frequently in opera houses, as well as in conventional musical theatres.

Not long after Oscar Hammerstein died on 22 August 1960, Richard Rodgers was invited to write an article called 'Opera and Broadway' for the magazine *Opera News*. The article was published on 25 February 1961 and in it, Rodgers examined the differences between the two art forms and also strongly made the case that the best of Broadway 'might be called, without apology or self-consciousness, American opera'. Whilst some might consider the article self-serving, it is a subject about which the composer spoke most passionately and for that reason, I think it is worthwhile quoting from it at length.

'Over the past two or three decades, it has become increasingly difficult to pigeonhole the works of our musical theatre into the convenient categories of opera, music drama, "play with music," or even "musical" and musical comedy. The line between them has grown elastic; there has been a healthy interchange of devices, ideas and themes among them. The one major difference seems to lie in where they are produced: opera house or theatre.

'Opera, states the *Harvard Dictionary of Music*, is "a drama, either tragic or comic, sung throughout, with appropriate scenery and acting, to the accompaniment of an orchestra." According to this flexible and useful definition, it is therefore, a play in which all the lines are sung rather than spoken. Dialogue interspersed with song was introduced with the development of comic opera, but such composers as Mozart and Beethoven used spoken dialogue even in serious operas. They made it legal, so to speak, for an opera even when not "sung throughout." In opera, then, all the arts combine: music, both vocal and instrumental, poetry, acting, design - and dancing. All of these are joined into a perfectly integrated (that is the popular word these days) whole. To the extent that the pieces mesh and match, so will the work be popular and successful. But what is even more important is that our latter-day definition of opera could serve equally well for *Carmen* - or *Show Boat, Porgy and Bess* and *Carousel.*

'Obviously, none of these falls into the category of traditional idea of an opera. As the form has developed over an even shorter period, it has become clear that the "plays with music" or musical comedies of our Broadway theatre might be called, without apology or self-consciousness, American opera'.

Talking about the development of early twentieth century musicals, Rodgers explained, '... during the twenties, we younger composers and lyricists - Irving Berlin, Jerome Kern, Oscar Hammerstein II, George and Ira Gershwin, Vincent Youmans, Lorenz Hart and I, were breaking ground for a native American musical theatre. We drew on everyday life for our themes, our musical ideas, our language. We did this unconsciously, for we were more concerned with doing our work as well as we could. Making history was incidental.

'A musical play completely in the American mould, with an American story, sung in American English to music characteristically American, was inevitably on its way'.

Rodgers was not afraid to defend his work, and those of his colleagues as an art form.

'Broadway and Tin Pan Alley have hardly been acknowledged as spawners of art - not at least, until fairly recently. Part of the problem may have been our inability to recognize our own art when it was presented to us. But like jazz, another purely American contribution, the musicals of Broadway, for all their commercial success, are just that. Aside from the songs, the developing maturity of the books has contributed to this artistic status, so has the close integration (opera-like in its way) of songs, dance and story. The attention given to the book of a musical led not only to the telling of stories that made sense, but to the choice of more varied and adult subjects'.

Rodgers then discussed the problems he and Hammerstein faced with their first two shows - and had a little dig at all those smart alecks who predicted that 'Helburn's Folly' would be a dire flop.

'In *Oklahoma!* (1943), the songs and dances flowed naturally out of the story while remaining natural to the personalities of our characters. Had it failed, *Oklahoma!* would probably have been dismissed as too experimental, but since it succeeded, it is called innovational instead. The very elements that contributed to its simple charm were those that brought objections from "Those Who Know". For example, who would open a Broadway musical with a slow song instead of a lively number with lots of girls? But we used the gentle *Oh What a Beautiful Mornin'* to open *Oklahoma!*

and we used dances by Agnes de Mille that were related to the story clearly expressing the state of mind of the characters. Some felt that one of the songs, *Lonely Room,* at once grim and poignant, did not belong in a light musical. It was too serious they claimed; but it did present an insight into the character of Jud and made him an understandable, less hateful villain.

'*Carousel* (1945), our next production, posed other problems. Not only did it lack a real villain, but its hero died long before the end of the show.[62] Since it was based on Ferenc Molnár's *Liliom,* we had the further complication of a European setting; we struggled with that for a long time until one day, the happy thought came to me to set it in New England. All the collaborators agreed, and we were able to go on with our adaptation. With some changes in the book, authorized by Molnár, we could adapt his universal theme to our American scene'.

After referring to some of the great shows of the era, including *My Fair Lady, Guys and Dolls, Kiss Me Kate, Fiorello!* and *West Side Story,* he concluded his article as follows.

'The distinctive form that has developed in our musical theatre is not, of course, grand opera in the traditional sense. It is rather musico-dramatic expression particularly native to us; to borrow a term from the industry, it is a product of American know-how. This implies a marriage, not only of the arts but also of technical aspects of modern stagecraft. When all those elements blend into a gratifying evening in the musical theatre, we can take pride in it and enjoy it. The labels don't matter at all'.

---

[62] I doubt that were he writing about *Carousel* today, Rodgers would have used the word 'hero' to describe Billy Bigelow.

Chapter 5

Crafting the Libretto

For Oscar Hammerstein, the early months of 1944 were taken up with work on *State Fair* which was expected to keep him busy either at home, or in Hollywood until June. Then, as he wrote to Jerome Kern, 'I am going back to Doylestown to keep a promise I have faithfully made myself to rest for from four to six weeks and do nothing at all. After that, I start work on the adaptation of *Liliom* which I am doing with Dick for the Theatre Guild. This will go into rehearsal in February and that would bring the New York opening not very much before a year from now'.[63] (He must have been psychic. The actual New York opening was a year and a day later).

As it turned out, just two weeks after writing that letter, Hammerstein's timetable was put in jeopardy when he was laid low by an attack of suspected appendicitis that was eventually diagnosed as diverticulosis, a condition that would require surgery at New York's Doctors Hospital. This caused the postponement of his trip to California but brought forward the planned period of rest at his farm, and his starting work on *Liliom*. He, and no doubt Dick Rodgers too, were substantially cheered up by the award that month of a special Pulitzer Prize for *Oklahoma!*

Despite his good intentions, in another letter, this time to his uncle Arthur on 31 August, he said he would be returning to Doylestown in a couple of weeks to start on *Liliom* which he had had to neglect. That is not to say there was no work being done on the new show. Hammerstein by then, had undertaken much of his preliminary research, something which he was fastidious about. He was a stickler for accuracy and meticulous about language and dialect, so for him, starting work on any new project meant doing his homework - and *Liliom* would require more than most.

Molnár himself had ensured that his play would be true to the people it portrayed. His biographer described his approach. 'The dialogue is pungent with idioms and the racy folksiness of the social class it represents. The warm, emotional tone is interspersed

---

[63] Letter, 18 April 1944, Oscar Hammerstein Collection, Library of Congress.

with pathos, delicate irony and rhapsodic passion. Carefully controlled comic relief is provided - the play permits laughter, but only occasionally and wryly. The humour is sardonic, evoking both delight and awe'.[64]

The challenge for Hammerstein was to find a way to preserve Molnár's literary integrity in the musical's new setting on the Maine coast where the people had their own idioms and racy folksiness. 'I was afraid of Molnár', Hammerstein admitted. 'He very generously and flatteringly turned his play over to us to do with what we would. We were determined to justify his confidence, but in our own way. We were certain that this should be truly a musical play based on *Liliom,* not *Liliom* with some songs added. We must sacrifice certain dialogue values and attempt to create musical compensations - singing and dancing expressions of the same story. This was the basis of my fear of Molnár - and incidentally, of all the original *Liliom* fans. Would he - and they - accept this compensation theory, provided of course that in our own medium, we would be faithful to the original story as well as to its characterisations'.[65]

As it turned out, so fortuitous was the choice of the Maine Coast, that Hammerstein had less reason to fear offending Molnár than he might have realised. The characters in *Liliom* live at the bottom of the social scale and their lives, choices and problems tend to be the same the world over. They certainly would have been familiar to the fishermen and mill workers in 1870s New England. Hammerstein had to get the dialect right, but he was able to retain far more of Molnár's play than he might first have imagined.

When George Gershwin started work on *Porgy and Bess,* in his quest for cultural accuracy, he was able to move for a while to Folly Island, South Carolina, to immerse himself in the lifestyle and music of the indigenous population.

Hammerstein could not travel back in time to visit 1870s Maine, so for his research into the dialects, speech patterns, and customs of that time and place, he did the next best thing. With the assistance of his twenty-two-year-old daughter Alice, he acquired

---

[64] Clara Györgyey, *Ferenc Molnár,* p154.

[65] Oscar Hammerstein. *Turns on a Carousel, New York Times,* 15 April 1945.

a collection of books, plays and other documents which would have to serve as his time machine.

Details of the books he obtained are among the collection of his papers in the Library of Congress. Some were used for what he termed 'color' some for 'dialect' and others for 'language'. They were also a source for the character names that would feature in the musical.

So it was, that *The Minister's Housekeeper,* a short story featured in an 1872 collection called *Oldtown Fireside Stories* by Harriet Beecher Stowe, provided the names 'Pipperidge', 'Snow', 'Bascome'[66] and 'Bigelow'. Stowe, who lived for a while in Bangor, Maine also inspired some of *Carousel's* dialogue and lyrics. Phrases such as 'corn poppin' on a shovel' and 'rustlin' of bonnets' were borrowed by Hammerstein from her story.

The 1923 Pulitzer Prize winning play *Icebound,* by Owen Davis, a native of Maine, was the source for the names 'Jordan', 'Nettie', 'Orin' and 'Seldon', whilst the 1926 play, *Ned McCobb's Daughter* by Sidney Howard, contributed the name 'Carrie' as well as samples of dialogue, "He don't say much but what he does say is awful pithy," for example, and Julie's pointed "'D ruther not say."

Another important source was *Mainstays of Maine,* a 1944 book by the lifelong Maine dwelling, Pulitzer Prize winning poet and author Robert P. Coffin. Described as a collection of essays about, and recipes from, Maine, Hammerstein used this book for his many references to food in the show, and as we shall see, cleverly incorporated Coffin's recipe for codfish chowder into the lyrics of *This Was A Real Nice Clambake.*

Edwin Mitchell's *Maine Summer,* a book about the coast and islands of Maine provided further material, as did *Our Way Down East* by Elinor Graham. Two books by Maine-born author, Mary Ellen Chase, *Silas Crockett* and *Mary Peters,* as well as her autobiography, *A Goodly Fellowship,* were consulted.

Other books that were mentioned amongst Hammerstein's papers were, *Time out of Mind* by Rachel Field; *Assignment Down East* by Henry Buckston; *Summer Yesterdays in Maine* by Willard

---

[66] Early drafts kept wavering between 'Bascome' and 'Bascombe'. It was not until the final version of the script that they settled on 'Bascombe'.

Sperry; *Maine* by Irvin Cobb, and last but not least, *American Sketches* by Charles Dickens.

Alice Hammerstein frequently assisted her father with his research and provided a lot of help to him on *Carousel.* In an interview in later life with theatre historian Amy Asch for *Playbill,* Alice spoke of how she researched what was going on in New England at the time the show was set, going into such detail as the type of trolley cars that were in use, the kind of policeman they had and much other peripheral stuff. She had even gone so far as to provide drawings of objects she was reading about.[67] Her father thanked her but told her he really didn't need all that and added that she had 'research poisoning', which Alice admitted was true.

Still, Hammerstein took his research seriously and consequently, he did not confine himself to the books and plays above. Julie and Carrie would be workers in the local mill so there are two pages of notes (presumably provided by Alice) on technical terms relating to cotton mills. He also learned about the extremely harsh, strict, and male-dominated conditions under which the girls worked, and which he would incorporate into the show.[68]

To make Mr. Snow appear even more pompous, Hammerstein found out all there was to know about herrings and sardines and gave him a half page of dialogue on the subject. Fortunately for Carrie, (and the audience), this was cut before the show opened in New Haven.

He spent time studying the demographics of Maine, its flora, fauna, industry, harbours and politics. Oscar even had Alice drop him a note outlining the history of the revolver, thereby ensuring that the replica prop used in the robbery scene was of a weapon that would have been available in 1874.

When Agnes de Mille devised her choreography for the *Blow High, Blow Low* dance, she wanted to incorporate some cries from the sailors. Once again, Oscar made sure that those cries would be the genuine cries used by whaler crews in the 1870s.

---

[67] *Playbill,* 19 September 2011.

[68] Nicholas Hytner made a special feature of the harsh condition in the mills in his version of the Prologue for the 1992 National Theatre production.

All this research not only helped with the details outlined above; it also provided the means by which he resolved one of the issues which bothered both Hammerstein and Rodgers so much when the idea of musicalizing *Liliom* was first put to them. What to do about the dark and gloomy interiors in which the original play was set.

Within the books he studied, he found references to both the loveliness of the Maine coastal region in June, and to the island picnics which accompany the arrival of spring. He read too about clambakes and treasure hunts. This material would prove invaluable. Not only did it provide the ideas for a couple of major songs, but it also enabled him to replace the dark interior scenes with more appealing exteriors.

Armed with the benefit of this research, he could think about how the new show might take shape. It was at this point that he and Dick Rodgers got together to begin the serious business of writing the musical version of *Liliom.* Rodgers, his wife Dorothy, and children Mary, thirteen and Linda, nine, decamped to the Hammersteins' Highland Farm in Doylestown, Pennsylvania for working weekends throughout the summer.

Meanwhile, other things had been happening in the background in preparation for the new musical. In April, the pair held early talks with Agnes de Mille about the show. They had also had discussions with Christine Johnson, a rising young star of the Metropolitan Opera, about what eventually would become the role of Nettie Fowler.[69] The full story of how she got her part is told in a later chapter, as is the story of how John Raitt had been signed up that Spring for the touring production of *Oklahoma!* but with the *Liliom* project in mind.

During those weekends in Pennsylvania, whilst their wives (Mrs. Hammerstein was also a Dorothy) swapped stories about interior design, the profession of them both, and the children played, (often with the Hammersteins young neighbour Stephen Sondheim, for whom Oscar would act as a surrogate father, and with whom Mary formed a lifelong friendship), the two writers set about their work. Their approach was as it had been for *Oklahoma!* with long sessions discussing every aspect of the show.

---

[69] Johnson was offered a contract in August 1944 at $300 per week rising to $400 if she stayed in the role for a second year.

Hammerstein explained this process more fully in his book *Lyrics.*[70]

'Dick and I stay very close together while drawing up the blueprint of a play. Before we start to put words or notes on paper, we have agreed on a very definite and complete outline, and we have decided how much of the story shall be told in dialogue and how much in song. We try to use music as much as we can …

'After we have passed the blueprint stage, we then work together on the interior problems. We approach the spots we have chosen for songs and we discuss each song very carefully. It is not at all unlikely that Dick will give me valuable lyric ideas and I, on the other hand, frequently contribute important suggestions for the music. I don't mean to imply that I give him ideas for melodies. I have no melodic gift whatsoever, but I have a feeling for treatment of a score, ideas for its structure'.[71]

This part of the process was spread over many weeks but once it was completed, they tended to work separately, Hammerstein staying on his farm to continue his work on the book and lyrics, before heading back to the city in the autumn. Rodgers could be found either at his summer home in Connecticut or at his New York apartment. He would not actually start composing until he had received a lyric, or preferably several, from Hammerstein, but based on his conversations with his partner, he would be thinking carefully about the musical challenges that lay ahead.

A copy of what Hammerstein referred to as the 'blueprint' for *Carousel* survives among the papers in his collection at the Library of Congress. It is headed 'LILIOM OUTLINE'. It is immediately recognisable as the musical we know today even though it still uses the names of the characters in *Liliom* to which it is remarkably faithful. Molnár's drab interiors have been moved outdoors. Spots are indicated where songs might be inserted and dances too. Possible song titles are suggested with outlines for their subject matter. All of this, the result of those weeks of discussion, is set out in this four-page outline. One character has been added, albeit temporarily, and of course other changes would be made, but the essentials are all there. The outline is reproduced in full at Appendix 1.

---

[70] Oscar Hammerstein II, *Lyrics,* p15.

[71] Ibid.

Although not always obvious, it is possible to identify many of the songs that appeared in the final version of the musical from their tentative descriptions in the outline.

As a result, *What's on Your Mind* became *You're a Queer One, Julie Jordan. The Wind Blows the Blossoms* developed into *The Bench Scene, (including If I Loved You.) Bustin' Out all Over* needs no clarification and the *Sea Chanty* of course, is *Blow High, Blow Low. Put Your Faith in Sardines and Me* became the introduction to *When the Children Are Asleep; I'm Going to Have a Baby* was the crucial song idea that Rodgers identified at the first meeting back in December and became *Soliloquy. A Song Drifts Over the Bay* turned into *A Real Nice Clambake. Female Duet* became *What's the Use of Wond'rin'* which in the 9 January draft is sung by Nettie and Julie before *You'll Never Walk Alone.*

The other song ideas fell by the wayside to be replaced by those that we now know. The positioning of some also changed as the full script developed.

The outline still retained some of Molnár's interior scenes and these were included in the 9 January script. Only during the try-outs were these eliminated, one, the interior of Nettie's Parlour after the robbery, at the suggestion of Molnár himself. The 'dirty hovel' that featured prominently in the original, was nowhere to be found.

The main characters in *Liliom* all reappear in *Carousel* and are to be found in the outline. Liliom is the Hungarian word for a lily, but in the context of the play, was used as a pejorative term for a tough guy, a bully, or a lout. Liliom's actual name in the play, though it is hardly used, is Andreas Zavoczky. In the musical, he becomes Billy Bigelow - note that the name Billy sounds like lily while Bigelow - the name Hammerstein chose for him from Stowe's book *Oldtown Fireside Stories,* has three syllables, and trips off the tongue just like Liliom. It also rhymes with gigolo, which may or may not have been a conscious choice. Though his name has changed, the character remains the same and his occupation continues to be that of a barker on a carousel. Hammerstein gave Billy more of a back story, suggesting that he originally came from New York and previously had worked as a barker on Coney Island. As we shall see, this history makes him even more of an outsider to the close-knit New England community amongst which he is now living. British Director, Jo Davies has directed

Carousel several times and believes it has an epic quality. In her highly regarded 2012 production for Opera North, she picked up on Billy's background detail and taking it further, she used the Prologue to show his growth from an abused, neglected child into the potentially violent fairground barker he became. It does not, of course, provide an excuse for his behaviour but knowing as we do today that a significant number of abusers were themselves abused as children, it does provide an understandable context.

Julie Zeller who was a maid of all work for a Budapest family in *Liliom,* is renamed Julie Jordan; she is now an employee at the local cotton mill; her best friend and co-worker, Marie becomes Carrie Pipperidge and works alongside Julie at the mill.

The carousel owner and Billy's employer in the play, Mrs. Muskat is now named Mrs. Mullin. Because we first see her threatening Julie and Carrie, and then dismissing Billy, it is easy to think of her as little more than a pantomime villain, but her role is much more nuanced than that. She has inherited the carousel from her deceased husband and now sees herself as something of an entrepreneur. She is hard and she is a fighter, as she must be to survive in a man's world; but as is apparent from the start, her interest in Billy is more than merely professional, and she is the only person in the play, other than Julie, who truly cares about him, a fact that Julie acknowledges when she allows her a moment besides Billy's body after his suicide.

Liliom's ne'er do well friend in the original is known simply as Ficsur, (The Sparrow), and has no apparent job. Hammerstein made him a sailor on a whaleboat and at first, gave him the name Tom Trainor. He then realised that name was too much like that of *Los Angeles Times* war correspondent Tom Treanor, who had been killed in France a few months earlier. The character was subsequently renamed Jigger Craigin.

Marie's fiancé in the original, Wolf Beilfield becomes Enoch (Wilbur in the first draft) Snow. Beilfield was an ambitious hotel porter in the play whereas Enoch Snow starts the musical as the owner of a small herring boat, but he is a man with big dreams.

Though names and occupations have changed, in terms of personality, the characters remained mostly as Molnár created them; one exception to this is the Wolf Beilfield/Enoch Snow character.

In *Liliom,* Beilfield is a Jew, (there are several unflattering references to Jews in the play even though Molnár himself was Jewish,) and is driven solely by his desire to get on in the world.[72] Snow, on the other hand, whilst on the surface might appear to be a figure of fun, is in fact, an ambitious, at times insufferably pompous control freak who regards Carrie as little more than a child-bearing machine. He is a stark reminder that abuse can take many forms.

There is a significant change to another of Molnár's characters. In the play, Mother Hollunder, Julie's aunt, is a most unlikeable character. Rather grudgingly, she has allowed Julie and Liliom to move in with her and she is constantly belittling him. Throughout the play, she tries desperately to persuade Julie to leave Liliom for a widowed carpenter. Julie, of course, has not the slightest interest in doing so, not even after Liliom dies.

In *Carousel,* Mother Hollunder becomes Julie's cousin, Nettie Fowler, a far more sympathetic character, who cares, not just for Julie, but for her entire community. There are obvious similarities between this character, and Aunt Eller in *Oklahoma!* Both are strong, proud women, compassionate and generous but at the same time no pushover: they have a firm belief that you must stand on your own two feet to fight for the life you want. These wise, sympathetic female characters are a feature of Rodgers and Hammerstein musicals and there is a probable reason for that. Hammerstein's own mother Allie, whom he adored, died at the early age of thirty-four when Oscar was just fifteen. Her death affected him deeply, and consciously or not, he honoured her memory in many of his shows. As well as Aunt Eller in *Oklahoma!* and Nettie Fowler in *Carousel,* there is Lady Thiang in *The King and I* and Madam Liang in *Flower Drum Song*. Finally, of course, there is the Mother Abbess in *The Sound of Music.*

---

[72] Why Molnár made these unflattering references to Jews is difficult to comprehend. Whilst not observant, he did not seek to hide his Jewishness and was most distressed when he learned the fate of the Hungarian Jewish population which was almost entirely wiped out in the Holocaust, and that of his many Jewish friends who did not escape. Perhaps, when writing *Liliom* in 1909, it was his way of showing how widespread anti-Semitism was in Hungary at that time.

The importance of the community is another prominent feature in Rodgers and Hammerstein shows and it is of particular significance in *Carousel.* Not only do the local millworkers and fishermen form the singing and dancing choruses, always an important consideration in a musical, but they have a dramatic function too. The easy togetherness of this tight-knit coastal community is in stark contrast to independent thinking Julie, *(You're a Queer One, Julie Jordan)* and especially Billy, *(He's a pretty fly gazaybo. Come up from Coney Island,)* who are perceived as outsiders, tolerated rather than welcomed by the majority. We will see during the ballet in Act 2 that this wariness of the unknown is passed down from one generation to the next and that fifteen years later, Louise, Julie and Billy's daughter is as much an outsider as her parents were.

In Hammerstein's original outline, there was one character added who definitely did not appear in *Liliom.* This is the guitar-strumming Dwight. He was created as an alternative suitor to Carrie but was quickly discarded when they realised that he would be part of a storyline that was far too similar to the Ado Annie, Will Parker, Ali Hakim triangle in *Oklahoma!*

***

It is often said that one of the ways in which *Oklahoma!* redefined the American musical was in its opening scene in which the curtain rises not on a glamorous set and a chorus line of beautiful girls, but on an elderly woman churning butter, sitting alone on a bare stage in front of a simple, painted backdrop.

Daring though that was, *Carousel's* is bolder still, opening as it does with a dialogue-free Prologue which grabs the audience's attention the moment the curtain rises on a teeming amusement park dominated by 'Mullin's Carousel' at right centre of the stage. A note to the libretto explains how the scene is to be played:

> This scene is set to the music of a waltz suite. The only sound comes from the orchestra pit. The pantomimic action is synchronised to the music, but it is in no sense, a ballet treatment.

Hammerstein's *Carousel* Prologue, which takes up four and a half pages in the final script, takes its cue from Molnár's in *Liliom.*[73] Whereas, in the original, the only accompaniment to the onstage action is that of a fairground organ, Rodgers and Hammerstein saw the possibility of using music to enhance the events unfolding on stage and to set the scene musically, as well as dramatically, for all that would follow.

Director Rouben Mamoulian spoke later about the dialogue-free Prologue. "The highest compliment I could get as a director is that no one has seemed to notice anything unusual about the prelude, but there it is - seventy people onstage for five and a half minutes, and not a word spoken. In a straight play, you couldn't think of getting away with that. But here it is so stylised that within its own framework, it is perfectly logical and right." [74]

Of course, Molnár (with Polgar's assistance) had succeeded perfectly well with his Prologue in *Liliom,* so Mamoulian, who was no slouch when it came to taking credit, was not strictly accurate in saying such a scene could not be done in a straight play. Furthermore, we shall see in Chapter 8 that the staging of the Prologue was at least partly the work of Agnes de Mille.

For all the superficial similarities between *Oklahoma!* and *Carousel,* the differences are considerable and best summed up in the frequently quoted comment by Stephen Sondheim, "*Oklahoma!* is about a picnic. *Carousel* is about life and death."

Hammerstein finished his first working draft of the script on 9 January 1945. There are two copies of this draft in the Library of Congress, both liberally marked with multiple revisions. Other than the final, published version of the script that is in use today, these are the only drafts available from which we can plot the changes between that date and the Broadway opening.

Just how early in the creative process this version of the script is, can be seen in the 'When the Children Are Asleep' scene. After Snow's initial refrain, Hammerstein inserted the following,

> (A second verse will be written for Carrie. They will then join in a duet refrain. There will probably be an encore. If not, the

---

[73] Molnár takes less than one page to describe the Prologue in his script for *Liliom.*

[74] Joseph P. Swain, *The Broadway Musical,* p104.

author and composer will probably jump in the Charles River ...)

Work on the script had been subjected to numerous interruptions, one of which was the opening of *I Remember Mama* on 19 October 1944. Another constant source of delay was the numerous war boards and charities on which he served. His papers for 1944 demonstrate the extreme demands made on his time that came with the fame and fortune associated with *Oklahoma!* It might well have been this frustrating period when he wanted to get down to work on *Liliom* but was prevented from doing so by these external forces that inspired him to write *Allegro,* a show which explores similar tensions, albeit those affecting the life of a young doctor.

Even by 27 November, Hammerstein was forced to respond to an actor called John Moore who had enquired about the possibility of a part in the show, '... not at the moment, but I haven't got very far into it'.[75] The bulk of the writing seems, therefore, to have been crammed into a relatively short period from October 1944 to early January 1945. Perhaps because he had to do so much writing in so little time explains why, in a letter of 18 January to his uncle Arthur, he indicated he was far from satisfied with the 9 January script and that he was worried that he would not have a more finished script ready for the rehearsals that were due to start on 12 February.[76]

One part of the script he had got more or less right by 9 January was *The Bench Scene*. We know how much Hammerstein liked Molnár's first act scene between Liliom and Julie, and how little he thought it needed to change. He remained true to that instinct and barely changed it at all, even while turning Molnár's prose into lyrics. This was Hammerstein's approach throughout. Keep as close to the original text as possible and make changes only when necessary.

How to soften Billy's character was one of the biggest challenges faced by Hammerstein. On first meeting Billy in the Prologue, we gain an immediate insight into both his flirtatious manner and the hint of menace lying not too deeply beneath the

---

[75] Oscar Hammerstein Collection, Library of Congress.

[76] Ibid.

surface. As the first act develops, we see these traits exposed still further, together with his disregard for the law and contempt for authority. In short, we are at a loss to understand what it is that Julie sees in him. Hammerstein faced a delicate balancing act in making Billy somewhat more likeable whilst not losing the essence of Molnár's tougher and rougher Liliom. Mostly, this would be achieved musically, but there were subtle little alterations to the book too. In the opening scene of both the play and the musical, Liliom/Billy threatens Mrs. Muskat/Mullin with a slap on the jaw. Only in the original, however, does Liliom admit to beating a woman so hard that she was hospitalised for three weeks, a line Hammerstein chose to omit from the musical. Today, directors such as Tim Sheader are faced with a similar dilemma, but this time in reverse; they feel a need to discard the few redeeming features that Hammerstein gave Billy, but how do you do that in a manner that can still enable us to believe that Julie would fall in love with him in the first place?

There are two major scenes where the musical does diverge from the play significantly, and not merely to accommodate songs or move action from gloomy interiors to more attractive exteriors. The first of these is the scene in *Liliom* which is referred to as 'In the Beyond', and which in *Carousel* is referred to as 'Up There'. 'In the Beyond' is a whitewashed courtroom to which Liliom is escorted by two heavenly policemen. There, he is confronted by a magistrate and asked to explain his actions, particularly beating Julie. Stubborn and defiant, Liliom refuses to express any remorse, and when offered the chance to return to earth to do something good, he refuses. He is sentenced to sixteen years to burn in the crimson fire for his pride and stubbornness to be burnt out of him; then he will be sent down to earth for one day to see how far the purification of his soul has progressed. If he can then do something good for his child, he may yet earn a place in Heaven. This rather stark and bare scene was clearly not to Rodgers and Hammerstein's liking, (It was part of the 'tunnel' about which they were so concerned early on), because even the latter's early outline indicated significant changes.

By the time he had drafted his 9 January script, Hammerstein laid out very elaborate plans for his version of this scene. Whilst Nettie and Julie are nearing the end of *You'll Never Walk Alone,* two men, unseen by the women, glide quietly into the room. (The scene initially was set in the bedroom Billy and Julie used in Nettie's cottage.) The two men, "heavenly policemen" in *Liliom,* are now "heavenly friends" in the musical, as Hammerstein emphasises in his script:

> The two men are casually and plainly dressed. They must not be in any kind of uniform. We are not headed for the "police court heaven" of *Liliom*. This is to be a "folk heaven."

The heavenly friends explain to Billy that they are there to take him to Heaven to see HIM, but the journey will take fifteen years so that he can see what the future holds for his daughter Louise during that time. Hammerstein intended that the story of those fifteen years would unfold in the form of a ballet, (described as an 'interlude' in the 9 January script), leading to the scene 'Up There'. The 'Interlude' is shown at Appendix II.

At the end of the ballet, the lights come up on a small New England sitting room circa 1885. Sitting on the left of the stage playing a harmonium and facing the audience is a plump, comfortable-looking little woman, identified in the script as SHE. Sitting next to a table centre stage is a larger man, rugged, yet gentle, identified as HE.[77] Both are in their fifties judged by earthly appearances. Billy is brought in to face them, the usual sullen, indignant Billy, when it suddenly dawns on him and the audience that he might be in the presence of Mr. and Mrs. God. He is questioned much as Liliom was in the play, often with the same dialogue, but whereas Molnár's magistrate was firm but fair, one can sense, even just reading off the page of an old, typewritten script, a warmth radiating from this odd couple. That it should do so is not surprising because Hammerstein had written it out of a deep and very private conviction. As Elliot Norton, then the famed critic of the *Boston Post,* and someone to whom writers and producers frequently looked for advice on how to fix a show, later wrote, 'he rejected out of hand the sentencing of Liliom to Purgatory and, in the belief that "there must be some feminine

---

[77] A large, rugged-looking man. That is just how Oscar Hammerstein himself was most often described.

principle in God' devised an afterlife presided over by both a man and a woman'''.[78]

That latter point is illustrated by this exchange early in the scene. It might have been fashionable to overlook women in 1945, but Oscar Hammerstein, again perhaps referencing his own mother, was having none of it.

Sir ... Who's the lady?

HE

I suppose you are like all the others. You thought, when you arrived here, you'd have to deal only with a man.

Billy

Yes, sir.

HE

Strange that the world doesn't realise it needs a mother as well as a father.

(Billy looks across at HER with new respect)

However well-intentioned the scene was, audiences in New Haven and Boston hated it; it stopped the show dead in its tracks and had to go. After several days of intense work in Boston, Hammerstein came up with the new scene with which we are now familiar.

The setting is still described as 'Up There', but it is now the Backyard of Heaven, the gates are only 'mother of pearly'. He and She have been replaced by a single character, the Starkeeper, who is polishing stars hanging on a clothesline stretching to infinity. The ballet telling Louise's story which originally preceded this scene, now follows it.

Agnes de Mille regretted the changes. In her autobiography, she stated that she felt the original version 'was extraordinarily

---

[78] Elliot Norton, *New York Times,* 16 September 1984.

imagined but shocked Calvinistic New Haven ... and had a dry toughness that the second lacked and a quality that Oscar has frequently had to yield before audience hesitation or surprise'.[79] Hammerstein himself, however, seemed rather more sanguine about it saying that 'the whole concept was pretty terrible'. [80]

In similar vein, he wrote to John Steinbeck after the New York opening, '... We cut Him and Her out of the play and put in a little old man who is a keeper of Heaven's back door - a sort of service entrance St. Peter who speaks New England dialect'.[81]

The entire original scene, as it appeared in Hammerstein's 9 January 1945 script is reproduced at Appendix III.

The other significant deviation from the original play was in the ending. When Liliom is given the opportunity to return to Earth for a day to help his daughter, he fails dismally and lashes out at her instead, just as he did with Julie. He is taken back to spend eternity in Hell. Neither Rodgers nor Hammerstein were prepared to let the musical end on that bitter note. There could not be a happy ending of course, but neither did they want it to be that downbeat.

So concerned were they, that during the summer of 1944, they became frequent visitors to the Imperial Theatre to catch the last ten minutes of Robert Wright and George Forrest's hit show *Song of Norway,* which had opened that August. Very loosely based on the life of composer Edvard Grieg, the operetta also had a teary ending, and Rodgers and Hammerstein wanted to gauge the audience reaction to it. Robert Wright, the lyricist, ran into Oscar Hammerstein on one of those visits. Wright remembered Hammerstein saying that they wanted to see whether a musical with such a melancholy ending could succeed. They saw the show several nights running and watched hard-bitten audiences wiping tears from their eyes. Only then, according to Wright, did Hammerstein decide to go ahead and make a musical of *Liliom.*

Of course, this is not quite true, as by that time, Rodgers and Hammerstein were fully committed to *Carousel.* The insight they

---

[79] Agnes de Mille, *And Promenade Home,* p234.

[80] David Ewen, *Richard Rodgers,* p236.

[81] Letter, 23 April 1945, Oscar Hammerstein Collection, Library of Congress.

gained from the audience's reaction though, did help them work through the problem of how to change *Liliom's* ending.

There had to be something positive, some glimmer of hope for audiences to cling to. This, they both firmly believed. In a profile written about the pair called *The Nicest Guys in Show Business,* Cleveland Amory suggested that their ending for *Carousel* was probably the best example of their daring to be optimistic and quotes Richard Rodgers' explanation for it. '*Liliom* was a tragedy about a man who cannot learn to live with other people. The way Molnár wrote it the man ends up hitting his daughter and then having to go back to purgatory, leaving his daughter helpless and hopeless. We couldn't accept that. The way we ended *Carousel,* it may still be a tragedy, but it's a hopeful one because in the final scene, it is clear that the child has at last learned how to express herself and communicate with others. The curious thing is, that when Molnár saw our final scene - which was the exact opposite of his - he told us it was the best scene in our play'.

Nonetheless, particularly with modern audiences, a frequently aired criticism of the show is that Billy gets off too easily relative to the wrongs he has done and that this results in a too sentimental ending.

But how, at a time when the World was still at war and families were losing loved ones every day, could Rodgers and Hammerstein end their show in the same downbeat fashion as Molnár? That Billy did wrong is a given and Rodgers acknowledges that. At the same time, however, there were thousands of grieving families mourning lost sons or brothers or husbands or sweethearts, and they needed to be reassured that God was compassionate, so even if their men had been less than perfect, there still was hope for their souls. To have suggested otherwise not only would have been disastrous for the show, but as Rodgers told Amory, was something neither he nor Hammerstein could do. They saw the same Billy/Liliom that Clara Györgyey described, and gave him a second chance which this time, he took.

They set the new final scene at Louise's graduation, but just before that, they adapted Molnár's final scene to give us a glimpse at the lives of Julie and Carrie fifteen years after Billy's death. Carrie has come to visit Julie who is now living in her own cottage with Louise. Whilst we sense that Julie gets by, it is immediately apparent that the Snows have prospered, and that Carrie has learned how to handle Mr. Snow, who is still as insufferably pompous as ever.

Billy, (John Raitt) hands Louise,(Bambi Linn) a star.
Courtesy of The Rodgers & Hammerstein Organization: A Concord Company, www.rnh.com

That beginning to the scene provides a little light relief before we gain a further insight into Louise's character which makes it even more imperative that Billy, whose ghost can now be seen watching Julie and Louise, finds a way to help her. He observes Louise talking to Enoch Snow Jr., who unfortunately, is clearly a chip off the old block. She tells him that she is going to run away to join a theatrical troupe. The young Enoch says he will stop her, and when she asks how, he says he will marry her, even if it will be hard to persuade his father to let him marry beneath his station.

Louise tells him not to bother, that she wouldn't have that stuck-up buzzard for a father-in-law for $1million. Of course, Junior responds in kind and reminds her that Billy beat her mother. At this, Louise throws him out, but as she does so, following Hammerstein's stage directions - (Giving JUNIOR a good punch). [In the first draft Louise gives him a quick, and effective box on the ear and a swift, well directed kick]. Having already seen in the ballet that Louise is, just as he was, alone and an outsider, Billy can see that she has inherited his temper and readiness to lash out too. He MUST help her. Now, once again, Hammerstein follows Molnár and Billy becomes visible to Louise and engages her in conversation saying that he was a friend of her father. But when he tries to give her a star he has stolen from Heaven, Louise becomes wary and when she refuses to take the star, he does what he always does and slaps her. Louise rushes back towards the house as Julie comes out and we sense that she caught a glimpse of Billy before he made himself invisible again.

Louise tries to tell Julie about her strange encounter and then poses that now infamous question:

> 'But is it possible, Mother, fer someone to hit you hard like that - real loud and hard - and not hurt you at all?'

> And the equally infamous answer -

> 'It is possible, dear – fer someone to hit you – hit you hard – and not hurt at all.'

This is where Molnár ended his play, with Liliom being led off to spend eternity in Hell. Rodgers and Hammerstein were never going to finish their version in that bleak fashion, but it was not until well into the Boston try-out that they finally came up with a satisfactory alternative.

What we now see is Julie discovering the star that Billy had left behind. Whilst she tries to make sense of what Louise has told her, and what she thought she saw, Billy, invisible to her, reprises *If I Loved You,* an addition that Rodgers fought for in Boston, before persuading his heavenly companion to give him one final chance and letting him attend Louise's graduation.

Writing that new graduation scene was not easy, and Hammerstein struggled to strike the correct balance, as can be seen by the difference between his 9 January version and the final version as we know it now.

Originally, the address to the graduation class was given by the local minister and read as follows:

> To you, children of our village, who are about to become its men and women, I wish good and happy lives. Try to stand close together always – as you stand today. For standing so, you are close to God. If those who are successful turn against those who fail, they too shall be failures in the eyes of heaven. If the strong and happy turn against the weak and lonely, they too shall be weak and lonely.
>
> (He turns and speaks directly to Louise,)
> And those of you who become desperate and need help, don't be ashamed to seek it.
>
> BILLY
>
> (Behind Louise, whispering sharply as if trying to breathe spirit into her.)
>
> Listen to him. Believe him!
>
> MINISTER
>
> Don't run away and hide like an animal in a cave. You all need one another.
> Weak or strong, no one is adequate all by himself. Stay side by side, children. No danger is unconquerable except the one you face alone. – or the one you run away from.
> (reciting,)
>
> When you walk through a storm …

Hammerstein clearly wasn't happy with that speech, and rightly so. It was far too preachy. Whilst the class would have listened politely, it is doubtful the children would have got the message and the entire point of the new scene is that everyone listening, especially Louise, (and the audience too), does hear and does believe. So, he worked very hard to get it right. In his papers at the Library of Congress, there are several scraps of paper with handwritten phrases which he thought might be incorporated into the scene. Some of them sadly, are so faded as to be almost illegible now, but one that I could decipher was *"Don't be afraid of the other feller - Don't make him afraid of you."* Finally, he got it right and wrote what some might call the gospel according to Rodgers and Hammerstein.

Instead of the local minister, the speech was now delivered by the town doctor, 'the best - loved man in our town'. In the 9 January draft, the minister was played by the same actor as HIM. In the final version, the doctor is played by the same actor as the Starkeeper.

> It's the custom at these graduations to pick out some old duck like me to preach at the kids. (Laughter) I can't preach at you. Know you all too well. Brought most of you into the world. Rubbed liniment on yer backs, poured castor oil down yer throats. (A shudder runs through them, and a girl laughs. All look mortified) Well, all I hope is that now I got you here this far, you'll turn out to be worth all the trouble I took with you! (He pauses, looks steadily at them, his voice earnest) You can't lean on the success of your parents. That's their success. (Directing his words to LOUISE) And don't be held back by their failures! Makes no difference what they did or didn't do. You jest stand on yer own two feet.
>
> BILLY (To Louise)
>
> Listen to him. Believe him.
> (She looks up suddenly.)
>
> DOCTOR
>
> The world belongs to you as much as to the next feller. Don't give it up! And try not to be skeered o' people not likin' you - jest you try likin' them. Jest keep yer faith and courage and

you'll come out all right. It's like we used to sing every mornin' when I went to school. Mebbe you still sing it – I dunno

(he recites)

"When you walk through a storm
Keep yer chin up high-"

(To the kids)
Know that one?

(They nod eagerly and go on with the song.)

ALL

And don't be afraid of the dark.

BILLY (To LOUISE)

Believe him darling! Believe.

(LOUISE joins the others as they sing …)

You know that this is what Billy would have wanted to say to Louise if only he could have found the words. He might have messed up first time round, but now he can ensure she hears Doctor Seldon's sage advice, just as he is able to finally tell Julie the words he could never say while he was alive. "I loved you, Julie. Know that I loved you!"

These final lines for Billy were another part of the script that Hammerstein struggled with. At one point, he gave Billy a longer final speech. On one of his scraps of paper, he jotted down under the heading, 'Last Scene':

I did love you, Julie –
And if I was alive today – I'd love her, too – and –
And I'd be awful proud of you both …!

And then, to the background of what Hammerstein described as a "Saintly Noise,"

You see? She can hear me.

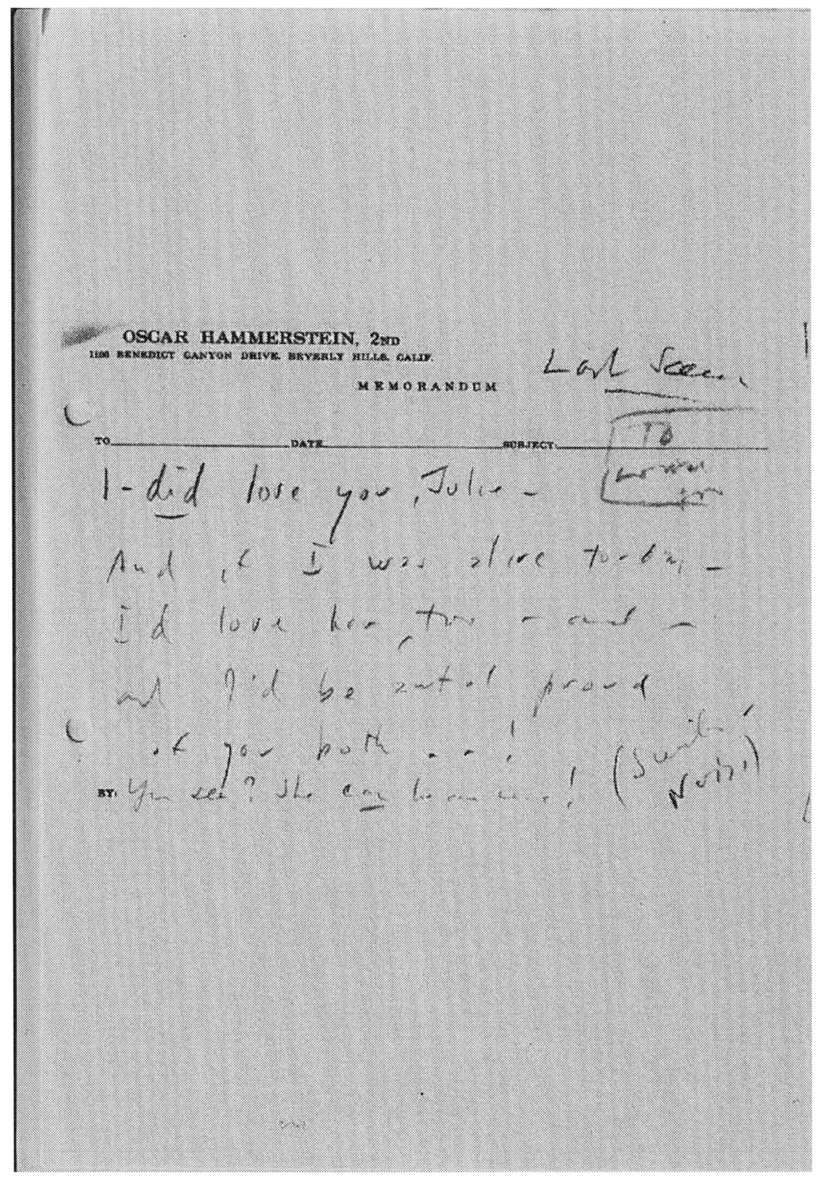

OSCAR HAMMERSTEIN, 2ND
[illegible] BENEDICT CANYON DRIVE, BEVERLY HILLS, CALIF.

MEMORANDUM

Last Scene

TO ____ DATE ____ SUBJECT ____

I did love you, Julie —
And if I was alive today —
I'd love her, too — and —
and I'd be awful proud
of you both...!
BY: You see? She can hear me...! (Saintly Noise)

One of Oscar Hammerstein's script notes from his collection in the Library of Congress.

The Graduation Scene in the original 1945 production.
Courtesy of The Rodgers & Hammerstein Organization:
A Concord Company, www.rnh.com

Chapter 6

And All the Rest is Talk

In his book *Lyrics,* Oscar Hammerstein set out this core belief about his art. 'There are few things in life of which I am certain, but I am sure of this one thing, that the song is the servant of the play, that it is wrong to write first what you think is an attractive song and then try to wedge it into a story'.[82] Consider how similar are Richards Rodgers' comments about the role of music in the theatre. He said, 'music must not only spring from character and situation, it must advance them'. This shared philosophy goes a long way towards explaining how these two very different men managed to work so well together to produce the extraordinary body of work they did.

Hammerstein's research applied not just to the show's book but also to the lyrics. This concern for accuracy may be one reason why some critics accuse him of writing simplistically and of lacking sophistication. Those critics, however, conveniently overlook the fact that Hammerstein was always writing for character. In *Carousel,* apart from Mr. Bascombe, none of the principal characters are well educated. Billy Bigelow is a barker, Nettie runs her spa, and the rest are millworkers or fisherman. Hammerstein's task was to ensure not just that their dialogue sounded true, but that their lyrics would do so as well.

He speaks as to how his characters struggle to find the right words in the lyrics of *If I Loved You,* one of the most popular love songs in the entire Broadway canon:

If I Loved You,
Time and again I would try to say,
All I'd want you to know

If I loved you,
Words wouldn't come in an easy way,
Round in circles, I'd go!

---

[82] Oscar Hammerstein, *Lyrics,* p19.

He does so again later when he has Julie sing,

What's the use of wond'rin'
If he's good or if he's bad,
Or if you like the way he wears his hat
Oh, what's the use of wond'rin',
If he's good or if he's bad?
He's your feller and you love him-
That's all there is to that.

Some might call these lyrics simplistic. Others would say the words reflect exactly what one would expect to hear from those characters given their social class and education in the 1870s.

Hammerstein, of course, could do sophistication. Contrast Julie's simplistic thoughts expressed above with the sophisticated feelings expressed by the well-educated Anna Leonowens in *Hello Young Lovers* from *The King and I.*

I know how it feels to have wings on your heels,
And to fly down a street in a trance.
You fly down a street on the chance that you'll meet,
And you meet – not really by chance.

Or again, consider Nellie Forbush's 'proud protestations' in the song *A Wonderful Guy* from *South Pacific.*

I'm as trite and as gay
As a daisy in May,
A cliché coming true!
I'm bromidic and bright
As a moon happy night
Pouring light on the dew.

Three different characters; a New England mill worker in the 1870s; an English governess in Siam in the 1860s; and an army nurse from Little Rock finding herself in the South Pacific in the 1940s: In each case, thanks to his research and his insistence on preserving the integrity of the play, Hammerstein found the perfect voice for each character.

Writing the lyrics first, obviously made it easier for Hammerstein to find those voices. He had a free hand to let each lyric flow naturally out of the dialogue so that maintaining the integrity of the language as it moved from speech to lyric was far less of a problem than it would have been had he been restricted by a previously written melody. That said, he still liked to have a dummy melody to which to set his lyric. Sometimes, he made up a melody of his own but mostly, he would find a classic tune to use, a Sousa march perhaps, or an aria from an opera or a folk tune. He might tweak them a little, but he found it helped him enormously; and he would never, ever tell Rodgers what tune he used. What frequently bemused Hammerstein was the fact that a lyric he was convinced would become a waltz in 3/4 time, came back from Rodgers composed as a ballad in 4/4.[83]

A good example as to how he would incorporate his research into his lyrics can be found in *When I Marry Mr. Snow.*

Hammerstein had made a list of phrases that caught his eye in the various books he read:

- From H.B. Stowe, he took the phrase, 'There was a rustlin' among the bunnets' and turned it into 'What a rustlin' of bonnets there'll be'.
- 'The great big elm tree over there would get perfectly rackety with birds' was translated as 'The birds'll make a racket in the churchyard trees'.
- Another Stowe line, 'There wa'n't a crimp nor a frill about her that wa'n't jest so', Hammerstein wrote in an early draft of the song as 'Not a crimp nor a frill on my wedding dress. That won't be pressed jest so'.

Hammerstein cared about every word. In his papers relating to *Carousel,* is an A4 sheet relating to this song on which he jotted down nothing but adjectives that Carrie might use to describe Mr. Snow. Among them are –

Eager	Gallant	Impulsive
Handsome	Bearded	Masterful
Slender	Darlin'	Exciting

[83] This is what occurred with *I Have Dreamed* in *The King and I.*

Strong and Tender	Dashin'	Whiskered
Daring	Muscular	

Another sheet contained this early lyric idea:

My lily-white hand bestowed
On that eager, ardent, handsome devil,
Mr. Wilbur Snow

Or,

Seaweedy, salty, eager Mr. Snow

Those final few bars really did cause him a lot of anguish before he got it just right.

***

Notwithstanding the changes Hammerstein made to the book of *Carousel,* until *The Bench Scene* begins, and Billy is given music of his own, he is still a remarkably unsympathetic character. This, in turn, creates difficulties for the actor playing Julie. Portraying the mixed emotions that come with being strongly attracted to someone whilst at the same time, knowing he is quite wrong for you, is not easy. Iva Withers, Broadway's second Julie and London's first, said that she understood Billy in a way that others didn't because she saw the poet in him, perhaps picking up on Mrs. Muskat/Mullins' description of him as an artist. Alexandra Silber, a more recent Julie, both in London and in Los Angeles, expressed similar thoughts, comparing Billy's heartbreak at losing his ability to do the one thing at which he excelled, with that of a violinist whose hands were crushed.

Initially, Billy is puzzled by Julie's decision to stay with him; doing so has already cost her her job. But, as the scene develops and his interplay with Julie continues, his usual swagger and assuredness turns to doubt, and hitherto unfelt emotions take hold of him. We hear uncertainty even before we see it when he whistles, "You're a Queer One" to himself. Without realizing what is happening to him, Billy finds himself wondering if she would marry someone like him to which Julie replies, as if she could see the future, "Yes, I would, if I loved you. It wouldn't make any difference what you ... even if I died fer it." Not only does this line, taken from Molnár, provide the title for the show's main love song, it also tells us that Julie knows exactly what she is getting into. She is aware of Billy's propensity for violence, his quick temper, and yet still she is drawn to him. When later, she sings *What's the Use of Wond'rin'* she is reaffirming this all-powerful love she feels for Billy - still against her better judgement. It is a feeling harder to understand today even though we know that many women still struggle to "Break and run away."

After Julie sings *If I Loved You,* Billy, afraid of previously unfelt emotions, is quick to seek reassurance by saying, "Well anyway - you don't love me. That's what you said."

In the 'Two Little People' section, he gives voice to all the frustrations he feels at the raw deal he has had so far from life; he looks at the sky and the sea and realizing how vast they are, considers how unimportant Julie and he are in comparison; "Just a couple of specks of nothing." He continues,

There's a helluva lot o' stars in the sky,
And the sky's so big the sea looks small,
And two little people-
You and I -
We don't count at all.

Initially, Julie was given a response to Billy's musings:

There's a feathery little cloud floatin' by
Like a lonely leaf on a big blue stream.
And two little people-
You and I
Who cares what we dream?

These lines appear in the original published version of the script but were removed from the updated version published in 2016.

It is not only in comparison to the vastness of the sea and sky that Billy and Julie are just a couple of specks of nothing. That is their place in society, right at the bottom of the heap. I shall discuss in a later chapter how it was this aspect of their story, their poverty and hopelessness that Nicholas Hytner would seize upon in his famed 1992 revival for the National Theatre.

Having agreed on the phrase that Molnár gave Julie, 'If I Loved You' as the title for the major refrain, this was Hammerstein's first stab at a lyric for that song.

If I loved you
I would tremble ev'ry time you'd say my name,
But I'd long to hear you say it just the same
I dunno jest how I know, but I ken see
How everythin' would be
If I loved you...
If I loved you
I'd be too a-skeered t'say what's in my heart
I'd be too a-skeered to even make a start
And my golden chance to speak would come and go
And you would never know
How I loved you –
If I loved you.

So how did the pair get from that first draft of the song to the version with which are now familiar? We know that this is one of the handful of Rodgers and Hammerstein songs for which the music was written first but from the draft above, it would certainly seem that that was not their original intention. Perhaps after that first effort, Hammerstein asked Rodgers to give him a melody to work to; perhaps Rodgers simply came up with the melody suggested by the title and fragments of Hammerstein's lyric. In the end, it does not really matter because whatever its true genesis, the song has become one of their most enduring love songs.

If I loved you,
Time and again I would try to say
All I'd want you to know.
If I loved you,
Words wouldn't come in an easy way –
Round in circles I'd go!
Longin' to tell you, but afraid and shy,
I'd let my golden chances pass me by.
Soon you'd leave me,

Off you would go in the mist of day,
Never, never to know
How I loved you –
If I loved you.

Jan Clayton and John Raitt performing the Bench Scene.
Courtesy of The Rodgers & Hammerstein Organization:
A Concord Company, www.rnh.com

Once again, through his lyrics, Hammerstein has warned his audience how the story will develop. Both Julie and Billy do indeed let their golden chances to say the words 'I love you' pass them by. Julie will only say the words over Billy's dead body, and it will take sixteen years before Billy's ghost expresses his true feelings to Julie.

It is hard to think of anyone who wrote a better conditional love song, one in which the lovers do not actually say "I love you," than Oscar Hammerstein. Apart from *If I Loved You*, there was *Make Believe* for *Show Boat, People Will Say We're in Love* in *Oklahoma!* and *Twin Soliloquies* in *South Pacific.*

Sometimes, Hammerstein's quest for accuracy in his writing must have seemed more trouble than it was worth. *June is Bustin' Out all Over* is a case in point. One chorus reads as follows:

The sheep aren't sleepin' any more!
All the rams that chase the ewe sheep
Are determined there'll be new sheep
And the ewe sheep aren't even keepin' score!

It was only after he had completed the lyrics that a friend pointed out that sheep do not mate in June but in winter: they give birth in June. At first, he was going to delete the offending lines.

In a letter of 2 March 1945, he wrote, 'I was delighted with the parts of your letter praising my work and thrown into consternation by the unwelcome news about the eccentricly [sic] frigid behaviour of ewes in June. I have since checked your statement and found it to be true. It looks very much as if in the interest of scientific honesty, I shall have to abandon the verse dealing with sheep'. [84]

However, much as he hated his lyrics to be inaccurate, Oscar decided not to change this verse. He wrote back to his friend, 'What you say about sheep may all be very true for most years, sir, but not in 1873. 1873 is my year and that year, curiously enough, the sheep mated in the spring'. [85]

The idea for the song that became *When the Children Are Asleep,* arose from a passage of dialogue in *Liliom.* Marie is explaining to Julie her view of ideal love - before marriage and children:

> I'll be sitting on the bench and Wolf, he holds my hand tight - and he puts his cheek against my cheek and we don't talk - we just sit there very quiet. - And after a while he gets sleepy, and his head sinks down, and he falls asleep - but even in his sleep he holds tight to my hand. And I - I sit perfectly still just looking around me and taking long, deep breaths ...

Whilst Molnár might have been wistfully thinking of the joys of life before marriage and children, Hammerstein's version of domestic bliss anticipated life after the arrival of the seven children

---

[84] Oscar Hammerstein Collection, Library of Congress.

[85] Letter, Oscar Hammerstein Collection, Library of Congress.

that Molnár gave the Beifelds, and then he gave the Snows two more!

One early lyric idea for the song, which made its way into the 9 January script, but was subsequently discarded is,

When we've tucked the kids in their downy beds,
And listened to each one pray,
We'll kiss the tops of their tousled heads,
And tiptoe quietly away.
We'll tiptoe into our sittin' room
Where we love to be by ourselves,
Where the flick'rin glow of the firelight
Makes the books wink down from their shelves ...
And there ev'ry evenin, we'll always be –
Me in my armchair, you on my knee.

We know that Hammerstein spent around a month working on the lyrics for *Soliloquy,* and from the pages of notes and discarded versions among his papers, it is easy to see how the time was spent.

Before even a word was written, Rodgers sat down at the piano with Hammerstein, not to give him a completed melody, but to suggest musical ideas, colours and tones that complemented the thoughts they had shared regarding what was one of the key moments in the entire show. Rodgers said later, 'I know this helped him when he wrote the words, and it certainly helped me when I wrote the music'.[86]

With these musical ideas in mind, Hammerstein could get down to work. One of his early attempts contemplating the birth of a son included this verse:

It ain't important what you do
Or what you want to be,
The thing that counts is to know that you
Are independent and free –
To turn around any time and tell
The world and his uncle to go to hell!
And to know that in order to hold a job

---

[86] Richard Rodgers, *Musical Stages*, p240.

You don't have to crawl
At the beck and the call
Of any old fat-bottomed slob!
No!
Nor work for his battle-axed wife!
Not on your life!

Note how in these early versions, Billy is addressing his unborn son directly. In the final version, he addresses him in the third person singular.

Some of his early drafts expressed real anger:

And not to have to say that a thing is so
When he knows damn well it isn't so
Or toady to people who think they know
What's right and wrong
Or false or true
I never met no one who really knew
And to hell with the people who <u>think</u> they do.

While entire verses were discarded like the one above, elsewhere only small changes were needed:

And he don't have to marry their la-di-da daughter
With eyes like marbles and blood like water,
Who'll give him a peck and call it a kiss
And look down at Bill through her lorgnette----
Say! Why am I takin' on like this?
The kid ain't even been born yet!

Became,

And I'm damned if he'll marry his boss's daughter,
A skinny lipped virgin with blood like water,
Who'll give him a peck and call it a kiss
And look at his eyes through a lorgnette-----
Say!
Why am I carryin' on like this?
My kid ain't even been born yet!

It took a while too before he was happy with what he had for the *My Little Girl* section. These early thoughts were all discarded:

In stylish white dresses
I'll see that she's dressed-
Her mother can starch 'em nice and stiff.
I'll send her to school
And I'll pick out the best
Of the young ladies' seminaries if -IF
That's it – IF!
I wonder what she'll think of me?
I'm kind o' sorry for the kid.
I don't know why she picked out
Such a good-for-nothin' father,
But she did!
Lord help her!
She did!

If she grows to be pretty and sweet like her mother
It wouldn't be hard to see
How I might even love her as much as her brother-
But what will she think of me?
Poor baby!
What will she think of me!

One final lyric that made it to the opening, but which was subsequently discarded is this introduction to the *My Little Girl* section:

When I have a daughter
I'll stand around in bar-rooms-
Oh, how I'll boast and blow!
Friends'll see me comin'
And empty all the bar-rooms-
Through ev'ry door they'll go,
Weary of hearin' day after day
The same old things that I always say …

Theresa Helburn recalled in her autobiography that she was present when Oscar Hammerstein first presented Rodgers with the lyric for *Soliloquy.* As Oscar read the words out loud, Dick

Rodgers' face seemed to light up, and from that moment, he was completely in love with the show.

Of all the songs in the score, none benefitted more from Hammerstein's research than *This Was a Real Nice Clambake* which opens Act 2. The chorus is pure Hammerstein. The verse, however, shows off the lyricist's remarkable skills at adaptation; it is taken from a recipe for a traditional New England clambake in one of the books he used as a source for information on the traditions of Maine coastal life. The book in question is *Mainstays of Maine,* a combined travelogue and recipe book by Robert P.T. Coffin. This is what Coffin had to say about a clambake:

> A good New England cook uses no book. "Put in what you think is right." ... CODSHEAD CHOWDER ... Catch the cod and cook them, still flapping, in an iron kettle. Onions, salt pork. Cook till the fish begins to flake apart ... Split sticks or bayberry and clamp them on clamshells, and these are the only proper spoons for this chowder ... After this comes the LOBSTERS. They have been broiling on the coals. Rake them out, split them down the back, pour in the butter, salt and pepper. After the lobsters come the CLAMS. Cook these in rockweed thrown over coals of driftwood.

This is how Hammerstein adapted that paragraph:

First come codfish chowder,
Cooked in iron kettles,
Onions floatin' on the top,
Curlin' up in petals!
Throwed in ribbons of salted pork-
An old New England trick-
And lapped it all up with a clamshell,
Tied onto a bayberry stick!
Oh-h-h
This was a real nice clambake ...

Remember when we raked
Them red-hot lobsters
Out of the driftwood fire?
They sizzled and crackled

And sputtered a song
Fitten for an angel's choir.

We slit 'em down the back
And peppered them good,
And dowsed 'em in melted butter-
Then we tore away the claws
And cracked 'em with our teeth
'Cause we weren't in a mood to putter! ...

Then at last came the clams –
Steamed under rockweed
And poppin' from their shells –
Jest how many of 'em
Galloped down our gullets –
We couldn't say oursel's!

Having used such an impeccable source for his lyric, Hammerstein was dismayed to be told by another busybody friend that you slit lobsters down the front. Once again, always wanting to be accurate, he sent for Alice and asked her to consult the head chef at the King of the Sea restaurant in New York who told her that he "slit them down the back - always." Oscar decided that people all slit lobsters the same way, but some called the back the front and vice versa. The lyric stayed unchanged.

During her research, Alice discovered that New Englanders referred to their clams as "manna from heaven." Hammerstein took that information and turned it into the 'fitten fer an angels', fitten fer an angels', fitten fer an angels' choir'. section of the song.[87]

While *What's the Use of Wond'rin* may give some people pause today, when Oscar Hammerstein sat down to write the words for the song all those years ago, his main concern was phonetics, which after rhyming, is the most important device used by a lyricist.

His belief was that proper phonetics not only made a song good but determined its popularity. A lyricist, unlike a poet, is required to find the right word and to ensure that it is a word that is clear when sung and not too difficult to sing on a given note. In

---

[87] Amy Asch (editor), *The Complete Lyrics of Oscar Hammerstein II,* pXi.

vocal climaxes and on high notes, singers are comfortable only with vowels that have an open sound. The word 'sweet' for example is not suitable for a high note for two reasons. Firstly, the '*e*' sound closes the larynx, and the singer cannot let go with his full voice; second, the '*t*' ending is a hard consonant which would make it impossible to sustain the note.

In writing *What's the Use of Wond'rin'*, Oscar broke this golden rule of ending a climactic word with an open sound. The last two lines are:

You're his girl and he's your feller –
And all the rest is talk.

'Talk' finished the song quietly and abruptly. The song worked well in the play but did not get as much airtime on the radio or as many record sales as it might have done. Oscar was convinced that it was the phonetics problem that was responsible. He said, "This is what I wanted the character to say … I realised that I was defying convention in ending with the word 'talk', but I had a perverse desire to do it anyway."

Phonetics aside, there is no doubting that some people listening to the song today, take issue with a lyric that seemingly brushes aside Billy's abuse. That though, as discussed earlier, is to miss the point. What Julie is saying in the song is that she knows she should walk away, just as she sensed she should walk away in *The Bench Scene*, but she cannot bring herself to do so. As Tim Sheader said, it is a problem faced by many women today, the world over and that is what gives the song its' relevance now. To outsiders, it would seem to be the easiest thing to do, to pack your bags and go; but for the women involved, it is far from easy. Not only can love blind someone to reality, but the sheer practicalities of leaving can appear overwhelming:

Common sense may tell you
That the ending will be sad
And now's the time to break and run away,
But what's the use of wond'rin
If the endin' will be sad?
He's your feller and you love him-
There's nothin' more to say.

Hammerstein's insistence on writing for character might not have impressed his critics. It did, however, impress Alan Jay Lerner, a master of the art of lyric writing himself, who paid tribute to Oscar's skill with these words. 'Whereas Hammerstein was never the wit that Larry Hart was, he was far superior as a dramatic lyricist, and certainly no one ever wrote a lyric that sang better'.[88]

[88] Alan Jay Lerner, *The Musical Theatre. A Celebration,* p153.

Chapter 7

Waltzes and Arias

From the moment the suggestion of a musical *Liliom* was first whispered across the table at Sardi's, Rodgers never veered from his initial belief that music would necessarily feature more in this show than in any other.[89] The man who as a student used to spend his Saturday nights at the old Metropolitan Opera on 39th Street and Broadway, enthralled by the works of the European masters, would now be employing some of their techniques on the kind of Broadway musical he had long dreamed of creating.

As in those great works he admired so much, he would use *leitmotifs* to enhance the dramatic effect on stage and help define characters; there would be the use of extended musical sequences, several of them; there would be underscoring, there would be dance, particularly the second act ballet; and all would be tightly integrated with the book and lyrics, to tell the story.

Of course, many of these elements had been seen before, most notably, in Kern and Hammerstein's *Show Boat* in 1927, arguably the most innovative and important musical until *Oklahoma!* and the first where there was a real attempt at integration. Composer Jerome Kern certainly used some of the above techniques in the score of that show. An obvious example is the extended musical scene early on in the show when Magnolia and Ravenal meet for the first time. Ravenal introduces himself with *Where's the Mate for Me?* which leads straight into the conditional love song, *Make Believe.* A degree of underscoring throughout the show was another feature. Whilst there was no formal ballet in *Show Boat,* Kern and Hammerstein did feature dream ballets in two later shows, *Three Sisters,* 1934, and *Very Warm for May* 1939. Rodgers himself had very successfully used dance to advance the story of his 1936 show, *On Your Toes.*

In 1941, musicals took another significant leap forward. Kurt Weill, who might easily have composed the musical version of *Liliom,* but for Molnár's stubborn refusal, gave us *Lady in the Dark,*

---

[89] Although it first appeared on Broadway, the Gershwins' *Porgy and Bess* is now universally considered to be an Opera.

with a book by Moss Hart and lyrics by Ira Gershwin. The entire score consisted of three extended musical sequences that told the dreams of the heroine Liza. The only song that did not form a part of one of those extended sequences was *My Ship,* and that was used throughout the show as a *leitmotif* for the central character, Liza.

And then of course came *Oklahoma!* to change everything for ever. If all those musical devices referred to above had been seen on Broadway before, why is *Oklahoma!* considered so revolutionary? The answer I believe, is that it was not until that show that all the disparate elements that constitute musical theatre came together to create a perfect whole; one where every note of music, every word of book and lyric, every dance step, the lighting, the scenery and the costumes, all blended so perfectly, nothing needed to be changed at all. One could argue, perhaps, that *Oklahoma!* represented not so much a revolution as the pivotal stage of an evolutionary journey that continues to this day.

The trouble with evolution is that it never stops, and now Rodgers and Hammerstein had to take the advances made in *Oklahoma!* still further. Musically, Rodgers knew what this challenge meant. He wrote, '… a score is more than a collection of individual songs. It is, or should be, a cohesive entity whose words and music are believable expressions of the characters singing them'. [90]

In an indication as to the importance Rodgers attached to the score he was creating for this show, he even insisted on having total freedom of choice when it came to the musicians to be hired for the orchestra. To that end, he wrote to Lawrence Langner and Theresa Helburn suggesting '… that whatever house LILIOM goes into, a stipulation be made that there be no interference on the part of the house management with the personnel of the orchestra. It may be necessary to accept the customary four house men but outside of this, it is imperative that we be allowed complete freedom of choice'.[91]

***

[90] Richard Rodgers, *Musical Stages*, p293.

[91] Letter, 22 December 1944, Theatre Guild Collection, Beineke Library, Yale University.

Composers sometimes write pieces of music which for one reason or another, could not be used for the purpose originally intended. If the music is good, it will be stuck in a drawer in the hope that an opportunity will arise later when it can be dusted off and put to good use.

This is exactly what happened with *The Carousel Waltz,* which is quite remarkable given how this piece establishes the musical tone for the whole show.

Bruce Pomahac, former director of music at the Rodgers and Hammerstein Organisation has set out its full history. He explained that according to one rumour, and it is no more than rumour as there is no documentary evidence to support it, Rodgers may have offered a waltz to Paul Whiteman for use in his famous Aeolian Hall concert in 1924, the same concert at which George Gershwin premiered his *Rhapsody in Blue*. It has been suggested that the waltz in question was an early version of *The Carousel Waltz*. However, there is no evidence that Rodgers offered any music to Whiteman at that time, nor significantly, is there any manuscript of the music dating from that time.

A story that has much more substance, is that Rodgers offered a waltz for Whiteman to use on a radio programme called *Music Out of the Blue*. The programme was to be broadcast in late 1944 and thirteen composers, including Richard Rodgers, Leonard Bernstein, Aaron Copland and Igor Stravinsky were to be commissioned to compose new instrumental pieces for the programme. They were to receive royalty advances for their work in return for which they would grant performance rights for a twelve-month period.

On learning of the commission, Rodgers offered a concert waltz called *Tales of Central Park,* a composition he had written a decade earlier and for which he had found no subsequent use. Currently of course, he and Oscar Hammerstein were engrossed in the writing of *Carousel.* They had already decided that their new show was going to open with a waltz which Rodgers would compose to accompany the onstage action of the Prologue. Before sending *Tales of Central Park* off to Whitman however, Rodgers must have played it to Hammerstein who saw at once how the music so perfectly captured the mood of the opening carousel scene, that he persuaded his partner to use it for the play rather than for the concert. That he already knew the music explains why

Hammerstein is so precise in his Outline, where he specifically describes the opening music as a 'Waltz Suite'. He also referred to it in a letter to his son Bill in August 1944, when he wrote about the opening and said, 'There will be no dialogue or lyric, only pantomimic action set to a Waltz Suite which Dick wrote'.

Why was the piece called *Tales of Central Park?* The answer is to be found in the Richard Rodgers Collection at the Library of Congress' Musical Theatre Division in Washington D.C. It is in a box with material relating to a film starring Al Jolson called *Hallelujah I'm A Bum*. The film was one that Rodgers worked on with Larry Hart in 1933 during their sojourn in Hollywood.

In the film, Jolson plays a hobo who sleeps on park benches in Central Park, hence the title suggested to Whitman. The manuscript is titled 'Park Notes' and it has references such as 'Zoo' and 'bears' over specific measures of music. There are three pages including a holograph sketch in pencil of the first waltz including the melodic line and chord symbols. Rodgers lays out all the melodic material, harmonic indications and a complete continuity for the entire suite of waltzes in the order we are used to hearing them.[92]

This, incidentally, is the way Rodgers nearly always worked: writing out his compositions first as one-line parts just with the main melody and harmonic indications noted as chord symbols. He would then write out full piano parts with complete harmonization and any counterpoint he wanted to indicate.

The fact that there is only the single line version here would indicate the idea of using the waltz in the film was abandoned and at that time, Rodgers had no need to expand on it. He did not forget it though, and if a request did come from Paul Whiteman sometime in 1944, Rodgers had an ideal composition immediately to hand, until Oscar Hammerstein's timely intervention.

The composition next appears in the collection of documents stored in the Library of Congress associated with *Carousel* 1945. Under the title *Intro Liliom,* it is a five-page holograph sketch in pencil. Again, it is a one-line melody score and is essentially, the

---

[92] A YouTube search will reveal a short film of singer and music historian Michael Feinstein talking about and playing the first waltz from this manuscript version in the Library of Congress.

same as that written out in 1933 but this time, without the references to 'Zoo' and 'bear'. There is also a thirteen-page holograph score, again in pencil, in Rodgers' hand, this time entitled *The Carousel Waltz*. This manuscript is a fully written out piano part, complete (except for one chord) with all the harmonies with which we have become familiar.

Does it matter that the waltz was not specifically composed for the show? Not according to musicologist, Joseph P. Swain who has emphasised its importance to the score as a whole and made light of its origins.

'*The Carousel Waltz* has an extraordinary relationship with the songs in the musical play. Like a classical overture, it sets the musical terms of the entire composition and is the main source of musical material, not tunes, so much as basic musical elements and procedures.

'In the end, of course, the dramatic effect of the music must stand or fall on its own terms in the context of the play, not on the facts of its origin. If a composer can make a successful adaptation, so much the better for him. In this case, the musical relationships between *The Carousel Waltz* and many of the other songs in the play are so compelling that it is difficult to believe that the waltz was not composed just for this purpose. Its unique tone, its vocabulary specific to the play, is established on the opening page'. [Of the score.] [93]

Whilst he talks about the high level of sophistication in Rodgers' music for the waltz, the chromatic juxtapositions, the multi-level harmonic rhythm, the emphasis on modal degrees, Swain nonetheless makes it clear that the piece is not too sophisticated for a show set in a New England mill town in the late nineteenth century. This, he suggests, is because of the slow, simple bass line of the waltz, emphasised by the tuba, an instrument Rodgers insisted on having in the pit. Also, Rodgers insisted that the musical tempo be maintained throughout. Agnes de Mille argued this point with Rodgers. "You've got to illustrate this a little bit more musically. You can't just go on playing a waltz in three-four time, unbroken without any punctuation from the

[93] Joseph P. Swain, *The Broadway Musical*, p101.

orchestra." Rodgers shot back, "I want those waltzes absolutely the way they were written".[94]

Fascinating though these academic discussions of Richard Rodgers' music are, do they give us any clues as to how he set about composing the music for *Carousel?* Probably not, for according to Bruce Pomahac, 'It wouldn't have made any sense to Rodgers. His work was instinctive and not academic'.[95] The truth of this point is borne out by Rodgers himself in a letter to John Steinbeck. 'I know very little about my own work. I feel a great deal, but I don't know much about origins'.[96] He surprised Stephen Sondheim too, one day, when the younger man commented on the fact that the melody for the release of *People Will Say We're in Love,* from *Oklahoma!* is the inversion of the 'A' section. It turns out Rodgers had been quite unaware of that fact. So well versed was he in the technique of composing, it just came naturally to him.

Rodgers expanded on his sense of musical feeling in a later letter to Steinbeck, written when he was working on *Pipe Dream,* based on the author's novel, *Sweet Thursday.*[97] 'I hesitate to start writing music', he said, 'until I have several lyrics at my disposal. It is the only way I can decide on the personality of the score and the direction I think it ought to take'.[98]

This correspondence helps explain why Rodgers so readily agreed to the lyrics first method of working. Having Hammerstein's lyrics, crafted carefully from the story, gave him the ability to create for each show, an individual score, each with its own unique musical personality. It enabled him to become the musical dramatist he always wanted to be.

---

[94] Stephen Citron, *The Wordsmiths,* p172.

[95] Bruce Pomahac. Email to the author. 24 September 2019.

[96] Letter, 5 August 1953. Richard Rogers Collection, New York Public Library, Performing Arts Division.

[97] *Pipe Dream* was Rodgers and Hammerstein's worst failure. Originally intended for Frank Loesser and set in a Monterey brothel filled with hookers and bums, it was a milieu about which they could not write with any conviction, and they should never have taken it on. "You have turned my whore into a visiting nurse," Steinbeck complained. Nonetheless, in my opinion, it does have a delightful score.

[98] Letter, 26 April 1954, Richard Rogers Collection, New York Public Library, Performing Arts Division.

In the 1930s, when most musical comedy scores were just a collection of (often wonderful) songs, a composer could very easily take one of his songs from one show and transplant it into another. You cannot, however, take a song from *Oklahoma!* and insert into the score of *South Pacific,* or one from *Carousel* and place it in *The King and I.* With the advent of the book musical, the song was indeed the servant of the play.

What must be so frustrating for academics is that apart from his finished scores, there is relatively little in the way of a paper trail one can follow to consider Rodgers' thought processes. Whereas Hammerstein left pages of notes relating to lyric and plot ideas, Rodgers left not much at all. Apart from his initial outline for what is now *The Carousel Waltz,* the only other sketch relevant to *Carousel* is a double-sided single sheet of manuscript for *Soliloquy,* in which the entire piece is mapped out; just the melody line, with the harmonies written as Roman numerals. The *My Little Girl* segment, which Rodgers notates as 'Girl Song', is shown at the bottom of the second page suggesting perhaps that it might have been an afterthought. Otherwise, his *Carousel* papers in the Library of Congress contain only Rodgers' fair, hand-written, three-line vocal/piano arrangements of each song, ready for orchestration.

We do know that Rodgers composed incredibly quickly, a trait that Oscar Hammerstein who laboured sometimes for weeks over a lyric, described as 'the annoying part of our collaboration'.[99] Perhaps, that speed is an indication that by the time he sat down at the piano with the lyric in front of him, having spent so much time discussing and thinking about characters and their situations, ideas for the music were already clearly formed in his head and once written out, hardly ever needed revision. According to his daughter Mary, Rodgers hated the work of writing out his music. He used to pray that one day, someone would invent a musical typewriter!

***

Where *Carousel* differs from most of its predecessors, is the extent to which it uses extended musical sequences through which the story is told, a seamless fusion of distinct musical themes defining

---

[99] Oscar Hammerstein, *Lyrics,* p17.

the characters and with underscoring highlighting the drama. The musical content of *Carousel* is some seventy-five per cent of the show, compared with the norm at the time of around fifty per cent. Much of the storyline that might have been told through dialogue, in *Carousel* is told in song, though definitely not in recitative. As discussed earlier, in trying to create a new style of American musical, imitating Italian grand opera by having their characters singing about such mundane matters as buying a bunch of bananas, was not something that appealed to either Rodgers or Hammerstein. In *Carousel,* it is lyrics that are set to music, not prose.

The very first extended musical sequence, *You're a Queer One, Julie Jordan/Mr. Snow* arises naturally from the preceding dialogue for which Hammerstein's stage directions state, 'From here the lines are synchronised to music'.

Stephen Sondheim considers *The Bench Scene (If I Loved You),* to be the most significant development in musical theatre. Writer and music historian Ethan Mordden on the other hand, argues that it is this earlier Julie/Carrie sequence, *You're a Queer One, Julie Jordan,* which serves as an introduction into *Mister Snow* that is even more significant. This is not a song in the conventional sense; it is a musical conversation. "Julie" says Carrie. "*Julie!*" she repeats, her voice backed by a solo violin. "Do you like him?" Mordden goes on to point out that without this first sequence, a mixture of musical conversation and conventional song, *The Bench Scene,* so much more intense than a relatively light conversation between two girlfriends, might have overwhelmed audiences.

In this sequence, we hear how Rodgers constructed his musical themes to define the characters singing them. Carrie and Julie each have their own distinct musical language. When Carrie sings the words, *"You are quieter and deeper than a well,"* she is singing a succession of even quavers indicating her steadiness and even temper. When Julie responds with the words, *"There's nothin' that I keer t'chose to tell,"* she does so with a mixture of dotted quavers and semi-quavers.[100] These dotted rhythms alongside a jumpy, uncertain melody are a sign of her restlessness, of her

---

[100] Rodgers used the same dotted rhythm device in the song *It Might as Well be Spring* for the character Margie in *State Fair.* "I'm as jumpy as a puppet on a string."

searching and yearning for something different. The dotted rhythms become Julie's *leitmotif* and appear throughout the show; in *The Bench Scene* which follows, and again in *What's the Use of Wond'rin'* though this time, Julie is in a quiet, accepting mood, suggested by a melody that consists of little more than scales. Whether Rodgers was being instinctive or deliberate, it is a musical device that works extremely well.

The second extended musical sequence is *The Bench Scene,* and whether you agree with Sondheim or Mordden, its iconic status in musical theatre history is not in dispute.

Again, it is a mixture of synchronised talking and singing but the essence of the scene is taken straight out of Molnár, as indeed is the title of the song at its core, *If I Loved You.* Following on closely from the previous extended sequence, it means that almost the entire first scene is set to music.

We have seen how Oscar Hammerstein developed his version from Molnár's original. Richard Rodgers' task was to set it to music, all twelve minutes or so of it. Having given Julie music which identifies her character, Rodgers had a different job to do for Billy. Apart from his helping her onto the carousel during the Prologue, nothing we have seen so far has explained Julie's attraction to him. His first song has to make the audience want to warm to him, and like Julie, ignore the policeman's dire warnings about his disreputable character.

Now we see the true genius of Rodgers and Hammerstein. Rather than begin by giving Billy a big self-declamatory number as many writers might have done, again taking their cue from Molnár, they start to reveal the real Billy. They show us that he is as bemused as we are at why this girl, so different from his usual type of female companion, has chosen to stay with him. Not only is he bemused; it bothers him too, this strange fascination he has for her, illustrated by the underscoring, a pianissimo *You're a Queer One, Julie Jordan,* a theme he suddenly finds himself whistling. There now begins a musical interrogation as Billy tries to find out more about Julie, asking her a series of questions about her former love life, all the while continuing to use themes from, *You're a Queer One, Julie Jordan* to do so, thereby indicating that he is falling further and further under her spell. To underline musically the rising level of conflicting emotions in Billy, Rodgers raises the key a semitone every time he asks her a new question.

Julie, meanwhile, appears to remain cool and calm throughout, her answers to Billy's questions ending in a natural musical cadence as if desiring to bring the interrogation to an end. Only as we move toward her singing *If I Loved You,* do we get a sense of the emotions stirring within her as she sings the song's introduction to the accompaniment of the weaving theme, once again, first heard in *You're a Queer One, Julie Jordan.*

The centrepiece of *The Bench Scene* is *If I Loved You,* one of the handful of Rodgers and Hammerstein songs for which the music came first. How this came about is not certain, but it may well have something to do with Hammerstein's struggle with the lyrics as described in the previous chapter. In the *Complete Lyrics of Oscar Hammerstein,* the author is quoted as answering a fan's query in 1951; 'In the case of *If I loved You* the melody - the entire melody- was written first and I set the lyric to it'.[101]

Rodgers' music tells the audience everything that is going on in the young lovers' minds. He does so first and foremost with the richness of his melody; this in turn, is set to a rhythmic pattern which makes skilful use of triplets which seem to capture the uncertainty the lovers are feeling, and the whole is enveloped in exquisite harmonies, none more so than the diminished seventh chords heard in the second and sixth bars of each 'A' section, chords which tug at your heart strings no matter how many times you hear them.

Rodgers's sense of musical drama is seen too in the way he finishes the song. The musical climax, comes not as one might expect with the final line of the song, but with the penultimate line, *"How I loved you."* Then there is the briefest of pauses before reality sets in and the song concludes quietly with the conditional *"If I loved you."*

It is only now, after Julie has sung *If I Loved You,* that we see the Billy that she has seen. Rodgers and Hammerstein created the Two Little People section in which he, perhaps for the first time ever, reveals his soul to another human being. Rodgers' music complements perfectly Hammerstein's reflective lyric, right down to the descending modal phrase on *"We don't count at all."* All Billy's frustration at the raw deal life has given him can be heard in those five notes. He knows that a *"couple o' specks of nothin"* like

---

[101] Amy Asch, *The Complete Lyrics of Oscar Hammerstein II,* p311.

them, don't really stand a chance, yet some power he cannot comprehend continues to propel him towards Julie; and just as it did with her, so the weaving theme underscore his inner turmoil as he introduces his reprise of *If I Loved You*.

Richard Rodgers' handwritten score for *If I Loved You* in the Library of Congress archives.

By the time he has finished his reprise, we know that Billy has fallen completely under Julie's spell. Had Rodgers and Hammerstein followed musical comedy convention, Julie and Billy would now sing a second reprise together emphasising their love for each other. In *Carousel,* the writers were not following convention. Instead, after a little more, typically awkward dialogue, and underscored by a thrilling, final harmonic progression, the lovers embrace beneath the falling acacia blossoms. The music has done its job. The audience may suspect that the affair will not end well, but in this moment, they are totally on Julie and Billy's side.

Not only did Rodgers and Hammerstein flout convention by not having that reprise; they went still further and denied Julie and Billy a duet at all, or indeed a single note to sing together, thereby emphasising their inability to communicate with one another - *"Longing to tell you, but afraid and shy."* Instead, the romantic duet is given to the more conventional couple, Carrie and Enoch in the next scene.

The second scene opens with another extended musical sequence, leading up to a song Hammerstein anticipated in his outline - *June is Bustin' Out All Over.* Music from this sequence will be heard again during the show, as underscoring and in the ballet, once more emphasising the use of music to reinforce the unfolding drama.

The next sequence features Carrie and Mr. Snow and was developed from the tentative 'Put Your Faith in Sardines and Me' title in the original outline. It begins by Snow setting out his plans for their future and the bright optimistic tone of this music is in stark contrast to the more subdued, reflective music associated with Billy. This optimistic mood continues when Snow and Carrie sing *When the Children Are Asleep.* A second verse was written for Carrie as Hammerstein promised in his 9 January draft and a form of duet was added too in that whilst it is primarily sung by Carrie, Snow keeps interrupting. This clever musical device reinforces the point that whilst Snow may not physically abuse Carrie, he does nonetheless, abuse her, by trying to exert absolute control over her to the extent that she cannot even voice her own opinions.

In his original outline, Hammerstein suggested a *Sea Chanty*[sic] to be sung by Billy, Jigger and the sailors. Originally *Blow High, Blow Low* was to come before *When the Children Are*

Asleep, but subsequently, it was moved to follow that song. Hammerstein's lyric inspired Rodgers to compose a jaunty hornpipe in 6/8 for which Agnes de Mille created a show-stopping dance.

Whilst Oscar Hammerstein agonised over the lyrics of the *Soliloquy* for some four weeks, according to John Raitt, Richard Rodgers completed the music in an afternoon. Apocryphal tale or not, it takes no account of the time Rodgers spent with Hammerstein when suggesting possible outlines for the music, or the time Rodgers had been thinking about it since.

When Rodgers said that they came very close to writing an opera, it may well have been this piece, more than any other that he was thinking of. A seven-minute aria (you cannot call it a song) that Billy sings as he ponders his impending fatherhood. Constantly switching keys and with numerous changes in tempo, nothing like it had been heard on Broadway before. Its numerous melodic themes provide the sense of wonder, the sense of pride and the fun that can be had with a son, followed by the bemused realisation that comes when he considers the possibility that the child might be a daughter. "You can have fun with a son, but you got to be a father to a girl." Here, Rodgers gives Billy a wonderful, tender melody, complete with dotted rhythms that match Julie's, ("Half again as bright, as girls are meant to be,") before reaching the climax when Billy, realising he has no money with which to feed and clothe his daughter, resolves to get some, no matter what.

Although he decided not to start the show with a conventional overture, it was always Rodgers' intention to have one with which to open the second act, "a big overture summarizing the main musical and dramatic ideas of the drama" as he told Olin Downes. Arrangements for overtures and entr'actes are usually prepared by the orchestrators. Sometimes, a composer may specify certain numbers they want to be included but that tends to be the extent of their involvement. When it came to prepare the *Entr'acte* for *Carousel,* Don Walker had so much to do with other parts of the score, he handed the task to Joe Glover who was one of a handful of arrangers Walker called in to help get the job done in time. Although still part of the published vocal score, it is hardly ever performed today. It may not even have survived long on Broadway because in a programme for the week commencing 13 May 1945, less than a month after its premiere, it is not listed among the musical numbers. [102]

Instead of the *Entr'acte,* the second act now opens with a brief orchestral reprise of *June is Bustin' Out All Over* before the entire ensemble sing *This Was a Real Nice Clambake,* a typically lilting Rodgers' waltz. There has been speculation, and it has appeared in at least one book, that this song was first written as *This was a Real Nice Hayride*, originally included in the score of *Oklahoma!* but later cut from that show.[103] However, numerous musicologists have pored over Rodgers and Hammerstein's original papers in the years since that book was written, and none of them reported finding any firm evidence supporting the suggestion.

Rodgers pokes musical fun at Enoch Snow in the next number, *Geraniums in the Winder*. The song follows an episode when Snow comes across Jigger trying to take advantage of Carrie's naiveté. Snow breaks off their engagement and sings about his regret at what might have been. The music Rodgers gave him is whiny and petulant and does not engender any sympathy for him at all.

After the spirited musical argument between the girls and the boys, *Stonecutters Cut It On Stone,* Julie has her only solo, the quietly reflective *What's the Use of Wond'rin?* This is a quite extraordinary song, which seems consist of little more than a series of scales. The reality is very different though because with its rich harmonies alternating between major and minor, and with its use of the dotted rhythms we have come to associate with Julie, it is far from simple; yet it works brilliantly in enabling the audience to understand Julie's decision to stay with Billy, even if it disagrees with her. Unusually, Oscar Hammerstein included a musical note in the stage directions relating to the song, saying that 'The Orchestration is light', and that is just what Don Walker gave him, very pianissimo, using just strings, harp and woodwind.

The next song we hear is *You'll Never Walk Alone* which I discuss in detail in Chapter 11.

---

[102] There is a recording of *The Entr'acte,* (quite possibly the only one in the public domain) on You Tube performed by the BBC Concert Orchestra for a 1994 radio broadcast of the entire show.

[103] Scott McMillin, *The Musical as Drama* (2006), p82.

The Highest Judge of All was the last song to be written and the last new song heard in the show. It was first added to the score to facilitate a scene change. In fact, it has an important role in explaining Billy's character. Even after his death, he is still the same confused person, one minute brash and bullying, the next tender and all too aware of his failings.

Rodgers accompanies this with music that is typically Billy, one moment bold and brassy in G major, and then as Billy becomes more reflective, modulating to E minor before finally returning to type in the major key.

Quite frequently, during rehearsals and the try-out runs of a new musical, songs were found not to work and would be replaced, often reappearing in a future show by the same composer. Whilst *The Highest Judge of All* was a late addition to the *Carousel* score, there is no evidence that any songs were cut. As noted elsewhere, in her memoirs, Agnes de Mille did refer to the cutting of a couple of songs after the New Haven first night, but she seems to have misremembered and the only significant musical cuts made were to the ballet, the dance that followed *Clambake* and some repetitions.[104]

***

Like most of his contemporaries, Rodgers did not orchestrate his own scores. By the time he had finished composing all the music for the show and it was ready to go into rehearsals, there was just not enough time to undertake what is a lengthy and specialist task. He would be busy overseeing the staging of the musical numbers, making sure they were in the right keys for the vocalists and that his songs were being performed as he intended. He much preferred being in a rehearsal room or theatre, to being stuck in an office copying out endless crotchets and quavers on sheets of manuscript paper. Additionally, there would be the inevitable writing and re-writing that is always required of the composer as a production takes shape during the frantic run up to opening night.

---

104 Although no evidence has been found in support of de Mille's claim of two songs being cut, it is a story that is still often repeated in articles about *Carousel.*

The man to whom Rodgers first turned to orchestrate *Carousel* was Robert Russell Bennett. Bennett had orchestrated the score for *Oklahoma!* and was renowned as one of Broadway's foremost exponents of the art. When the invitation came, Bennett was heavily involved in lucrative work for the advertising industry and told Rodgers that he did not feel able to do the show. Rodgers, who according to Bennett, did not seem inconsolable when told of his situation, nonetheless asked Bennett if he would at least work on those parts of the show that were ready for orchestration, *The Carousel Waltz* and *Mr. Snow* and said he would hand the big contract over to Don Walker. Bennett agreed and later wrote that no one could shed any tears over having Don Walker's arrangements, and that his work on *Carousel* was one of the finest jobs ever done.

At first glance, the choice of Walker for the *Carousel* orchestrations might have seemed strange as his background was very much non classical. Born in New Jersey the son of a small-town grocer, he started learning piano at age nine. At school, he quickly learned to play the drums, the flute and the saxophone. By the time he graduated high school at age fourteen, he was too young to go to a music conservatory, so his parents sent him to a business college instead.

He got his first break whilst studying accountancy at the Wharton School of the University of Pennsylvania. On learning that Fred Waring was visiting Philadelphia, Walker engineered a meeting and persuaded the renowned bandleader to listen to a couple of arrangements he had made for a local band. So impressed was Waring with what he heard that he hired Walker on the spot. He stayed with Waring for a couple of years before moving to New York where during the 1930s he built up a reputation as an arranger on Broadway. Richard Rodgers hired him to orchestrate the score for what would be his last complete show written with Larry Hart, *By Jupiter* in 1942 and the revival of *A Connecticut Yankee* a year later.

Apart, however, from some work he had done with Sigmund Romberg, Walker's growing reputation was for his jazzy, swing-influenced arrangements. It was he who began to give saxophones much more prominence in the pit. In 1941, for a show called *Best Foot Forward* by Martin and Blane, the orchestra had three trumpets, three trombones and five reeds, all doubling on saxophone.

Carousel was going to be a very different task. Though not quite an opera, the orchestrations that Richard Rodgers required would be more akin to those heard at the Met than the usual fare on Broadway. By the time the score was completed, Rodgers had decided on the instrumentation he wanted:

2 Flutes (doubling Piccolos)	1 Harp
1 Oboe (doubling English Horn)	1 Percussion
2 B flat Clarinets	9 First Violins
1 Bassoon (doubling Bass Clarinets)	4 Second Violins
3 French Horns	4 Violas
2 Trumpets	3 Cellos
3 Trombones	2 Basses
1 Tuba	

Not a saxophone in sight. This was the challenge Rodgers set his new arranger. Walker was not fazed and shared Rodgers' view about the score: 'I always thought it was an opera. It should sound different from other shows'.

When he was asked to take over *Carousel,* Walker was busy with a show he was writing himself called *Memphis Bound*. He did not want to stop work on this, but because, like almost every other arranger at the time, he was under contract to the Chappell Music Publishing Company, when they insisted that he had to take on a job, he had no choice. When he was summoned into Chappell's boss Max Dreyfus's office, Walker recalled he was told, "Don, the next two weeks could be the most important in your career. Russell Bennett was supposed to be the orchestrator of Rodgers and Hammerstein's new production, but now after scoring two numbers, he is suddenly ... out of the picture. Hans Spialek is busy with his own show ... He might be able to score one number for you but that is all. What we need right now is someone to be responsible for the whole score of CAROUSEL and the only one we have available right now is *you,* DON WALKER!"[105]

Walker's worry was not that he could not handle the score for such a large orchestra. His concern was the paucity of time,

105 Don Walker, *Men of Notes*, p224.

only two weeks remaining to put all those notes on paper and then have them copied and played.

"*Carousel* was about one week into production," Walker said, "I would have to accept responsibility for a production with as much music as an opera to be played by an enormous orchestra, for Broadway, of forty men ... It was a monster. I was able to score the first act myself but got into trouble with the second act. I called in Hans Spialek for one number, (*When the Children Are Asleep*) and Stephen Jones for another, (*You'll Never Walk Alone*) and was able to complete the rest myself in time for the opening in New Haven, scoring the final number in the Hotel Taft while rehearsals were going on."[106] Stephen O. Jones was also responsible for orchestrating *This Was a Real Nice Clambake.*

Such was the pressure on arrangers as opening night drew ever closer, that it was common practice to bring in colleagues to help, particularly once a show opened out of town. Depending on audience reaction and how the creative team saw it, existing musical numbers and dance routines might be cut or re-ordered, new ones added or the composer or musical director might request changes of key or instrumentation: there might also be a requirement for extra underscoring or music to accompany scene changes; and of course, with music making up seventy-five per cent of *Carousel,* that made the pressure even greater. Arranger Irvin Kostal described just how great the pressure was at that time by saying that staying up all night was an absolute necessity when trying to meet a Broadway show premier. Writing in 1982, Walker recalled other details.

'Rodgers was delighted with the orchestrations, with the exception of the two numbers that Russell had done. He made me promise to re-score *The Carousel Waltz* and *Mr. Snow* in the style I had established with the rest of the score. The show went on to Boston, but I had to go back to New York to take care of *Memphis Bound.* Before that went into rehearsal, I was able to score *Mr. Snow.* [The extended opening sequence, *You're a Queer One, Julie Jordan* is still Bennett's original, and has never been replaced.]

'I was too busy with *Memphis Bound* to restore *The Carousel Waltz* until after the *Memphis* opening. By that time, Rodgers not only wanted me to re-score it, but to score it for a full symphony

---

106 Stephen Suskin, *The Sound of Broadway Music*, p359.

orchestra, capable of being reduced to play with the forty men in the pit of the show. That was a most difficult assignment, but I did it and from then on, my orchestration of the "Waltz" was played not only in the show, but in all concert presentations'.

Stephen Suskin quotes a letter from Walker in which he explains that Rodgers was asked for a symphonic version of the 'Waltz'. By having him do it in a manner that was reducible to pit orchestra size, Rodgers was able to get his new 'Waltz' for the theatre but have the Symphony foot the bill.

Ten years later, in 1955, when they were about to make the film version, Walker wrote to Rodgers and referred back to the original production. '... I was preoccupied, to say the least. Nevertheless, after I read the book and heard the score of *Carousel,* I could not help myself. I gave it my whole heart and I know the result showed it. I feel today that *Carousel* was the best job I have ever done. There was something about the story and your wonderful music that inspired me ...'[107] In the end, because 20th Century Fox had overall control of the production, Walker did not get to arrange the score for the film.

Although Rodgers used an orchestrator, he nonetheless retained control of the sound of his music. This was illustrated by a story told to author, Ethan Mordden by production associate, John Fearnley who recalled that one day, during *Carousel* rehearsals, he was particularly struck by the underscoring in *You're a Queer One, Julie Jordan,* which has the 'weaving theme' unexpectedly embellishing the main strain. Fearnley mentioned this to Robert Russell Bennett (who had orchestrated just that scene before leaving the show) and complimented him on his imaginative arrangement, only to be told by Bennett that it wasn't

---

[107] Back in the 1940s, once a production had finished its run the various orchestral parts were scattered to the winds. Wanting to ensure that future productions of *Carousel* sounded as Richard Rodgers intended, in the year 2000, the Rodgers and Hammerstein office began the task of restoring all the parts of the entire score. Led by their musical director Bruce Pomahac, it was a massive undertaking. As an example, *The Bench Scene* alone has two-hundred and ninety-four bars of music. Although Don Walker orchestrated most of them, Hans Spialek and Stephen O. Jones contributed fifty bars between them. Tracing all the various sources required a great deal of research.

him, "it was all laid out in Rodgers' parts."[108] As previously noted, this 'weaving theme' *leitmotif* is heard frequently during the show.

***

The job of the dance arranger, another particularly important member of the backstage team on this show, was to work with the choreographer and perhaps the composer, to create the music for the many dance sequences. It is a Broadway role that Trude Rittmann more or less created.

Trude (Gertrude) Rittmann was born in 1908 in Mannheim, Germany. At the age of six, she began taking piano lessons at the local conservatory. At fourteen, she started formal studies in composition and then at seventeen, she moved to the Hochschule fur Musik in Cologne where she continued her studies in composition and piano.

So talented was she that by 1931, Rittmann had begun to build a successful career as a soloist, performing in her native Germany and in England, Holland, France and Switzerland. She was also gaining a reputation as a composer, once being described as 'Germany's most brilliant woman composer'. However, her dreams for the future were about to be shattered. Two years later, in 1933, after being told not to perform any pieces by Jewish composers, she fled Germany and arrived in England via France and Belgium.

In England, she found work teaching piano, theory, harmony, and counterpoint at Dartington Hall School near Totnes in Devon. It was during this period, while at Dartington Hall which also housed the Kurt Jooss School of Dance, that she began to learn about the relationship between music and dance.

In 1937, armed with recommendations from friends, she left England for the US where she was hired as concert accompanist and pianist for the American Ballet Caravan, later to become the New York City Ballet. Her mother managed to join her in America, but her father died in a Nazi prison. Over the next couple of years, Rittmann composed two ballets, *Charade* and *The Debutante,* and subsequently became the company's musical director, a role that

---

[108] Ethan Mordden, *Anything Goes: A History of American Musical Theatre.*

brought her into contact with other composers such as Leonard Bernstein, Aaron Copeland and Marc Blitztein.

Shortly after this, she began working with choreographer Agnes de Mille who enlisted her services as her concert accompanist and then to work with her on Kurt Weil's *One Touch of Venus.* It was this association that really changed the entire course of her career.

De Mille then hired Rittmann to work on *Carousel.* Whilst a show's composer would nearly always choose his orchestrator, the choice of dance arranger was left to the choreographer who more often than not, had the right to make that choice written into his or her contract. De Mille exercised that right in the case of *Carousel.* The work that Rittmann did for the show was so impressive that Rodgers used her on many of his subsequent shows, whether or not Agnes de Mille was the choreographer. Amongst her outstanding future works for him would be *The Small House of Uncle Thomas* ballet in *The King and I* for choreographer Jerome Robbins, and the *Do Re Mi* and *Laendler* sequences in *The Sound of Music.* All told, she worked on over fifty shows. Although her name is now becoming a little better known, she still does not receive the credit her contribution to Broadway's 'Golden Age' deserves.

***

For a show in which the music was so important, the choice of music director was a vital one. Whoever was to be chosen would have to have the approval of Richard Rodgers and Theresa Helburn seemed to be aiming high. A memo in the Theatre Guild Collection indicates that she had spoken to Fritz Reiner who recommended his former pupil, Ezra Rachlin who was now conducting the Philadelphia Opera Company and also, Anton Dorati who at that time was with the American Ballet Theatre.

When neither of these became available, the job was given to Joseph Littau who had been the conductor at Radio City Music Hall and lately, on *Carmen Jones* which had just completed its run.

Chapter 8

The Dances of Carousel

By 1943, dance had become an essential component of Broadway musicals. It had become almost a cliché that shows in the 1920s and 1930s opened with a chorus of scantily clad girls dancing in a tightly synchronised routine to a bright, jaunty tune. This set the tone for the evening to come, reassuring those in the audience that wanted nothing more than an undemanding evening of light entertainment, they were in the right place. That is why, when the curtain rose on the opening night of *Oklahoma!* to reveal nothing more than an elderly woman churning butter, it created such amazement.

This new development did not go down well with everybody. The respected critic, George Jean Nathan, who had encouraged playwrights such as Eugene O'Neil and William Saroyan, was most unhappy that the traditional chorus line of beautiful girls had been replaced by classically trained and fully clothed dancers. He demanded, maybe with tongue firmly in cheek, a return to the frivolous, glamorous musicals of the 1930s.

Whilst *Oklahoma!* correctly was considered the catalyst for so many changes in musical theatre, so far as dance is concerned, Richard Rodgers had anticipated himself in his 1936 show *On Your Toes*. It was in this show that choreography was used for the first time as an integral part of the story and that the term 'choreography' was introduced on Broadway. Choreographers Albertina Rasch and Harry Losee subsequently received similar credit for the Kern and Hammerstein show, *Very Warm for May*. Before then, it was 'Dances by ...' or 'Dances arranged by ...' *On Your Toes* employed a genuine, world-renowned choreographer in the person of Georges Balanchine and he was credited accordingly, as he was on Rodgers and Hart's next show, *Babes in Arms*, for which he created a dream ballet.

The choreographic revolution that began with *On Your Toes*, continued apace with Agnes de Mille's revolutionary dances for *Oklahoma!* and now would develop still further on *Carousel*.

De Mille was the daughter of screenwriter William C. de Mille and the niece of film director Cecil B de Mille and so grew up in a household rooted in the arts. After being told she was not pretty enough to be an actress, she switched to dance and fell in love with ballet. She spent some time in London with the Ballet Rambert. Whilst there, she also gained valuable theatrical experience working with producer C.B. Cochran on a number of shows and reviews including staging dances for Cole Porter's *Nymph Errant.* On returning to New York shortly before the outbreak of the Second World War in 1939, she joined the American Ballet Company. Her first big break came in 1942 when she choreographed Aaron Copland's ballet *Rodeo* for the Ballet Russe de Monte Carlo. Amongst those in the audience for the first night, at the invitation of Theresa Helburn, were Richard Rodgers and Oscar Hammerstein.

They saw at once that she had considerable talent, but Rodgers wondered if she could make the crossover from ballet to Broadway. Would she be able to create choreography for a Broadway musical, that was integral to the story, reveal character and advance the plot? It took some time before he finally was able to set aside those doubts and give her the job. She did not let him down, but his initial concerns meant that their relationship would always be prickly.

In her autobiography, *And Promenade Home,* de Mille writes how from hardly knowing Rodgers and Hammerstein at all when she signed up for *Oklahoma!* during rehearsals and afterwards, their friendship deepened. When work properly got underway on *Carousel,* she was able to add, 'By the winter of 1944 - 1945 I was going to Oscar not only for professional advice but for personal reaffirmation ... The relationship grew to be one of the joys of my life. He had talked for more than a year about his plans for *Liliom* and I looked forward to the opportunity of working on a second R.& H. production as the happy reward for being a good girl. Plans ripened that spring'.[109]

Her relationship with Rodgers, however, was more complicated. Whilst always respectful of each other's talent and professionalism, on a personal level, they found each other increasingly difficult. De Mille thought Rodgers changed after *Oklahoma!* and became harder, arbitrary and autocratic. She thought his success corroded him.

---

[109] Agnes de Mille, *And Promenade Home*, p228.

According to Dorothy Rodgers, her husband liked to quote Irving Berlin when speaking of de Mille. Berlin was reputed to have said of Ethel Merman, "I'll never work with that Merman again as long as I live - until I need her," and that was exactly how Rodgers felt about de Mille. Rodgers' daughter Mary reinforced her mother's opinion saying that her father thought she was a pain in the ass. De Mille was convinced that she was severely underpaid and undervalued on *Oklahoma!* and was determined not to be so treated on *Carousel*. Perhaps the tension was simply Rodgers' response to the continual demands that de Mille was making and his own determination to ensure that the show would be known as Rodgers and Hammerstein's *Carousel* and not Rodgers, Hammerstein and de Mille's.

Given that Richard Rodgers had composed the spectacularly successful *Slaughter on Tenth Avenue* ballet for *On Your Toes,* it is perhaps surprising that he did not compose a specific score for either the *Oklahoma! Dream Ballet* or the second act ballet for *Carousel.* Trude Rittmann suggested the reason might have been that the composer could not face the prospect of being stuck in a small rehearsal room for days on end, alone with Agnes de Mille.

Unsurprisingly, with the astonishing success of *Oklahoma!* everyone associated with it found themselves in high demand and de Mille was no exception. Offers of work poured in. The one she eventually accepted was the Kurt Weill musical, *One Touch of Venus,* starring Mary Martin. She had a much higher profile on this show than on *Oklahoma!* Now she had a chance to influence much of the production, not just the dances. The credits described the show as being 'Staged by Elia Kazan, Music staged by Agnes de Mille'.

Her progression continued in her next show, *Bloomer Girl,* music and lyrics by Harold Arlen and E.Y. Harburg, the latter also being credited with the show's staging whilst William Schorr was credited as director of the book and de Mille as choreographer.

Her dances in both shows were well received, particularly the *Sunday in Cicero Falls* number in *Bloomer Girl*. This prompted Rodgers and Hammerstein to contact de Mille in the Spring of 1944 about working on what would become *Carousel*. In April, she wrote to her husband, Walter Prude, 'Dick Rodgers told me I was a really important person in the American Theatre ... This was apropos of his wanting me to do *Liliom*'.[110] Rodgers no doubt meant that compliment, whatever reservations he might have had about her as a person. Knowing how important dance would be to the new show, getting her on board, was one of the first decisions he and Hammerstein made regarding the *Liliom* project, even before they had overcome all their reservations about doing the show. [111]

By November 1944, de Mille was having regular lunch meetings with Rodgers and Hammerstein. She learned, to her dismay, that as he had on *Oklahoma!* Rouben Mamoulian was going to direct the new show. The extent of her anguish can be discerned from another letter to her husband (serving in the Army in Europe.) She wrote, 'Mamoulian is going to direct. Oh Hell! Oh hell! Oh hell!' [112]

To eliminate potential conflict between the two temperamental creative talents, Richard Rodgers got them together at an emotionally charged reconciliation and as added insurance, arranged for the dance rehearsals to be held some forty blocks away from the theatre.

Peace may have reigned but de Mille's feelings about Mamoulian did not change. In a later letter to Walter, she said that the director 'was behaving like a lamb and his direction is just about as intelligent'.[113] Perhaps she had harboured hopes that she might be allowed to direct this new show, but as much as Rodgers and Hammerstein admired her choreography, they clearly did not think her ready for that big leap of faith, although she would get her chance to direct their next project, *Allegro*.

For now, though, not only would she miss out on directing *Carousel*; she would not even get to stage the Prologue, a task given her recent successes, she considered well within her capabilities. That opening sequence, it was thought, would not require choreography. It involved movement and pantomime but no dance whatsoever. In fact, as discussed earlier, Hammerstein's stage directions specifically stated that it should not be a ballet

---

[110] Agnes de Mille correspondence, Special Collections, Smith College.
[111] However, much she might have infuriated him, Rodgers would not let that stop him using her once he knew she was the right person for the job.
[112] Agnes de Mille correspondence, Special collections, Smith College.
[113] Ibid.

treatment. As such, all the producers felt it would be better staged by Mamoulian.

Dancer Bambi Linn, however, in an interview with Carol Easton for the latter's biography of de Mille, had no doubt that de Mille contributed significantly to the Prologue. Linn said that Mamoulian just could not get the scene right, changing it continually throughout the out-of-town try-outs. Finally, Linn recalled, with the Broadway opening looming, Mamoulian turned to de Mille and said, "All right Agnes, you do it," which is what she did, thereby saving the Broadway opening.

Linn has remained adamant that this version of events is true and said, "Mamoulian didn't know what to do with the Prologue." There is further evidence in support of Linn's claim; It takes the form of an annotated score together with detailed notes prepared by dancer, Gemze de Lappe, describing every piece of action in the Prologue. De Lappe's association with de Mille began when she was given a small part in the original production of *Oklahoma!* When the show opened in London in 1947, she created the role of Laurey in the dream ballet. Over the years, she became something of a muse for de Mille who created several dances for her. Later, de Lappe devoted herself to faithfully preserving de Mille's choreography in any productions of her shows all over America.

Her notes came to light when Bruce Pomahac was engaged in the restoration of the *Carousel* score. He met regularly with de Lappe who had retained her original copy of the score in which were written many stage cues at specific points in the Prologue. None of those cues appeared in any other version of the script or score that Pomahac had seen. Although no specific date can be put on these insertions, de Lappe's recollection was that they were written when Mamoulian finally turned the Prologue over to de Mille. De Lappe then produced a detailed summary from all the notes she had acquired and her memory of what de Mille had accomplished.

The notes that de Lappe produced are headed 'CAROUSEL CHOREOGRAPHIC NOTES PROLOGUE'. These are not the four and a half pages of stage directions written by Oscar Hammerstein but with bar numbers added. De Lappe's notes were created to solve a problem that Mamoulian seemingly could not; namely, to enable the Prologue to be performed as a pantomime synchronised to a pre-written score. Why Mamoulian struggled to get it right is uncertain, but de Mille's experience as a choreographer meant that when he turned to her, she was ready to step up.

She was used to devising movement, dance or otherwise, to fit existing music. From her notes, as annotated by de Lappe, one can see Hammerstein's storyline remains the same, as does the way the characters relate to each other. What de Mille was able to do, was to take Mamoulian's ideas for staging the story but place them in such a way that they would coincide precisely with the most suitable dramatic moment in the score. So, 'At measure [bar] 117, Billy gets up on his stand. Mrs. Mullins goes back to her stand to sell tickets'. 'At measure 225, Julie enters'. Billy first becoming aware of Julie is described at measure 291. '... The carousel starts again. Billy notices Julie and comes down from his stand. He coolly circles around her as Mrs. Mullins, having noticed his manoeuvre, has come downstage to confront him. This girl may be different - she may be the first one Billy is actually interested in. Mrs. Mullins doesn't like that'. All of this carefully staged action is completed by measure 307 and of course, the story is conveyed without a word. The drama continues with the action described between measures 357 to 393.

'At Measure 357, Mrs. Mullins gets back on her stand and the girls rush forward to buy tickets. Julie tries to buy a ticket but is pushed out of the way by the other girls. Billy notices this. He smiles and with exaggerated gallantry, he walks over to her and offers his arm. He leads her towards the carousel. But Mrs. Mullins strides over to Julie, demanding her nickel. Julie fumbles in her purse. Billy stops her. Mrs Mullins is furious. Billy takes a ticket from Mrs. Mullins, tears it in two and escorts Julie to the carousel, which has already started (for the third and final time) at measure 377. At measure 393, Billy picks Julie up and puts her on the only remaining horse on the carousel'. As the Prologue moves towards its finale, there is a reminder 'that the center [sic] must remain clear enough for the audience to see Billy and Julie on the carousel and Mrs. Mullins, down stage of her stand, reacting to them'. By the time the lights black out at measure 461, the Prologue has told us everything we need to know to be able to understand the scene that is about to follow.

Although it seems quite clear that in the end, Agnes de Mille made a very significant contribution to the staging of the Prologue, when *Carousel* was premiered, it was Mamoulian alone who received the credit.

De Mille's role ostensibly was to be limited to the Second Act Ballet and three other planned dances; *June is Busting Out All Over, Blow High Blow Low* and *This was a Real Nice Clambake.* That last dance at the start of Act 2 would fall by the wayside in New Haven as part of the changes necessary to cut the show to a reasonable running time, although she fought very hard to keep it in.

The first dance in *Carousel* appears in Act 1, Scene 3. It is now spring and from the moment the curtain opens, there is a sense of excitement as humorous dialogue leads into *June is Bustin' Out All Over,* a full-scale chorus number extolling the joys of the season and reminding everyone, that this is the time when all God's creatures, as Cole Porter so eloquently put it, "do it." The song features almost the entire company and is led by Julie's cousin, Nettie Fowler who we meet for the first time.

Rodgers and Hammerstein decided that this would be the perfect spot for the show's first dance. In his initial outline, Hammerstein referred to a 'sand dance' at this point. By the time of his draft script dated the 9 January 1945, he included a more detailed description of the dance he had in mind. Being set on the seashore, he decided to make use of the sand to be found there and envisaged a humorous dance where the boys would track sand back from the beach and the girls would come on stage with 'a variety of brooms and brushes that they would force sternly into the dancers' hands and the rest of the dance is performed with the sand being actually swept off the stage'. He described it as a 'shuffling sand dance' in a 'soft - shoe' kind of style, a light-hearted production number for the girls and boys of the chorus.

Agnes de Mille saw here an opportunity to add to Hammerstein's vision. A 'sand dance' might be entertaining but it would not advance the narrative.

We are fortunate that the dances she created, and her thinking behind them have been recorded on video for posterity, thereby giving us a detailed account of their creation. How those videos came to be made is itself an interesting story.

Part of the history of *Carousel* is the long running dispute between Agnes de Mille and Rodgers and Hammerstein that arose because de Mille felt that the significant contributions she made to both *Oklahoma!* and *Carousel* were never properly acknowledged, either artistically or financially. The dispute was exacerbated when de Mille was overlooked for the film and was, therefore, unable to recreate her choreography for the big screen. Nor was it resolved during the lifetimes of either Richard Rodgers or Oscar Hammerstein. In fact, it was only resolved in 1990 when Ted Chapin, former president and C.E.O. of the Rodgers and Hammerstein Organisation, saw a production of *Carousel* performed by the Houston Grand Opera Company who had hired Gemze de Lappe to recreate the original choreography.

Seeing those dances performed so perfectly made him realise how important it was that they should be preserved for future generations. With the blessing of Richard Rodgers' and Oscar Hammerstein's families, he approached Agnes de Mille who by then was in her mid-80s and recovering from a stroke. He told her that he wanted to record on video all her dances from the two shows. Furthermore, he hoped she would talk about them and explain how each dance should be staged. In return, she would now receive ongoing royalties for her work and all future productions would acknowledge her original choreography.

De Mille agreed and shortly after that, the *Carousel* dances were recorded when de Lappe staged the same production in Nashville. She and de Mille then sat down in front of the camera and discussed the work in detail, providing a unique insight into how Hammerstein's brief notes on a page were turned into arguably some of the finest dances seen on a Broadway stage.

The video is introduced by Richard Rodgers' daughter Mary Rodgers Guettel who had no doubt as to how important the dances are to the play. She expressed the opinion, that to do *Carousel* without the de Mille dances is like reading a great book with one of the main characters missing.[114]

The first dance demonstrated in the video is *June is Bustin' Out All Over,* which is followed by Agnes de Mille describing what she was trying to achieve. Initially, she decided to choreograph the dance for the female dancers alone. She described them as "just on the verge of bursting into bloom … ready for love, ready for life, ready for fruition." Indeed, fruition is a word she used frequently when talking about this number.

---

[114] This video is available to view in the Theatre on Film and Tape archive of the New York Public Library for the Performing Arts.

Whilst she did retain an element of Hammerstein's 'soft shoe' idea, she made the dance far more sensual, in keeping with the lyrics of the song. She gave the girls movements reminiscent of the season, hands rising and falling with shimmering fingers, like moisture, almost visible in the air. They gazed at the sky, opening their arms to embrace the warmth of the sun, and smelling it on the wet grass.

It is only when this expression of youthful, female sensuality has finished that Julie appears onstage for the first time since *The Bench Scene*, and the contrast between her and the other girls could not be starker. Far from being '*fresh and alive and gay and young*' we see that life has not been kind to her. She is completely oblivious to the joy and promise of the day. Billy is out of work, and worse he has hit her. We already knew that Julie was different from the other girls. By now changing the 'June' dance to a purely female dance, that difference has been highlighted still further.

Like the 'June' dance, the choreography for the *Blow High, Blow Low* hornpipe was given a narrative function by de Mille serving to further help the audience to identify the community in which the two principal characters lived. Having taken the decision to set *Carousel* in a New England coastal town, the authors anticipated their male chorus would be sailors for whom there would be an appropriate song and dance. Sure enough, a Sea Chanty [sic] is indicated in Hammerstein's first outline.

The pair duly came up with *Blow High, Blow Low,* a rousing hornpipe in 6/8 time. How predictable it would have been for a choreographer to create a spirited, masculine dance which would feature just the sailors. Such a dance, well performed, would always guarantee a respectable round of applause at its conclusion. That was never going to be enough for de Mille. The song is sung by Billy, his ne'er-do-well friend, Jigger and sailors from Jigger's whaler. At its conclusion, de Mille had them form into the shape of the bow of a ship before leaving the stage to the male dancers.

In the video, de Mille explained that the narrative she created for the *Blow High, Blow Low* dance was that "the sailors are in port, and they want to meet the girls. And the girls want to be met." To ensure that we don't lose the sense of the community, the music for the dance was cleverly arranged by Trude Rittmann to incorporate the 'Weaving Theme', reminding us that these are all girls who work at the mill with Julie. The girls act shyly at first but are soon swept up in the moment. They are all too aware that before long, the men will have to leave again. De Mille continued, "... and when they go, they go. And the women are left, they're abandoned. Most New England houses have that little railing at the top called the 'widow's walk'. And it wasn't called that lightly." It was that sense of loss that de Mille wanted to tap into, aware no doubt, how it would resonate with audiences in a country still at war. But even as she did so, she created for the dance, the character Hannah, a little spitfire who could handle that loss.

The role was played by former American Ballet Theatre principal, Annabelle Lyon who was only 4'6" tall. Dancing opposite her was 6'4" tall Peter Birch as the Boatswain. When they moved towards each other it was as de Mille put it as if she "looked up a mast." Indeed, the dance is peppered with dialogue and numerous sailor cries such as "Looks like a sailboat ridin' up to a lighthouse!" All these calls are what would have been heard on whalers in the 1870s and are the result of Hammerstein's detailed research. The index cards on which he noted them down can be seen among his papers at the Library of Congress. When the two begin dancing together, another sailor cries, "Climb aloft!" As Hannah more than holds her own in the frantic jig, one of the girls shouts, "Go it Hannah!" De Mille said, "The height, the power, and the maleness of this man, against the tiny little spunkiness of the girl was the fun of the dance." But the dance was not just to entertain. As the dance winds down, all the men leave to board their ship. The women, backs to the audience, wave their sad goodbyes, a scene repeated thousands of times during the war. But tiny Hannah, dancing against her giant partner, was representative of the strength of the women left behind and she demonstrated the strength that we know Julie will need to survive her own battles. She continues to dance alone, stomping on the ground like a stubborn child, fists clenched. Suddenly, her sailor returns and sweeps her off stage, so at least this couple are assured a happy ending.

Important though the first two dances were, de Mille knew that her most important task, the one by which she would always be judged, was the second act ballet.

Although Richard Rodgers had schmoozed de Mille early on to ensure she would be available to choreograph *Carousel,* when her choreography for *Bloomer Girl* received rave notices, he began to have second thoughts. He asked her to "step off her own bandwagon," perhaps a sign that he was concerned she was becoming over-confident and that her ego might get in the way of her giving the team the ballet they needed.[115] Hammerstein, however, seemed to have no such doubts and had talked to her throughout 1944 about his plans for the show and especially, the ballet. Shortly after completing his first draft of the script, he invited de Mille to Doylestown for the weekend. 'While the snow fell softly outside his Pennsylvania farmhouse, Oscar talked as only he can, transforming the material of our common craft into hopeful and lyric enchantment'. [116]

A few days later, she wrote to her husband Walter, 'I've been in most today and the evening "mauling" over the *Liliom* (now called *Carousel)* dances ... this time I've met a real challenge ... Also, they've given me the damndest thing to do. Liliom's perception of the first fifteen years of his child's life while he's climbing up the stairs for his interview with God'. [117]

Hammerstein's thoughts for this remarkable concept began with the idea that Billy's spirit would see his daughter for the first time from the vantage point of a 'flying horse'. The ballet was intended to depict the 'growth and development of Louise against a background of evil that constantly threatens her. [Billy] is tortured by the dangers that result from his retreat from earth and his responsibilities'. Hammerstein planned for the 'union of ballet, opera, drama and pantomime' to have several innovative elements. He insisted that there would be 'no ballet substitutions', meaning that unlike in *Oklahoma!* the characters in the ballet would be portrayed by the same actors who played them throughout the musical; he attached great importance to continuity. His original intention was that the ballet would include dialogue and Billy in particular, would have 'spoken lines and lyrics to sing'. By telling the story of Louise's first fifteen years in this way, the action would allow Billy to understand that 'the child is his in a deep and real

---

[115] Agnes de Mille correspondence, Special collections, Smith College.
[116] Agnes de Mille, *And Promenade Home*, p228.
[117] Agnes de Mille correspondence, Ibid.

way'. Hammerstein's script continues, 'When she is tempted, he knows why. He knows she has his weakness as well as his strength and revolutionary defiance to society'.

This was the bare blueprint that Hammerstein outlined for de Mille during that cold January weekend. As she wrote to her husband, she had the 'details of the narrative'. Her job now was to bring that narrative to life.

Trude Rittmann was de Mille's constant companion in this process. Together, they would pore over Richard Rodgers' score, experimenting with different pieces of music, a phrase here, a few bars there, as they sought the perfect match for the choreography that de Mille was devising. Sometimes, they would bring in one or two dancers to test the ideas they were developing. When things got fraught, as they often did, it was Rittmann who calmed 'Agschen' down. Finally, when they had settled on the form of the ballet, and the music to accompany it, Rittmann produced a piano score which was then given to Don Walker to orchestrate.

In a letter to Beverly Sills dated 8 April 1945, de Mille summed this lengthy process up in what was surely a rather understated manner. 'The music for the Act 2 Ballet was composed in the rehearsal room as I worked. It follows the action in almost Mickey Mouse style'.

Rodgers gave de Mille and Rittmann total freedom to create the music for the ballet for which, in its final version, they used eight different themes from the score, skilfully weaving those individual melodies into one piece that told Louise's story in a most compelling way. Some of their music choices seem inspired; who, for example, could have imagined how perfectly the music of the *I wonder what he'll think of me* section in *Soliloquy* would work as the background for the pas de deux? Accompanied by Trude Rittmann's intense yet tender arrangement, it provides a heart stopping moment.

Taking Hammerstein's broad outline, de Mille began sketching her own ideas for the story. A copy of this outline scenario survives amongst her papers in the New York Public Library. As Hammerstein suggested, it included dialogue and many of the leading actors from the cast, including Jan Clayton, who was to be shown giving birth to Louise on stage. 'It's wonderful" she said later, "I give birth to Bambi right on stage!'[118]

De Mille's scenario began - again as per Hammerstein's suggestion - with Julie weeping beside Billy's dead body. Billy then rises and mounts a carousel horse while heavenly attendants ride on either side of him. Julie stands alone, and Billy cries out 'Must she face this alone? Will nobody go to her? Will nobody help her?'[119]

Reports vary as to how long the ballet actually ran at the New Haven premiere (which famously did not finish until 1.30 a.m.), but the consensus seems to be around an hour and fifteen minutes. It was not well received. A devastated de Mille wrote to her husband, 'I was in such disgust with the way it went that I found Oscar Hammerstein and said, 'I've things to say so stringent about my work that I don't know whether my pride will permit me to stand up in a meeting with Mamoulian and the Guild Board and say them." He smiled, and put his hand on my shoulder, "You watch out what you say. You're talking about the woman I love.'"[120]

By the time the show reached Boston, ruthless pruning had reduced the ballet to some forty minutes. That was still far too long. Further drastic cuts led to de Mille complaining to her husband that it had been truncated to about ten minutes before she put her foot down and forced the producers to think again.

De Mille and Hammerstein met for breakfast and discussed how they could bring the ballet down to an acceptable length while still conveying the message it was meant to convey. (This was just one of the many problems Hammerstein had to work on in those frantic three weeks leading up to the New York opening. He was putting in five or six hours of creative writing every day from dawn on.) First of all, they decided to move the ballet to a different position in the second act. Instead of following Billy's death, it would now be positioned after the 'Backyard of Heaven' scene which Hammerstein created to replace Billy' meeting with Mr. and Mrs. God. The dialogue makes it clear that fifteen years have passed enabling the entire early part of the ballet, including the

---

[118] Carol Easton, *No Intermissions,* p244.

[119] Kara Anne Gardner, *Agnes de Mille,* p98.

[120] Agnes de Mille correspondence, Special Collections, Smith College.

birth scene to be cut. Day by day, throughout the Boston run, they inched their way towards a final version of the ballet, which at approximately twenty minutes, still fulfilled its intended purpose. It leaves Billy, and the audience, in no doubt that this is a troubled, lonely young woman, still suffering the consequences of her father's deeds fifteen years ago. And of course, it provides Billy's motivation, having turned down all previous offers, to finally take the opportunity to return to Earth for one day.

Now the ballet worked. 'My version brought the house down and we got the first genuine audience response of the run', de Mille wrote Walter. 'Oscar found me in the lobby and threw his arms around me. I cried. He thanked me for holding out and making dramatic sense. Later, Dick embraced me. And Mamoo, who had argued and argued ... said "Didn't I tell you?' ... When will people trust me to handle my own department?"' [121]

The drastic shortening of the ballet was not the only casualty de Mille had to endure. The show was still far too long. *This Was a Real Nice Clambake* was originally followed by a big waltz which according to the detailed notes made in conjunction with the restoration of the entire *Carousel* score, was set to music which Trude Rittmann had arranged from the melody that accompanies the lines *Fust come codfish chowder ...* De Mille argued that it should stay. "Convince Me," Hammerstein said and de Mille tried to do just that. Hammerstein responded that she argued well but that he did not agree.

"I don't agree too." de Mille replied.

"That makes us even. But I have the choice."

De Mille acknowledged, "That's candid. I can accept that."

But Hammerstein had the last word. "My dear," he chuckled, "you'd better. You have to."

The final version of the ballet begins with Louise, danced by Bambi Linn, just as Hammerstein had envisioned in his first outline, 'standing alone on the beach in full morning light. To the music of *If I Loved You,* she runs and leaps and tumbles in animal joy'.[122] At the conclusion of her solo dance, she turns a somersault and lies down on the sand to stare at the sky. Then two young urchins appear, and to music from the introduction of *June is*

---

[121] Carol Easton, *No Intermissions*, p245.

[122] Carousel Vocal Score

Bustin' Out All Over, she joins them in their game of leapfrog. She is forced to play boys' games because she has no girlfriends. After a while, the music changes to *When I Make Enough Money Out of One Little Boat,* and the six, well-scrubbed, well-dressed children of Enoch Snow, now a prosperous businessman, enter the stage. They stop and stare in amazement at this bawdy behaviour, their disapproval, very apparent. There is a momentary change of music to *My Little Girl.* When Louise invites them to join in her game, they snub her and start to leave but a young Miss Snow lingers behind out of curiosity and regards Louise's poor dress and bare feet with barely disguised contempt.

Now, as Hammerstein suggested, there is a little dialogue. De Mille stresses that this dialogue has to be delivered in a musical rhythm in time with the music, something quite hard to do:

> MISS SNOW: My father bought me this pretty dress.
> LOUISE: My father would have bought me a pretty dress too. He was a barker on a carousel.
> MISS SNOW: Your father was a thief!
> Louise chases her in rage and steals her fancy hat to the BOYS' approval.

A carnival troupe now appears to the strains of themes from *The Carousel Waltz* led by a young man who appears exactly how Louise has always imagined her father to be; handsome, bold and charismatic. She is enchanted by the troupe's costumes and 'snitches' the Leading Lady's gold parasol. The troupe dance a frenetic waltz at the end of which the lady demands her parasol back. The handsome young man, approaches Louise and tells her not to mind. The other carnival people exit but the young man stays behind, and they dance the pas de deux. Suddenly, as their dance ends, he becomes alarmed by her intensity and realises she is only a child. For him, it is a mild flirtation but for Louise, it is much more; her first experience, overwhelmingly beautiful, painful and passionate. He leaves her abruptly with a smile and a gentle pretend punch on the chin, the sort a father might give a child. She's too young. Thwarted, humiliated once more, she weeps alone. But Louise's heartache is not yet over. A group of children dressed for a party appear. This is to Carrie's solo in *When the Children Are Asleep.* Louise tries to join them, but they constantly push her away. Eventually, she tries to play by herself outside the party, to the sound of the original *June* theme, but still, they shun her and make fun of her until her heart breaks. She turns on them in a fury they never expected and cries "I hate you! I hate all of you!" The other children back away, leaving Louise heartbroken and very, very alone.

Seeing his daughter's pain from 'Up There', Billy cries "Somebody ought to help her," before realising that he is the only one who can.

All the midnight oil that was burned in Boston, all the heartache, the arguments and the compromises were worth it in the end. After the New York opening, once again de Mille wrote to Walter, this time to tell him about the reception the show received.

'The ballet - got tremendous applause at the end - at least, Bambi got it - the actors who came to the curtain to continue the play had to stand for about a minute and a half before they could speak. Then, in the next scene on Bambi's entrance, the noose broke. I've never seen anything like it in the theatre. They gave her an ovation, and no one could speak a line until she stepped out of character and with the grace of a dove inclined her head to acknowledge the glory'.[123]

The critics shared the audiences' enthusiasm for Linn's dancing, but even more pleasing was that they nearly all understood that the dances arose out of the plot and served the purpose of advancing the story. Accordingly, Lewis Nicholas of the *New York Times* wrote, 'The dances are not offered as individual dances, but as part of *Carousel*'.

Mary Rodgers was right in emphasising how important de Mille's choreography was to the show. Liliom the play is about the title character. With her imaginative choreography, de Mille made Carousel the musical, less about Billy, and much more about Julie and Louise and the consequences of Billy's behaviour on them, thereby providing a countermeasure against Hammerstein's softening of Billy.

The dream of a fully integrated musical in which book, music, lyrics and dance would all play an essential part, had finally come true.

---

[123] Agnes de Mille correspondence, Special Collections, Smith College.

Mayara Magri, Mathew Ball, Royal Ballet *Carousel* 2020.
©Bill Cooper / ArenaPAL

Chapter 9

Onstage and Backstage

Two years earlier, it was so difficult to find anyone prepared to invest in the $83,000 production cost of *Oklahoma!* that Rodgers and Hammerstein had to suffer the indignity of trawling the Park Avenue penthouse circuit seeking $1,000 here and five hundred dollars there from Manhattan's wealthiest residents. Rodgers accompanied at the piano while cast members sang and Hammerstein narrated the story.

There was no need for a repeat of that humiliating experience this time. Raising the $180,000 budget for *Carousel* could not have been easier. 20th Century Fox, who owned the movie rights to *Liliom,* put up thirty per cent of the cost. The remainder divided into tranches of 0.9% or $1,620 came from the producers, their families and friends.

As with *Oklahoma! w*hen it came to casting *Carousel,* Rodgers and Hammerstein decided that the show would be the star. So again, they sought relatively unknown actors and singers, sticking to their belief that nothing should come between the audience and the characters on stage.

No sooner had news of the forthcoming production been confirmed in October 1944, than they both began to receive letters from actors hoping there might be parts for them in the new show.

One such letter received by Oscar Hammerstein was from a young Hollywood actress called Judy Tuvin. She asked if she might be considered for the role of either Julie or Marie. 'Was 'legitimate' singing needed?' she wondered. 'Do you have any use for a Sunkist [sic] ex comedienne?' In response, Hammerstein answered, 'the bad news is that both Julie and Marie have to sing "legitimate" but just how illegitimately do you sing?' Miss Tuvin did not get either part in the new show, but she would go on to achieve considerable fame under her stage name, Judy Holliday.

Notwithstanding their preference for unknown artists, some big names were put forward as possibilities. Betty Jane Watson, Virginia Simms, Anne Blythe and Kathryn Grayson were all considered for Julie, Grayson still being in the frame as late as the 23 January 1945. Among those being considered for Billy was José

Ferrer but any interest in him ended when he was drafted. Another name being floated was that of French born baritone, Martial Singher who had recently made his debut at the Met.

The very first cast member to be signed up was John Raitt, and he was lined up for the role of Liliom even before Rodgers and Hammerstein had signed contracts to write the show.

A native of Santa Ana, California, Raitt began his career performing in operas and operettas with the Los Angeles Civic Light Opera. He then began appearing in musicals. A tall, handsome man blessed with a powerful baritone voice; he was obvious leading man material. The story of how he became one is worth telling. Lawrence Langner and his wife Armina Marshall were in California when they met with Armina's niece a very tall lady known by the soubriquet 'Little Armina'. She had seen Raitt perform and was so impressed by him that she recommended him to her aunt who served as the Guild's casting director. They did not see Raitt on that visit but sometime later, in January 1944, Marshall was back in California on a very short visit looking for someone to replace Alfred Drake as Curly in *Oklahoma!*

Because she was on a tight schedule, through Raitt's agent, Marshall arranged to meet him outside her hairdresser in Beverly Hills. Then, in a taxi between the hairdresser and David Selznick's office, she proceeded to interview Raitt. She did not hear him sing, but on a hunch, on her return to New York, persuaded the Guild to bring Raitt East to audition.

In March, Raitt received a registered letter from the Guild offering to pay his fare to New York (including the return if things did not work out). He did not think twice about it. He gave up his apartment, sold his car and set off on the four-day train journey to Broadway.

He was met at Pennsylvania Station and whisked to the St. James Theatre for his audition It was 15 March 1944. Waiting in the stalls were Dick Rodgers, Oscar Hammerstein, Lawrence Langner, Theresa Helburn, and a very anxious Armina Marshall sitting on the edge of her seat. The entire cast of *Oklahoma!*, currently playing at the St. James, were also waiting expectantly. If he was nervous, there was no hint of it when Raitt strode on to the stage, his six-foot two-inch frame towering over the writers, producers and actors sitting below him. He asked them if he could sing the Barber's song from *The Barber of Seville* to loosen up his voice. He moved forward onto the apron of the stage and dazzled his audience with the beauty of his voice and the clarity of his diction. Richard Rodgers who was sitting behind Lawrence Langner, leaned forward, and whispered, "There's our Liliom."

John Raitt, recalling that audition, said that the choice of the *Figaro* aria was pure cockiness and he recalled that he followed it up by singing virtually all the songs from *Oklahoma!* after which there was a deathly silence which seemed to last a lifetime. Having found their leading man, they were not going to take a chance on losing him. Raitt was immediately put under contract and took over the role of Curly on tour in Chicago in May 1944 and continued in that role until rehearsals for *Carousel* started the following February.

He found out later that he almost did not get the part because he was so much taller than Alfred Drake. Apparently, it was Oscar Hammerstein who came to his rescue. "I am a tall man" he proclaimed. "Why can't Curly be tall?"

There were, however, certain obstacles to overcome. First, when he signed his contract with the Guild, probably more out of naiveté than a deliberate intention to mislead, Raitt omitted to inform them that he had already signed an option agreement with a film company. When the film company decided to exercise their option in the summer of 1944, all of the Guild's plans for Raitt were thrown into disarray. After weeks of legal arguments, the matter was eventually resolved by a $5,000 payment to the film company, half by the Guild and the other half by Raitt.

Of even greater concern regarding *Carousel* was Raitt's acting ability. At a meeting in August with Armina Marshall when the possibility of his playing the lead role in *Liliom* was raised, Raitt himself voiced concerns. He knew that he was a very fine singer, but he had serious doubts about his suitability for such a demanding acting role. He had no problem with Curly for which he felt he was a natural, but Liliom was a different matter altogether. Marshall agreed with this assessment noting that Raitt did not think like an actor.

The extent of the concern over his acting ability (and the desire not to have star names) can be seen from a Western Union telegram of 21 September 1944 sent by Theresa Helburn to leading theatrical agent Louis Shurr:

> WE HAVE NOT FOUND SATISFACTORY LEADS FOR THE RODGERS HAMMERSTEIN LILIOM. ARE LOOKING FOR GOOD YOUNG ACTOR NO ACCENT EXCELLENT BARITONE VOICE. ALSO, YOUNG SOPRANO LEAD AND SOPRANO COMEDIENNE. PREFER NOT TO HAVE STAR NAMES. HAS STEVE BEKASSY GOOD ENOUGH VOICE AND SLIGHT ENOUGH ACCENT TO BE A POSSIBILITY. REGARDS[124]

In November 1944, Raitt returned to New York to read for the part. Doubts concerning his acting must have persisted, because it was not until rehearsals started, a year after Marshall first saw him, that he was finally confirmed as Billy. When Marshall informed Raitt of the decision, she told him "I have heard the music of the first act, and you have the most wonderful song I have heard in years. It has everything!" No doubt, she was referring to *Soliloquy*. Two days into rehearsals, Raitt recalls Richard Rodgers came on stage and handed him a huge piece of paper folded like an accordion. It was fifteen feet long and this indeed, was the *Soliloquy*. This song alone was enough to ensure that even though he was an unknown going into the show, his status as a star would be assured after it.

Another early cast signing was budding opera star, Christine Johnston. She was chosen to play Nettie Fowler and of course, would introduce *You'll Never Walk Alone*. How the role came to her is told in Chapter 11.

To play the role of Julie Jordan, the producers eventually found a talented twenty-seven-year-old actress called Jan Clayton. By the time she auditioned for the role, she had appeared in several MGM films all of them unremarkable. Slender and blonde, she had a clear, expressive soprano voice which obviously appealed to Rodgers and Hammerstein notwithstanding her lack of Broadway experience. After an initial audition with Theresa Helburn in Los Angeles, she flew to New York for a further audition with Rodgers and Hammerstein. She sang *The Trolley Song* from *Meet Me in St. Louis* but perhaps because of nerves, she did not perform as well as she would have liked. Fortunately for her, those listening still saw her potential, so Rodgers taught her *What's the Use of Wondering* and Rouben Mamoulian spent some time working with

---

[124] Theatre Guild Collection, Beineke Library, Yale University.

her; after her next audition, they took her to Sardi's and signed her up.

Whilst Clayton's future in the show was still in doubt, Oscar Hammerstein received a letter dated 2 February from friend and playwright, Sig Herzig:

> Dear Oc,
>
> Far be it from me to advise the Old Master on casting, nor is it the old gag about getting a girlfriend into a show, but I feel impelled to write you a short note about Jan Clayton, whom I understand is being considered for Julie ... She's got that quality of pathos about her which, I believe, is exactly what you're looking for in the character of Julie, beside which she has a good voice and knows how to sing.

Herzig went on to remind Hammerstein that he cast Clayton in the L.A. production of *Music in the Air.* 'Wouldn't it be rather redundant to have to discover your own discovery all over again?'

Hammerstein sent a brief reply a few days later:

> Dear Sig,
>
> Thank you for your letter. We are auditioning Jan Clayton now and she looks very promising ...
>
> If this note seems cool and brief, it is because I am very hot and bothered since I am on the threshold of rehearsals.
>
> All good wishes[125]

A pleasant postscript to Jan Clayton's involvement with the show occurred in 1954 when *Carousel* was given a revival at the New York City Center. Auditions for the new production were being held at the Majestic Theatre where Rodgers and Hammerstein's *Me and Juliet* was running. Rodgers invited Clayton to join him to watch one of the sessions. Arriving early, the pair were sitting in the deserted stalls when they suddenly remembered that this was the theatre where *Carousel* had first played all those years ago.

---

[125] Oscar Hammerstein Collection, Library of Congress.

'The idea occurred to us simultaneously', recalled Rodgers. 'Jan stood on the same spot on the stage where she'd stood nine years before, and I went to the piano. She sang *What's the Use of Wond'rin* to the empty seats. I don't mind saying we were both a little teary'. [126]

For the role of Carrie Pipperidge, Rodgers and Hammerstein settled on twenty-two-year-old Jean Darling. In a way, this was a break from their 'No Star' rule as Darling had been a child star as a member of the *Our Gang* series. She also appeared in Laurel and Hardy's *Babes in Toyland* and as the young Jane in the 1934 film version of *Jane Eyre.* She then decided to study singing and in 1940, won a scholarship given by the New York Municipal Opera Association. After turning down an offer to appear alongside Mickey Rooney in an *Andy Hardy* movie, she appeared in the 1942 Broadway musical *Count Me In* before being chosen to play Carrie.

Eric Mattson, a highly regarded operetta singer was chosen to play Enoch Snow while Murvyn Vye, who had played Jud Fry in *Oklahoma!* was signed to play Jigger Craigin. Experienced actress and *Pal Joey* and *By Jupiter* graduate, Jean Casto, won the part of Mrs. Mullin. The Starkeeper role went to another Broadway veteran, Russell Collins.

***

Once Rodgers and Hammerstein had committed to the show, Langner and Helburn turned their attention to the rest of the production team. They had fallen out spectacularly with Rouben Mamoulian, the director of *Oklahoma!* so their first choice for director was Elia Kazan.

He had directed two recent successes on Broadway: Thornton Wilder's play, *Skin of our Teeth* in 1942 and in 1943, the Kurt Weill musical, *One Touch of Venus.* Indeed, Kazan had been an early choice to direct *Oklahoma!* but as he put it, "I just don't click with it."

When Helburn contacted Kazan, he was in Hollywood directing the film, *A Tree Grows in Brooklyn.* Not only did she write to him about the *Liliom* project but also all the Guild projects in the pipeline. Kazan expressed particular interest in *Liliom* but was

---

[126] David Ewen, *Richard Rodgers,* p241.

afraid to commit to anything because of his draft status. He already had received one deferral and was uncertain that he would obtain another.

Joshua Logan was another director who could not be considered because of the war. He was stationed in Normandy when he received a letter from Dick Rodgers telling him that in the end, they could see no alternative to Rouben Mamoulian. Logan wrote back thanking Rodgers for his letter and said, 'the news of [sic] Mamoulian will do Liliom and make me writhe with envy. I think it's by far the right decision though and agree with you that his job will be terrific, headache or no. I hope he doesn't get 'arty' the way he did with Porgy and Bess and sticks to the style he got in Oklahoma [sic] I would love to put one carping remark in but I'm drooling green'.[127]

The reason Mamoulian had not been the automatic first choice for *Liliom* was because of that spectacular falling out referred to above.

The trouble was that the success of *Oklahoma!* had seemingly gone to Mamoulian's head. Even though the Guild had its own press office through which they promoted all their productions, shortly after the show's opening, Mamoulian engaged his own press agent and suddenly articles were appearing everywhere suggesting that everything new and innovative in the show together with its subsequent success was largely down to him.

The final straw came in an article in the *Mirror* which gave Mamoulian the credit for just about everything; the quiet opening, the placement of two of the best songs in the opening moments of the first act, the clothing of the dancers in period costumes without the usual display of legs, the casting of Alfred Drake and Joan Roberts as leads, and the overall integration of drama and music without resorting to specialty numbers. The article appeared on 13 June 1943, a shade less than three months after its New York opening.

So incensed were Rodgers and Hammerstein that two days later, Rodgers, on behalf of them both, wrote a vehement letter to the Guild demanding that it make Mamoulian cease his actions and institute a rigorous campaign to rectify the damage to their

---

[127] Letter, 22 August 1944. Richard Rogers Collection, New York Public Library, Performing Arts Division.

reputations. Rodgers also threatened they would go to the press themselves and publicly denounce Mamoulian if they did not receive immediate assurance that the Guild would do so. Furthermore, they would, with great reluctance, sever their amicable relations with the Guild, which would include the cessation of their attendance at the Thursday luncheons at Sardi's.

Immediately upon receipt of Rodgers' letter, Langner called Mamoulian. A transcript of the conversation is in the Guild files:

M. How are you?
L. I am not well at all.
M. What's the matter?
L. As a matter of fact, I am fed up with you and your lousy publicity! It's got to stop.
M. What publicity?
L. The stories you have been giving out *in PM, Sunday Mirror, Christian Science Monitor,* etc. You are just aggrandizing yourself at the expense of everyone else ...
M. What do you mean?
L. And what's worse, you told a damn lie in *PM,* saying that you were going to direct *Porgy and Bess* in the pictures when this had fallen through, and also saying that I had tried to cut out a scene in *Porgy* and you told me I could either take it out or you would go. I have never been so insulted publicly in my life.
M. Why, I didn't say that.
L. Saying you hired Alfred Drake and Joan Roberts, in the *Mirror* when you know that contracts were signed with them long before you were even asked to direct the play - Saying in the *New Yorker* that you had resuscitated The Theatre Guild ...
M. (Shouts) Wait a minute!
L. I won't wait a minute. You can go straight to hell!
(Langer then slams down the phone.)[128]

The following day, Langner and Helburn informed Mamoulian by letter that the sole right to exploit *Oklahoma!* lay with the Guild's press department and warned him that the

---

[128] Theatre Guild Collection, Beineke Library, Yale University.

improper exploitation of the show could result in serious damage to the property. They specified the particular instances referred to above where they felt Mamoulian had claimed credit to which he was not entitled, for example, the quiet opening, the period costumes and the positioning of the first two songs which were clearly set out by the authors in the script.

Finally, they implored him in the strongest possible terms to desist in making false statements about his involvement in the show; if not, the Guild would have to publicly deny any future statements made by him. Rodgers and Hammerstein affixed their signatures to the letter and registered their approval of its contents.

Mamoulian replied on 23 June referring to their "extraordinary letter", and mysteriously suggesting that the Guild had ulterior motives consistent with its behaviour in recent months. He went on to say:

> As you well know, in spite of the disingenuous assumptions of your letter, I have not been exploiting Oklahoma! but have been discussing for the press my own professional activities, which are what I have to offer, and the means of my livelihood.
>
> Oklahoma! happens to be only one of the many notable and successful productions which I have directed on the stage and on the screen; as the direction of the entire production of Oklahoma! is my most recent work, it is perfectly obvious and natural that in any discussion of my professional activities with the press, Oklahoma! has its proper place. [129]

The letter continues for several more paragraphs, justifying his actions, explaining that whilst he may grant an interview, he has no control over what eventually appears in the final article and even finishes by alleging that the Guild had been making false, defamatory and derogatory statements about him. He did not deny, however, that he appointed his own press agent.

All this was a far cry from the time in 1932 when Mamoulian worked with Dick Rodgers and Larry Hart on the film, *Love Me Tonight.* Rodgers recalled that 'At that time, Mamoulian was God

[129] Theatre Guild Collection, Beineke Library, Yale University.

at Paramount. Whatever he wanted to do, he did. He believed in Larry and me, and we believed in him, and we got along beautifully'.

In the end, Mamoulian accepted the demands made of him, and by September, his working relationship with the Guild was sufficiently harmonious for him to be offered the job of directing *Carousel*.

This episode again clearly illustrates the extent of the power that the success of *Oklahoma!* had delivered to Rodgers and Hammerstein. That they were prepared to break with the Guild with whom they had such a good working relationship over this issue, underlines this fact.

It is almost certain too, that if the Guild had not acted so swiftly and so decisively in dealing with Mamoulian, thereby preventing that break, *Carousel* would not have been written.

Mamoulian was born in Tbilisi, then part of Tsarist Russia in 1897, to Armenian parents. His mother was a director of the Armenian theatre. After spending a year in England, he arrived in the US in 1923 where he was engaged to teach at the Eastman School of Music and direct theatre and opera.

His first Broadway production was Dubose Hayward's *Porgy* in 1927 for the Theatre Guild and in 1935, he directed the Gershwin's opera based upon that play.

In 1929, Mamoulian directed his first Hollywood film, *Applause,* and during the thirties and forties this was followed by several more, including *Dr. Jekyll and Mr. Hyde, Queen Christina, Becky Sharpe, Love Me Tonight, The Mark of Zorro* and *Blood and Sand.*

Then in 1942, the Theatre Guild invited him to return to Broadway once more to direct their new musical version of the Lynn Rigg's play, *Green Grow the Lilacs.* This, of course, would become *Oklahoma!*

Agnes de Mille was the next recruit from the team that had worked on *Oklahoma!* As we have seen, her selection for *Carousel* was almost inevitable, notwithstanding her difficult working relationship with both Richard Rodgers and Rouben Mamoulian.

Costume Designer, Miles White was yet another graduate from *Oklahoma!* to join the *Carousel* production team. His experience in the ballet and his understanding of the need for dancers to be able to move freely in their costumes made him an ideal choice for these productions, notwithstanding his previous

Broadway experience was with more conventional shows such as *Ziegfield Follies* and *Best Foot Forward*.

Whilst many of the *Oklahoma!* team were asked to repeat their roles on *Carousel,* one significant change was the hiring of Jo Mielziner who was brought in to design the sets and lighting for the new show. Mielziner had already gained a reputation as one of the very best designers around. He was born in 1901 in Paris, the son of émigré artist parents. His mother was the Paris correspondent for *Vogue,* reporting on fashion, fine arts and theatre from the French capital. His father, Leo was a portrait painter. Apart from the talent he inherited from his parents, they encouraged him to get the best possible professional training as an artist. He was educated in England and Europe and studied at the Pennsylvania Academy of Fine Arts and the National Academy of Design. He got his break when his brother, the actor Kenneth MacKenna, recruited him to work as a stage manager in a summer stock production in Michigan. From that moment, he knew what he was destined to do.

By the 1920s, he was working for the Theatre Guild and by the end of the decade had become one of the most sought-after designers on Broadway. In the late 1930s, he worked on nearly all the Rodgers and Hart shows from *On Your Toes* to *By Jupiter.* During World War II, he worked on camouflage design for the Army Air Force and the O.S.S.

Mielziner wrote about his work on *Carousel* and believed he might have done a better job. 'Even the most finished of musical-comedy manuscripts is difficult for a scenic artist because a musical is a true collaboration. The action is developed not only through a text but through lyrics, music and choreography. Before a designer can create anything, he has to confer at length with the author, composer, lyricist, director, choreographer.

'When I was asked to design *Carousel,* only the first half of the script had been completed. But Rodgers and Hammerstein, good friends of mine, were concerned with the galloping calendar. They needed estimates of costs and time schedules speedily. Had I been able to read a finished manuscript, I would have tried, for one thing, to eliminate the realistic merry-go-round that opened the production. It was effective. A lovely carousel revolving on the stage and filled with glamorous young people makes a charming Prologue to the romantic drama. But when I finally got the script of the second act, weeks after I had started the designs, I knew that the backstage of even our largest New York musical theatre was going to be far too crowded. In the end, it meant that the producers had to employ an excessively large number of stagehands. As I grew more experienced in these matters, I refused to design piecemeal. Now, until I have the entire working script (as far as settings go), I will not commit myself or the management to the risk of overdesigning. If I were doing *Carousel* today, either the merry-go-round would be sacrificed, or I would try to develop a scheme that would employ a turntable as the basic mover of the sets'.[130]

Mielziner would go on to work on several other Rodgers and Hammerstein shows and win five Tony awards including two for his sets for *South Pacific* and *The King and I*. He was also responsible for the interior design of the Vivian Beaumont Theatre at Lincoln Center.

***

Auditions for the remainder of the cast started in December. The vocal demands of the score which Rodgers was composing, made casting rather more difficult than was the case on other shows. The original *Playbill* has only brief cast biographies compared with those we see in programmes today, but even in that abridged form, it is apparent that the common factor among the cast was the number of operas and operettas they had appeared in; *HMS Pinafore, Carmen, The Marriage of Figaro, The Barber of Seville, The Merry Widow, The Chocolate Soldier, Rigoletto, Il Trovatore, Das Rheingold*. The priority was clear. They sought singers who could act, rather than the other way around.

If finding singers who could act was one problem, finding dancers who could also act was another; yet these were the just the dancers that Agnes de Mille required. As we have seen, the narrative-advancing choreography she devised for the show was as much about portraying character as it was about dancing, so she too was trawling in a smaller pool. This was particularly so when it came to finding male dancers. The still raging war meant that what might have been a sizeable array of talent from which to

---

[130] Jo Mielziner, *Designing For The Theatre*, p8.

choose had been greatly reduced. Stage manager, John Fearnley complained about the situation to Richard Rodgers. The composer quickly explained the wartime policy designed to resolve the problem. "We hold a mirror in front of their face and if it clouds up, they're in."

Chapter 10

Rehearsals, Try-outs, Broadway

Rehearsals started one week later than originally intended, on Monday, 19 February. Actors and singers rehearsed at the theatre, whilst to preserve that uneasy peace between de Mille and Mamoulian, the dancers rehearsed at a studio several blocks away. Other than that, the rehearsals seemed to go smoothly enough.

The only recorded drama during the rehearsal period was about halfway through, when Lawrence Langner invited Ferenc Molnár to see how the show was developing. Oscar Hammerstein was furious with Langner for inviting him. "We're not ready for Molnár. Why not get him to come next week when we can give him a better show?" Oscar was also terrified that Molnár would hate all the changes he had made, particularly the ending. He went over to Molnár and apologised for the rough performance he was about to see. Molnár smiled and assured Hammerstein, "That is theatre. That is the part of theatre I like. Good, rough rehearsals."

During the run through, Hammerstein could only see the show through Molnár's eyes; hear it through his ears. At the end of the performance, he remained rooted to his seat. So nervous was he that he hoped Molnár would leave the theatre if he wanted to, without the need to talk to him. Suddenly, he was aware that Molnár was standing next to him, his eyes wet with tears. Molnár told him how much he enjoyed the show. "What you have done is so beautiful," he said. He understood the reasons for the changes that had been made; he liked the music. "And you know what I like best? The ending." According to Rodgers, hearing Molnár saying that "... was better than a rave notice in the *Times*."[131]

After a month of rehearsals, as was the custom in those days, the production went on the road for its pre-Broadway try-out. This is when the cast and orchestra perform together for the first time on stage with the sets and props, and where the authors and producers would first be able to gauge an audience's reaction to the show. The first port of call was the Shubert Theatre in New Haven, Rodgers' favourite venue for trying out his shows,

[131] Richard Rodgers, Musical Stages, p241.

although his daughter Mary was not so fond of it, pointing out its many disadvantages, 'the miserable Taft Hotel (lumpy beds and lousy room service) and Kasey's (a greasy spoon theatrical hangout across the street from the Shubert Theatre where the food was so terrible, I got sick once just from eating the pickles.)'[132]

Whatever those disadvantages, it was at the Shubert Theatre on the night of 22 March 1945, that *Carousel* had its world premiere. Before the performance could take place however, several seats had to be removed from the auditorium to make room for the larger than usual orchestra.

That first night was one of those occasions that stayed in the memory of everyone who witnessed it for a very long time; and not for the right reasons. Not only was the show not working as intended, but the final curtain did not come down until one-thirty the following morning. The first act went well enough, but the second act was far, far too long. What followed when the curtain did finally fall is now the stuff of theatrical legend and is described by Agnes de Mille in her autobiography.

'The staff repaired to a hotel room where sacrifice and a cold supper awaited. There followed the kind of conference that professionals seldom see; in two hours, we made a plan, throwing out or drastically altering the better part of Act 2, half my ballet, five complete scenes (and with one, the services and hopes of an elderly actress who had come out of retirement for the first real chance of her life), a couple of good songs[133] and several verses in the remaining ones.

'At the end of the two hours, we were all well exercised. Although neither of the authors could have foreseen the audience reaction that night, they must have been to some extent prepared, because they set to rewriting with alacrity and organisation that bespoke foresight.

'One of the assistants, (John Fearnley, production stage manager) said as we left the room after that dreadful first *Carousel* conference, "Now I see why these people have hits. I have never witnessed anything so brisk and brave in my life." And indeed,

---

[132] Mary Rodgers, *Musical Stages*, Introduction.

[133] If the songs were as good as de Mille suggests, they almost certainly would have reappeared in some other vehicle, as did songs cut from other Rodgers and Hammerstein shows.

not three minutes had been wasted pleading for something cherished. Nor was there any idle joking. We cut and cut and then went to bed'. [134]

(Left to Right) Rouben Mamoulian, Oscar Hammerstein, Theresa Helburn and Richard Rodgers.
Courtesy of The Rodgers & Hammerstein Organization: A Concord Company, www.rnh.com

Nobody was more surprised at the audience reaction than set designer, Jo Mielziner. He thought the show was the best musical comedy script he had ever read and that it had been beautifully directed. He could not understand why it had not come off as expected.

In the audience for that first night was Stephen Sondheim. It was his fifteenth birthday and Oscar Hammerstein had invited his young protégé to the premiere. Sondheim recalls that he found the first act so moving that at the end of it, he just bawled buckets of tears into Dorothy Hammerstein's fur coat. It was the lucky coat

---

[134] Agnes de Mille, *And Promenade Home,* p238.

she always wore at Oscar's first nights, but the poor boy's salty tears stained it so badly, she never wore it again.

A major part of the effort to put things right, necessarily fell on Hammerstein who had an enormous amount of rewriting to do. He was up before dawn each day, no matter how late he had gone to bed the night before, working on the revisions they had agreed upon, one of which was suggested by Molnár, moving Billy's death scene from his bedroom at Nettie's house to the dockside scene of the robbery.

Not that Rodgers was idle. From auditions through to opening night, he and Hammerstein assumed control over every detail of their shows. Usually they would be together, but as was the case now, with Hammerstein busy rewriting, it would fall to Rodgers to oversee everything happening on stage. They had the final say on everything, whether it was a prop, a costume, a vocal inflection, or the tempo of a song. The formidable reputations they had earned before *Oklahoma!* were even more formidable now, so if either of them suggested "We'll do it this way," that's the way you did it; and you did not think twice about it. Undoubtedly, they were demanding, but only as demanding of others as they were of themselves; everyone knew that they spoke from their years of experience, and as tough as they were, they usually achieved what they wanted through a combination of patience and good humour.

This desire for perfection never left them. Whilst rehearsing *This Was a Real Nice Clambake* for the 1965 Lincoln Center revival, Rodgers was becoming increasingly annoyed with how the chorus, many of whom were of Italian origin, kept pronouncing the word 'good', when singing the line, *"... and we'll all have a real good time."* To his ears, it sounded as though they were singing, *"... and we'll all have a real good-a-time."* Rodgers finally pounded his cane on the orchestra rail and exclaimed, "Gouda is a cheese!"

On Tuesday, 25 March, the show moved to the Colonial Theatre in Boston, another favourite try-out venue, and where, again according to Mary Rodgers, the accommodation, (at the Ritz Carlton), and the food (at Locke-Obers) was a considerable improvement on New Haven.

It was in Boston that most of the revisions to the show were made. The result of the hours and hours of work was that they injected more of Billy and Julie into the first act whilst cutting some of the lines of other characters. (Enoch Snow's discourse on the herring family, for example). More severe changes were required for the second act. Hammerstein made it sound simple when he wrote, 'We shortened and dove-tailed Act Two, integrated the ballet, and entirely changed our conception of God'.[135] The reality, particularly where the Heaven scene was concerned, was far from simple. Elliot Norton recorded what happened.

'When the show opened for its try-out run in New Haven, it simply did not work and by the time it got to Boston, they knew it had to be changed.

'The original Heaven of *Carousel* was a New England parlour, bare and plain. In it sat a stern Yankee, listed on the program as 'He'. At a harmonium, playing softly, sat his quiet consort, identified as 'She'. Later, some observers, Rodgers included, referred to this celestial couple as Mr. and Mrs. God ...

Walking back from the Colonial Theatre to their hotel after one more performance when the scene died a death, Rodgers put it bluntly to Hammerstein.

"We've got to get God out of that parlour."

Hammerstein agreed readily.

"I know you're right, but where shall I put him?"

"I don't care where you put Him,' Rodgers replied. 'Put him up on a ladder for all I care, just get Him out of that parlour."[136]

Hammerstein went back to his room at the Ritz Carlton, locked himself in, and ten days later remerged with an entirely new scene, this one set in the backyard of Heaven. "SHE" was gone completely, and 'HE' became The Starkeeper, an altogether softer, more empathetic character; furthermore, picking up on Rodgers' off the cuff remark, Hammerstein did put him on a ladder. Rouben Mamoulian suggested having him polishing stars and hanging them on a clothesline strung across the floor of infinity. Hammerstein's decision to make this new character a Starkeeper is an interesting one. Was it a deliberate reference back to the "Two Little People" segment in the Bench Scene, and Billy singing, "There's a helluva lot o' stars in the sky ...?" The Starkeeper may have become less awe inspiring than 'HE', but that did not mean he was any more tolerant of Billy's sullen responses to his

---

135 Letter, 23 April 1945, Oscar Hammerstein Collection, Library of Congress.

136 Elliot Norton, *New York Times*, 16 September 1984.

questions and the result was the same; Billy was persuaded to take his day on Earth to help Julie and Louise.

Whilst most of the revisions to the second act involved cuts, there were a couple of additions. The song, *The Highest Judge of All* was added, as was a reprise of *If I Loved You.* Rodgers felt there was a need for more music, and he proposed not a new song but a reprise of *If I Loved You.* Lawrence Langner agreed, but elsewhere, there was considerable resistance to the idea on the grounds that the show was too long, and an audience will not want to hear a previously heard song again; even one as good as *If I Loved You.* "Once you do this" they were told, "the members of the audience will reach for their hats and will never wait for the end of the play." Langner, however, was insistent, and the reprise went in.

However, when he saw that the audience was indeed reaching for their hats, Langner knew that he and Rodgers were wrong. At the end of the show, he went backstage to admit his error when he was suddenly confronted by an excited Dick Rodgers who asked him to guess what sheet music was selling most copies in the lobby. Langner had no idea, so Rodgers told him. "*If I Loved You*, and it is going to be the hit song from the score." Langner still insisted that the reprise had to be taken out. It just wasn't working, and people were ready to leave. Rodgers though was not going to be so easily deterred. "If it is not working," he countered, "we shall just have to find a way to make it work so that people don't want to leave." It took a few days, but they found a way, and the reprise stayed in.

Not only did the reprise stay in, but it became a key moment in the show. Julie has sensed that Billy's spirit was there. She is almost convinced she saw him. Now, as she takes the star he brought down from Heaven and holds it to her breast, Billy sings:

Longing to tell you,
But afraid and shy,
I let my golden chances pass me by
Now I've lost you;
Soon I will go in the mist of day,
And you never will know
How I loved you,
How I loved you

What was a conditional love song has become an unambiguous declaration of love. More than that, Billy knows Julie has sensed his presence, heard his words. It is a beautiful piece of theatre.

Other problems were easier to resolve, such as one involving John Raitt and *Soliloquy.* As first staged, at the opening of the number, during the minor key vamp introduction, Raitt would walk downstage and begin singing. One night during rehearsals, Joseph Littau, the musical director, came backstage to tell him that he was spitting on one of the two bass players in the orchestra pit when he started to sing. At first, Raitt scoffed at this, maintaining that he was still upstage at this point. At the next performance though, Raitt became aware that he was indeed moving downstage during those opening four bars. Not only that, but as he began to sing, he realized he was standing directly over the two bass players, one of whom was holding a toy paper umbrella over the bald head of his colleague.

Once all the revisions were in place, Rodgers felt able to write to his wife Dorothy on 3 April:

> Darling,
>
> Now I can write to you because last night we had a SHOW! I'm a very cautious kid, as you know, but there are certain bits of evidence that cannot be refuted. Best of all, I know how I feel, and I feel that there are many moments of extreme beauty here and that the public will want to see and hear them."[137]

The sudden death of President Roosevelt on 12 April cast a long shadow over the final few days of the Boston run. Richard Rodgers described it as one of those days you can never forget and how the loss felt so personal. He was in the middle of understudy auditions when he got the news; he did not want to interrupt them but inevitably, the word did get out and everyone was so upset, they had no choice but to cancel. When he finally was able to speak to Dorothy, all they could do was cry down the phone.

---

[137] Richard Rodgers, *Musical Stages*, p242.

The final Boston performance was on 15 April and then it was back to New York and the Majestic Theatre for a final dress rehearsal and opening night. One major task had to be undertaken beforehand, however. As with the Shubert Theatre in New Haven, the Majestic orchestra pit was too small to accommodate the forty-piece orchestra. Increasing the size of the pit necessitated the removal of the entire front row of the stalls.

John Raitt and Jan Clayton ride the carousel.
Courtesy of The Rodgers & Hammerstein Organization:
A Concord Company, www.rnh.com

Not that Richard Rodgers knew much about what was going on at that time. Returning home to Fairfield from Boston, on leaving the train at Bridgeport, there were no porters available, so he had to carry his two heavy suitcases to the car where Dorothy was waiting for him. He suffered no ill effects that night, but next day, when he coughed, he was in agony. He had wrenched one of his lumbar vertebrae. His doctor advised bed rest, but of course, that was impossible, so Dorothy took him to their home in the city at the Volney. For the dress rehearsal, he was laid out on a stretcher in the centre aisle, from where he watched as best he could. It was not an easy watch because the dress rehearsal did not go at all well.

Later, Langer recalled that on leaving the theatre after that dreadful rehearsal, he felt thoroughly discouraged, and that he was in the most absurd of professions. Months had been spent on creating the musical, still more months and $180,000 were spent on producing it, and in the end, based on a single evening's performance, it could all turn out to be for nothing.

The dress rehearsal might have gone badly, but the following night, opening night, 19 April 1945 was triumphant. Rodgers again had to be taken to the theatre by ambulance. He was placed in a box hidden from view by a curtain. He could only see part of the stage, but he was so heavily sedated with morphine that he could not have appreciated what was happening wherever he might have been seated. He was unaware of the laughter and applause and was convinced the show was a dismal failure. He was even unaware of the rapturous reception the ballet received. It was only after the final curtain call, when people came up to congratulate him, that he knew he had another triumph on his hands.

That it was a triumph was confirmed when the first editions of the papers came in. Lewis Nichols in the *New York Times* said '… One of the most beautiful Rodgers' scores and some of Hammerstein's best rhymes'. In similar vein was John Chapman of the *New York Daily News*, '… One of the finest musical plays I have ever seen and I shall remember it always. It has everything the professional theatre can give it and something else; besides, heart, integrity and an inner glow … The score and lyrics are by Rodgers and Hammerstein and the musical theatre does not have two finer creative artists …'.

Robert Coleman in the *New York Daily Mirror* put it simply. '… beautiful, bountiful, beguiling'. Ward Morehouse of the Sun wrote, 'Something memorable in the theatre', while in the *New York Journal American*, George Jean Nathan said, '... Welcome in almost every way, and I herewith help to spread the doormat'. That from the man who two years earlier had regretted the lack of a chorus line to open Oklahoma!

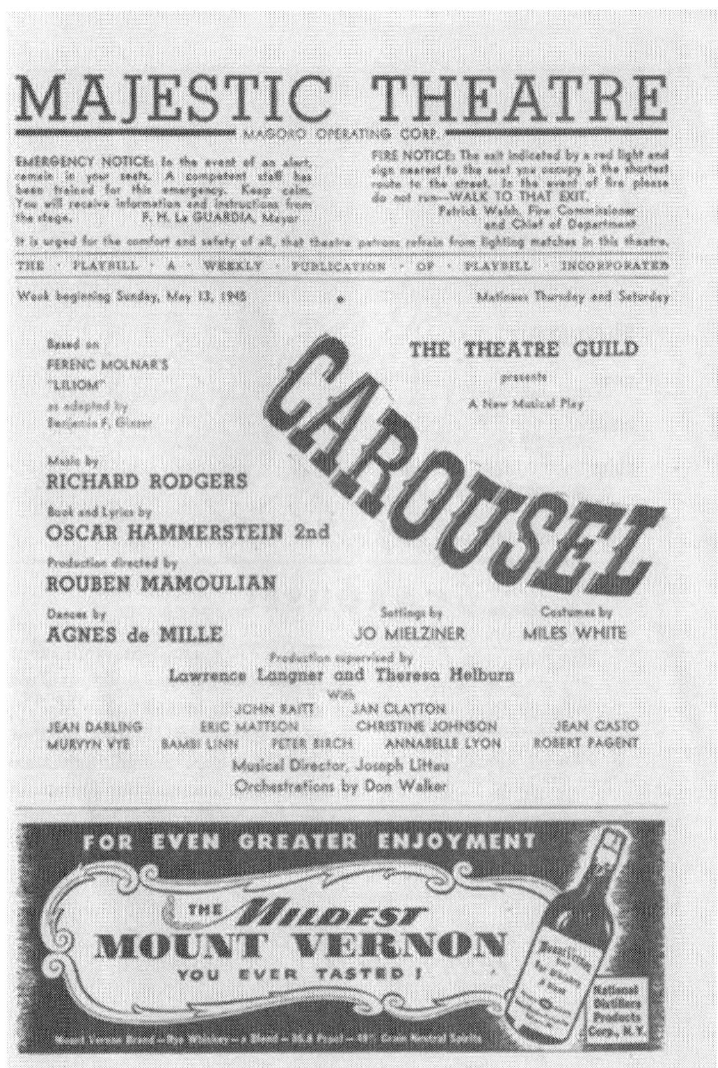

MAJESTIC THEATRE

MAGORO OPERATING CORP.

EMERGENCY NOTICE: In the event of an alert, remain in your seats. A competent staff has been trained for this emergency. Keep calm. You will receive information and instructions from the stage. F. H. La GUARDIA, Mayor

FIRE NOTICE: The exit indicated by a red light and sign nearest to the seat you occupy is the shortest route to the street. In the event of fire please do not run—WALK TO THAT EXIT.
Patrick Walsh, Fire Commissioner and Chief of Department

It is urged for the comfort and safety of all, that theatre patrons refrain from lighting matches in this theatre.

THE · PLAYBILL · A · WEEKLY · PUBLICATION · OF · PLAYBILL · INCORPORATED

Week beginning Sunday, May 13, 1945 • Matinees Thursday and Saturday

THE THEATRE GUILD
presents
A New Musical Play

CAROUSEL

Based on FERENC MOLNAR'S "LILIOM" as adapted by Benjamin F. Glazer

Music by
RICHARD RODGERS

Book and Lyrics by
OSCAR HAMMERSTEIN 2nd

Production directed by
ROUBEN MAMOULIAN

Dances by AGNES de MILLE — Settings by JO MIELZINER — Costumes by MILES WHITE

Production supervised by
Lawrence Langner and Theresa Helburn

With
JOHN RAITT JAN CLAYTON
JEAN DARLING ERIC MATTSON CHRISTINE JOHNSON JEAN CASTO
MURVYN VYE BAMBI LINN PETER BIRCH ANNABELLE LYON ROBERT PAGENT

Musical Director, Joseph Littau
Orchestrations by Don Walker

Programme from 1945 Majestic Theatre production

Louis Kronenberger in *PM* had 20/20 foresight. 'I suppose a comparison between *Carousel* and *Oklahoma!* is inevitable ... The high spirits of *Oklahoma!* the meadow freshness of it at its best, its fetching qualities as a "show" have no counterparts in *Carousel* ... but *Carousel* ... may yet seem more of a milestone in the years to come'.

Only Wilella Waldorf of the *New York Post* had anything negative to say. '... rather a long evening. The *Oklahoma!* formula is becoming a bit monotonous and so are Miss de Mille's ballets. All right, go ahead and shoot!' Oscar Hammerstein lost no time in accepting that invitation and in a letter to John Steinbeck a couple weeks after the premiere, he opened up with both barrels. He wrote of Waldorf that she was someone '... who clings desperately to the protection of not liking anything so that she might like herself a little better than she knows she ought to'.[138]

Perhaps more than any other, the review Dick and Oscar would have enjoyed most was one that appeared in *Time Magazine* which apart from heaping praise on the book and on the score, added this, '... More than a succession of tunes, the music helps interpret the story ... Hammerstein has caught the spirit with his lyrics'. Confirmation that they not only had created another hit but had done so whilst also achieving their ambition of doing so with a show that utilised all the theatrical arts, book, music, lyrics and dance. Years later, on 31 December 1999, *Time Magazine* presented its selection of the Best of the 20th Century. When it came to musicals, the winner was *Carousel* by Rodgers and Hammerstein. The citation read, 'They set the standards for the 20th century musical, and this show features their most beautiful score and the most skilful and affecting example of their musical storytelling'.

The morning after that first night, Jan Clayton wrote to Oscar Hammerstein:

> Oscar dear,
>
> Last night meant so very much to all of us but I'd like you to know how deeply I feel about it - and how grateful I am to you for what you have done - but somehow there aren't any new ways - just the same old thank you. Please know how much I mean it -
>
> Jan[139]

---

[138] Letter, 23 April 1945. Oscar Hammerstein Collection, Library of Congress.

[139] Jan Clayton, undated letter, Oscar Hammerstein collection, Library of Congress.

Oscar Hammerstein and Richard Rodgers
celebrate two triumphs on Broadway.
Courtesy of The Rodgers & Hammerstein Organization:
A Concord Company, www.rnh.com

There were no Tony awards in 1945; they were first awarded two years later, but *Carousel* won the New York Drama Critics Circle Award for best musical, and eight Donaldson awards: Best Musical; Best Performance in a musical, male, John Raitt; Best Direction, Rouben Mamoulian; Best dancer male, Peter Birch; Best Dance Direction, Agnes de Mille; Best Book, Oscar Hammerstein II; Best Lyrics, Oscar Hammerstein II; Best Score, Richard Rodgers.

Later, when writing his autobiography, Rodgers would answer the question that is most frequently asked of all artists - of all your works, what is your favourite? Rodgers wrote, "My answer is Carousel. Oscar never wrote more meaningful or moving lyrics, and to me, my score is more satisfying than anything I have ever written. But it's not just the songs; it's the whole play. Beautifully written, tender without being mawkish, it affects me deeply every time I see it performed."

The show ran for a very respectable eight-hundred and ninety performances before going on a lengthy national tour and then on to London.

Chapter 11

You'll Never Walk Alone

There is nothing to suggest that either Richard Rodgers or Oscar Hammerstein ever saw a game of soccer (or football as it is known in every country other than the U.S.). Rodgers' sport was croquet, which he took very seriously and at which he was very good, though by all accounts, his wife Dorothy was even better. They had a beautiful croquet lawn laid out beside a specially designed lake at their summer home in Connecticut, where according to the US Croquet Association, they kept the state croquet flame alive.

Hammerstein's sport was tennis. He played frequently and had a highly competitive streak, always striving to win, even when playing against his own children. So, football, or soccer was not a sport that held any interest for them and yet partly because of it, *Carousel's You'll Never Walk Alone,* has become one of the best-known songs in the world and in the process has acquired an additional name - 'The Football Song'.

Of course, it is not just its association with football that has made it a global favourite. That did not begin until 1963 by which time, it and several other songs from the score, had become established standards.

The popularity of *You'll Never Walk Alone,* however, is different; it has an uplifting quality that has made it a favourite choice of song for grand state occasions such as Royal Jubilees and Presidential Inaugurations, and yet is equally at home sung in a Sunday church service or providing comfort to mourners at a funeral.

That it achieved instant popularity is hardly surprising considering what was happening in the world when it was first performed. America had been at war for almost three and a half years, and the war in Europe had been raging for even longer. There would not have been many people in that first night audience who were untouched by the conflict in some way or another. As the Allied forces were closing in on Berlin bringing the war in Europe to a close, the full extent of the Nazi terror was only now becoming clear; Auschwitz had been liberated just three months earlier and only four days before the show's New York opening, the British Army had liberated Belsen revealing to the world scenes of unimaginable horror. Moreover, the war in the Pacific seemed far from over, with America preparing for an invasion of Japan, an operation that inevitably, would have exacted a horrendous loss of life; the existence of the terrible weapon that would bring about Japan's surrender so much sooner than expected was still a secret, known only to a tiny handful of people. Finally, as was noted earlier, President Roosevelt had died unexpectedly leaving America in a state of shock and still further uncertainty.

No wonder, therefore, that Hammerstein's deceptively simple, homespun words, combined with Rodgers' hymn-like music fell on receptive ears that first night and every night thereafter. In the show, the song is introduced by Nettie Fowler midway through the second act. It is sung to comfort Julie after Billy's suicide, reminding her that she is part of a community, one that will care for her and her unborn child.

In *Liliom,* the precursor of Nettie is Mother Hollunder. When Julie asks her what she is to do without Liliom, her response is - "He is better off, poor fellow - and so are you. He was a bad man." Nettie, a much more sympathetic character provides real comfort to Julie. Her reply to Julie's question is that she will stay with her so that she can help care for her unborn child and then reminds her that the main thing to do is "Keep on livin' - keep on keerin what's goin' to happen." She reminds Julie of a sampler that she gave her and asks if she remembers the words. Julie tries to sing them but breaks down and then Nettie sings ...

When you walk through a storm
Keep your chin up high
And don't be afraid of the dark
At the end of the storm
Is a golden sky
And the sweet, silver song of a lark.
Walk on through the wind,
Walk on through the rain,
Though your dreams be tossed and blown.
Walk on, walk on with hope in your heart,
And you'll never walk alone!
You'll never walk alone.

In the first draft of the script, Julie then sang a reprise of the song with, as Hammerstein wrote, 'a light of courage in her eye'. This reprise was one of the many cuts and changes that were required to make the second act more manageable.

The song is, however, heard again in the show's finale, the added scene that moved Ferenc Molnár to tears. The reprise follows the simple yet inspirational address to the class by the town's doctor. Go out and find your own happiness, he tells them; don't rely on your parents' success or be held back by their failures; stand on your own two feet. Then, he leads the entire cast in singing *You'll Never Walk Alone.*

On this occasion, it is sung not to provide comfort at a time of loss, but to reinforce the message Louise and her fellow high school graduates have just heard, before they take their first tentative steps as young adults.

When the song ends and the curtain falls, the audience knows that both Julie and Louise will be okay. Rodgers and Hammerstein's message, however, was intended for an audience far beyond the confines of the Majestic Theatre.

Christine Johnson, who created the role of Nettie Fowler, recalled for the BBC how she came to get the part and consequently, introduce *You'll Never Walk Alone* to the world.

She had just landed her first role at the Metropolitan Opera, Erda in Wagner's *Das Rheingold.* - the youngest person ever to sing that role at the Met. That performance was on 8 February 1944, and it brought her to the attention of Jules Glaenzer, head of Cartiers and renowned socialite, party giver and theatrical angel. Glaenzer asked her if she knew his good friend Richard Rodgers. When she replied that she did not, he invited her to a dinner party that he was hosting for Rodgers and his wife Dorothy. A week or so before the party, Johnson and a friend visited a nightclub called One Fifth Avenue, which featured all types of music, both classical and popular. One singer that night particularly caught her attention, Loulie Jean Norman who performed Rodgers and Hart's *He was Too Good to Me.* Johnson especially admired the singer's phrasing and kept it in mind.

At the dinner party, all the guests were still excited about *Oklahoma!* even though it had been running on Broadway for a year by then. As the drinks flowed, everyone was soon on first name terms. Then, Dick Rodgers sat at the piano and started playing and invited Christine to sing. She chose the song she had heard sung by Loulie Jean Norman, *He Was Too Good to Me* and sang it exactly as she had heard a few nights earlier. Rodgers was duly impressed. Over dinner, Dorothy suggested that Rodgers tell Christine about the new show he was working on, *Liliom.* Rodgers did so and Johnson told them that she knew the play and thought that the idea of a musical version was fascinating. Rodgers, displaying even then his operatic thoughts about the score, then astonished her by saying "Could we wean you away from opera?"

"I heard myself saying yes without a moment's hesitation," Johnson recalled.

"Good" Rodgers replied, "I'll be in touch."

The role seemed to be hers, 'Offered on a silver platter'. Some months later, that silver platter was almost snatched away. On 1 September 1944, Bettina Cerf, the Theatre Guild's casting director, sent a memo to Theresa Helburn regarding Johnson's contract. 'We have agreed on salary but Oscar and Dick feel that considering her price, they would prefer not to sign any contract with her until they have heard her read an actual scene which Mr. H. is in fact writing'.[140] She was worried that they could lose Johnson because of script delays and explained the situation to Johnson's agent after promising to keep on at Hammerstein to deliver something for her to read.

That material was duly delivered, and Johnson's reading was obviously satisfactory because a few weeks later, Johnson received a call from Rodgers. Could she come to his office to enable him to set the key for a 'little' song he had written for her character? She arrived to find Rodgers sitting alone at an old Bechstein piano. He handed her a copy of the lyric but as he did not have a lead sheet, he asked her to watch his hands to see the notes and pick out the tune. As this was rather awkward, she asked Rodgers if he would write out the melody and the words on a piece of scratch paper she saw on the piano. This he did and they went through the song a few times, Johnson singing *sotto voce* to make sure she was singing the correct notes. At that point, Oscar Hammerstein came into the room along with Louis and Max Dreyfus, of Chappells. Hammerstein stood by the window 'as was his way', and then she and Rodgers performed *You'll Never Walk*

---

140 Theatre Guild Collection, Beineke Library, Yale University.

Alone in full voice for the very first time. When she finished, there was a moment of complete silence. She felt perspiration pouring down her back. Rodgers' eyes were glassy, Hammerstein was wiping his eyes and then as one, they burst into spontaneous applause.

They all knew that this was not a 'little' song but one that was here to stay, adding that she too was almost in tears on that special day: she was so honoured to have had the privilege of introducing *You'll Never Walk Alone* to the world.

Christine Johnson as Cousin Nettie in the original 1945 production. Courtesy of The Rodgers & Hammerstein Organization: A Concord Company, www.rnh.com

There would be more tears too when she performed the song during the show's run. This was particularly true of matinee performances, which she recalled, tended to attract mostly female audiences. As she sang, Johnson became aware of sobs coming from the audience and clumps of white as ladies took handkerchiefs out of their handbags. Then, she sensed that the audience did not know whether to applaud or not, such was the emotion in the theatre. Strangely, she always felt that she had done a better job when they did not applaud.

The version of the lyric printed above is the version published in Hammerstein's own collection of his works *Lyrics by Oscar Hammerstein*, the first edition of which was published in 1949. This version of the lyric is also to be found in the published version of *Carousel*. Therefore, one may assume it is the definitive version of the lyric Hammerstein wrote for the play. That view is reinforced by the fact that on the original cast album, these are the words that Christine Johnson, the original Nettie Fowler recorded.

Yet in the vocal selection, published by the writers' own publishing company, Williamson Music, the second line is printed 'Hold your head up high' and that version has been recorded as frequently as the original.

Which version is correct? Ted Chapin suggests that because the latter version was used so frequently, and because it is easier to sing, Hammerstein changed it himself. He also suggests that as you cannot keep your chin up high if you do not hold your head up high, that version is more logical.

Equally puzzling is that a little further on, Nettie sings "... and the sweet silver song of a lark." Yet when the song is reprised in the final scene, the graduation class sing "... and the sweet silver song of the lark" and that is how it is written in the published version of the play.

Why the change? I fear that is a question to which we shall never find the answer, particularly as there are no handwritten copies of the lyric to be found, even amongst Hammerstein's papers in the Library of Congress.

One person who was quite definite about what Hammerstein intended was Christine Johnson. She wrote to Ted Chapin as follows, 'You shall have proof that the original lyric Mr. Hammerstein wrote and never changed was "Keep your chin up high" -- he was a purist about the words he wrote -- had he wished to change it; he had many opportunities to do it. You know if you sang a 'the', and Hammerstein wanted an 'a', you'd hear about it backstage as soon as the performance was over!'

Johnson, reprising her role as Nettie on the original cast album, was the first of some five hundred artists to record *You'll Never Walk Alone* but she was quickly followed by many others. Among the earliest was Frank Sinatra, whose version was the first to make the record charts. Judy Garland recorded a version, as did Perry Como, Andy Williams, and Doris Day. Others who recorded it over the years were singers as diverse as Barbra Streisand and Johnny Cash; Louis Armstrong and Bernadette Peters; Elvis Presley and Mahalia Jackson; Placido Domingo and Kiri te Kanawa. Domingo would also perform the song with Luciano Pavarotti and Jose Carreras in a live concert in Rome before the World Cup Final in 1990 and again before the final in Paris in 1998. By then, it had long been established as 'The Football Song', a story that began when it was recorded by a very different singing group.

***

That recording was made on 2 July 1963, at the famous Abbey Road Studios in London by an English pop group called Gerry and the Pacemakers and it is this slightly up-beat version that is sung by tens of thousands of soccer fans in stadia all around the world.

The group had been formed in Liverpool in 1959, one of more than three hundred such groups performing in local clubs and dance halls, playing what became known as Merseybeat or the Mersey sound. Heavily influenced by the likes of Buddy Holly and Chuck Berry, and by the music of the city's large Irish population, it was a sound that dominated the world's airwaves during the nineteen-sixties.

The group's eponymous lead singer was Gerry Marsden a twenty-year-old Liverpudlian, and under his lead they quickly became an early rival to the Beatles, whose career they emulated by playing in some of the same venues in their home city and in Hamburg and Cologne in Germany. They became the second group (after The Beatles) to sign with manager Brian Epstein, and he secured for them a contract with Columbia Records. Their first big hit *How Do You Do It?* was released in early 1963 and went to number one in the UK. This was followed by another number one hit, *I Like It.*

A few years earlier, Gerry Marsden had seen the film version of *Carousel,* and from that moment *You'll Never Walk Alone* had been one of his favourite songs. He was attracted by the strength of the words, and he thought the melody was beautiful and the dramatic effect strong. He liked the song so much that he had added it to the group's repertoire when they were performing in Hamburg. Many pop stars, aware that their careers might be short lived, looked to become all-round entertainers and to achieve this, needed to prove that they could do more than just sing rock and roll. The Beatles, with Paul McCartney as lead vocal had been singing *Over the Rainbow* for some time and the song had always gone down very well. Not wanting to be outdone by their local rivals, Marsden quickly thought of *You'll Never Walk Alone* as the ballad to show off the group's versatility.

Gerry and the Pacemakers
©Topfoto/ArenaPAL

By mid-1963, they had achieved two successive number ones and they now needed to find a song for their next record. After two rock and roll numbers, Marsden wanted it to be a ballad and he argued strongly for *You'll Never Walk Alone.* Both Epstein and leading record producer, George Martin had severe reservations, but Marsden won the argument. "Be it on your own head" was the response from Epstein.

Having accepted defeat, George Martin then suggested adding a gentle offbeat on the drums, which he felt would add an extra element to the recording and Marsden agreed to this. Then, Martin proposed adding strings. At first, Marsden thought this idea was crazy, but Martin did it anyway, and when the group heard the final version, they knew he was right. Marsden commented, "I nearly died on hearing the strings, they were so incredible. Good old George!"

The new record was released on 29 October 1963 and rose quickly to number one making them the first group to have three successive number ones in the UK, fully justifying Marsden's insistence on a ballad and on that choice of song. Poignantly, it was still at number one on that fateful Friday when President Kennedy was assassinated.

That though, was just the beginning of the song's new life.

In the early 1960s, Liverpool Football Club installed a new sound system at their Anfield stadium. They also employed a public address announcer who in the hour before the game, played the top ten from that week's hit parade. Spectators would sing along with the records, particularly the current number one, which would be played just as the two teams came onto the pitch for the start of the match. In October 1963, Gerry and the Pacemakers' recording of *You'll Never Walk Alone* was released; this was followed by its rapid rise to the top of the charts, and it first being sung at Anfield. Then, something strange occurred. Normally, as songs began to drop down the charts, spectators stopped singing them, but with *You'll Never Walk Alone* that did not happen; the fans continued to sing it week after week. It did not take long for the announcer, whose name was Stewart Bateman, to realize that Liverpool supporters had taken the song to their collective hearts, so instead of ending his pre-game session with whatever might be the current number one, he decided to finish it with *You'll Never Walk Alone.* In those days, the stand at the Kemlyn Road end of

Anfield, a huge terrace known as the Kop, which had highly effective acoustics that propelled sound around the stadium, held some twenty-eight thousand people. When those massed voices were raised in unison, singing along to Gerry and the Pacemakers' record, they became a truly potent force; in this way was born *You'll Never Walk Alone's* status as Liverpool's anthem. There are, no doubt, scores of music industry executives who are paid a fortune for promoting newly published songs. Few will have been more successful at their jobs than Mr. Bateman whose sharp wits in recognizing the special qualities of *You'll Never Walk Alone,* helped make it one of the most recognized songs in the world.

Before long, Celtic Football Club in Glasgow had also adopted the song as its anthem. European competitions meant that as Liverpool fans followed their team all over the continent and sang their song wherever they travelled, so one club after another, followed suit. In Holland, three clubs use it as their anthem: Feyenoord, FC Twente and SC Cambuur. In Germany, Borussia Dortmund, FSV Mainz05, FC Kaiserslautern and Borussia Monchengladbach among others have adopted it, as have Belgium's Club Brugge and Spain's CD Lugo. Even in Japan, FC Tokyo use it as their anthem.

Truly, it has become 'The Football Song' but as much as it has become a worldwide soccer favourite, nowhere is it cherished more than in Liverpool; not just because Gerry and the Pacemakers were a local group; nor because Liverpool was the first to adopt it as their song, but because of a tragic event that took place on 15 April 1989.

On that day, Liverpool were playing an F.A. Cup semi-final match against Nottingham Forest at the neutral Hillsborough stadium in Sheffield. As crowds built up in the minutes prior to kick off, in an attempt to ease overcrowding outside the stadium, too many people were allowed into the stand reserved for Liverpool supporters. When safety barriers gave way, ninety-seven Liverpool football fans, men, women and children, were crushed to death. Numerous enquiries were held over the years to establish the exact cause of the disaster, but it was not until 26 April 2016 that a second coroner's inquest absolved supporters of any blame and returned a verdict that the victims were unlawfully killed as a result of gross negligence by the police and ambulance services, and the faulty design of the stadium.

Throughout the twenty-seven years that the families were fighting for justice, *You'll Never Walk Alone* was the song that kept them going and inevitably, became a part of every memorial service held on anniversaries of the tragedy. On the evening the inquest concluded, thousands of Liverpudlians gathered in the city centre to sing it as part of a vigil to remember the victims. This was followed by a spine-tingling rendition of the song at Liverpool's next home game when visiting supporters from Spain's Villarreal joined in to create a very special atmosphere.

In another indication as to how enshrined the song has become at the club, the words 'You'll Never Walk Alone' now appear on its official badge, and on the Bill Shankly Gates, the main entrance to the stadium, named after a former, highly successful manager. Shankly himself included the song as one of the eight records he could take with him as a castaway on the BBC's long running radio programme, *Desert Island Discs.*

Do football anthems such as *You'll Never Walk Alone* have the power to inspire a team to victory? There is evidence to suggest that they do. In 2005, Liverpool were playing in the Champions League Final against AC Milan in Istanbul. At half time, they were 3-0 down having been completely outplayed in the first half. As their captain Stephen Gerrard recorded, "You've been totally played off the park for forty-five minutes. And then you hear the chorus of *You'll Never Walk Alone*, probably the loudest and most emotional rendition I've ever heard as a player." History will record that against the odds, Liverpool fought back to level the match at 3-3 and went on to win the penalty shoot-out.

***

How is it that a song from a Broadway musical, written by two non-observant Jews has acquired such a religious, spiritual identity? Irving Berlin, on hearing it played at a funeral, said that it made him realize what an extraordinary composer Rodgers was, because in that context the song had all the power of the twenty-third Psalm. This spiritual quality was endorsed by Justin Welby, the Archbishop of Canterbury who, like Shankly, when he was the guest on *Desert Island Discs,* chose the song as one of the eight that he was allowed to have with him on the island. Unsurprisingly, the song has been the choice of many of the guests on the show during its seventy-five-year history. It continues to be one of the most popular choices at funerals. On another BBC radio programme, *Soul Music*, it was ranked alongside *Abide with Me* and *Silent Night* in terms of its impact and iconic status. Its total acceptance as a hymn, appearing in modern hymnals around the world, makes it unique for a song originating on Broadway.[141]

As stated above, neither Rodgers nor Hammerstein were at all religious in the traditional sense. According to Rodgers' wife Dorothy, whilst she and her husband both considered themselves a part of the Jewish community, Dick was an atheist who thought that all religions are based largely on fear and contribute heavily to feelings of guilt.[142]

In his autobiography, Rodgers wrote that whilst his parents maintained an element of Jewish life until his bar mitzvah as a gesture to his maternal grandfather, from then on, his parents, brother and he were Jewish for socio-ethnic reasons rather than because of any deep religious conviction. Oscar Hammerstein was not totally convinced by his partner's professed lack of religiosity. 'In his heart', he wrote, 'Dick is far more of a mystic than he knows'.

During the production of *The Sound of Music,* actress Mary Martin introduced Rodgers to her good friend, Sister Gregory of Rosary College, Illinois with whom he too would develop a close relationship. Sister Gregory wrote a moving letter to Rodgers on receiving news of Oscar Hammerstein's death. In his reply, Rodgers wrote, 'The afternoon we met at Mary's apartment, we discussed the fact that formal religion was not the beginning and end of faith. I have never been able to become a formalist, but I think you know that I have deep and abiding faith. It happens to be in people'.[143] Formalist or not, Rodgers had joined New York's Congregation Emanu-El in March 1951.

Hammerstein too had no religious convictions in the conventional sense. He was, however, a man of deep moral convictions who believed very strongly that all men are created equal; he believed in democracy and human rights, and he longed

---

[141] Ian Bradley, *You've Got to Have A Dream,* p79.

[142] Dorothy Rodgers, *A Personal Book,* p32.

[143] Letter, 31 August 1960, Richard Rodgers Collection, New York Public Library, Performing Arts Division.

for a world that was no longer threatened by war. That was his religious creed. He had a strong belief that somewhere, even in the worst of us, there has to be some good. Nor was he afraid of expressing those views on stage. When asked in an interview by Arnold Michaelis why he changed Molnár's ending, Hammerstein replied, "It was not the anxiety to have a happy ending that made me shy away from that original, but because I can't conceive of an unregenerate soul - and to indulge myself, I changed the ending."[144]

Further, in that same interview, Hammerstein gave an insight into his faith. "Our interest, our belonging to one another, the oneness on earth is the same thing as our oneness with God. God is that oneness, in my conception. He is all of us, and we all are Him."

Michaelis then asked, "Isn't that the feeling that you tried to get across in *Carousel* in the song *You'll Never Walk Alone*?"

Hammerstein replied, "I think that is in there, yes. I think that the faith I think we should all have in ourselves and in one another is in there, illustrated by these words: 'When you walk through a storm, hold your head up high and don't be afraid of the dark. At the end of the storm is a golden sky and the sweet silver song of a lark. Walk on through the wind, walk on through the rain, though your dreams be tossed and blown. Walk on, walk on, with hope in your heart, and you'll never walk alone. You'll never walk alone'."[145]

Hammerstein reinforced these comments in a television interview with Mike Wallace recorded on 15 March 1958 in which he told the following story. "I was jaywalking, ran across eighth avenue and fifty-seventh street. When I was half-way across the street, I heard a voice calling to me and it was a policeman, and I thought well, here it is, I'm wrong, he's right. I can't defend myself I have to take a bawling-out. When I reached the curb, he came over to me, he was a young cop, and he didn't bawl me out at all. He said, 'Aren't you Oscar Hammerstein?' I said, 'Yes.' He said,

---

[144] Stephen Citron, *The Wordsmiths,* p175.

[145] Note that by the time of that interview, 9 November 1957, Hammerstein is himself using 'Hold your head up high' rather than 'Keep your chin up high'.

'Well, I want to tell you how much my family, my wife and I and my kids enjoy all your songs. We have a record of *Carousel* and we've worn it thin. We can hardly hear it anymore, it's scratchy but we love it and I want to thank you.' And I thanked him for telling me so and I felt very good, and I started to go, and he said, 'Just one thing. Do you mind if I ask you a question?' and I said, 'No.' He said, 'Are you religious?' and I said, 'Well, I don't belong to any church,' and then he patted me on the back, and he said, 'Ah, you're religious alright.' And I went on feeling as if I'd been caught and feeling that I was religious. He had discovered from the words of my songs that I had faith, faith in mankind, faith that there was something more powerful than mankind behind it all. And faith, that in the long run, good triumphs over evil. If that's religion, I'm religious, and it is my definition of religion."

Sister Gregory, who began to get to know Oscar on *The Sound of Music* did not need to know him long to appreciate his qualities. In her letter to Dick Rodgers when Oscar died, she wrote, 'Mr. Hammerstein was not only a gifted artist but also a man of stature; his integrity, gentle warmth and luminous spirit were reflected both in his work and in his life'.

But let Richard Rodgers have the last word on Oscar Hammerstein. Speaking after Hammerstein's death in 1960, Rodgers said, "Almost to the day he died, everything about Oscar was an affirmation of life ... He was infused with a faith and an optimism that only grew stronger as he grew older." Seven years later, Rodgers reflected on his partner again. "His view of life was positive. He was a leader, a man willing to do battle for whatever causes he believed in. He was not naïve. He knew full well that man is not all good and that nature is not all good; yet it was his sincere belief that someone had to keep reminding people of the vast amount of good things that there are in the world."

Some may complain at Hammerstein's sentimentality. No-one though, could doubt his sincerity or that of Richard Rodgers for that matter. They may not have been observant in the traditional religious sense, but they did have the spiritual depth necessary to write what has become a hymn of inspiration to people of all faiths and none.

***

Musically, *You'll Never Walk Alone* is one of Rodgers' simpler melodies. For someone renowned for the speed with which he worked, it was one over which he laboured for some time. It is written in the key of C major, a strong, positive key and there is only one note, the B flat on the word 'sweet', that is not natural to that key.[146] Rodgers again uses an arpeggiated accompaniment repeating musical patterns found earlier in the score. The emotion of the piece is established by a steadily rising chromatic progression, a common Rodgers' device, until the climax, a succession of repeated notes, Cs and Es, supported by a harmony of augmented chords that once again, echo musical themes heard before. When the song is first sung to comfort Julie, it concludes with a quiet fall to the dominant fifth in a simple affirmation of the fact that she will not walk alone. When it is reprised in the final scene, it again finishes on the dominant fifth, but this time, acknowledging that Billy has finally managed to express his love for Julie and Louise, it is a joyous octave higher. Rodgers employs a powerful musical device here, having that final high G on the second syllable of 'alone' harmonized as a unison. Had he followed the expected route and harmonized it in C Major, it might have been bogged down. As it is, the unison choral voicing sends that high G and the word 'alone' straight to Heaven. Bruce Pomahac told me that in a Rodgers and Hammerstein show, the music was as choreographed to the drama as seamlessly as was the dancing.[147]

Ian Bradley, former Reader in Practical Theology at the University of St. Andrews, Scotland has made a study of the spiritual dimension to be found in musical theatre. Writing about the climax of *You'll Never Walk Alone,* he said, 'It is of course, possible to take several different meanings from these words, sung to Rodgers' deliberate pulsating minims. Do they simply imply that there are other humans treading the road of suffering and offering some kind of companionship and solidarity, even if it is unseen? Or do they suggest the companionship of some divine being and convey a similar message to the much loved and quoted poem "Footprints" that when you are least conscious of his [sic]

---

[146] On the original piece of manuscript, he used to write out the melody for Christine Johnson, he wrote it out in the key of A Major, not C Major.

[147] Email to the author, 9 September 2020.

presence, God is carrying you? That, is certainly how they have been interpreted by many people and it is certainly an interpretation that both the words and the tune bear very easily'.[148]

In today's more cynical times, Rodgers and Hammerstein's intuitive perennial optimism can be all too easily thought of as corny and sentimental. Science, however, suggests that their belief in the value of hope should not be so readily dismissed. The renowned Viennese psychiatrist, Viktor Frankl, a survivor of Auschwitz, recorded in his bestselling account *Man's Search for Reason,* first published in 1946, that it was not necessarily the physically strongest who survived the horrors of the camps but those who clung to the hope that one day, their torment would end and that they might yet see their loved ones again beyond the barbed wire. Similarly, Dr. James Groopman, Chair of Medicine at Harvard Medical School, discovered and described in his 2004 book *Anatomy of Hope,* how hopeful attitudes actually can alter neurochemistry and block pain by releasing endorphins. He said that they were only at the beginning of their endeavours to understand the full power of hope, but he saw in it the very heart of healing. Other studies have confirmed these findings.

Whatever the cynics may say, the public, perhaps precisely because the song can mean whatever the listener wants it to, have taken it to their hearts. It has now become a regular fixture at the Last Night of the Proms, the annual music festival held at London's Royal Albert Hall. It was sung quite spontaneously at a concert in 1990 at Wembley Stadium to honour Nelson Mandela. In the introduction to an updated edition of her father's autobiography, Mary Rodgers relates the story of her own daughter who was walking in New York's Upper East Side a few days after the 9/11 attacks. A vigil was being held outside the Metropolitan Museum of Art and the assembled crowd was singing hymns and patriotic songs. After a moment's silence, someone began singing the opening lines of *You'll Never walk Alone* and at once, everyone began to join in. A year later, Renée Fleming sang it a Concert for America on the first anniversary of the attacks. She sang it again at the inauguration of President Barack Obama. Back in London, in 2012, tens of thousands of people gathered in the Mall, the broad, tree-lined boulevard leading to Buckingham

---

[148] Ian Bradley, *You've Got To Have A Dream,* p80.

Palace, and burst into song in tribute to the Queen's diamond jubilee. Still today, *You'll Never Walk Alone* is being used for inspiration, as the world finds itself engulfed in the corona virus crisis. It is being sung particularly to show gratitude to the thousands of frontline health workers in hospitals the world over, letting them know that our hearts and prayers are with them just as they are for the patients whose lives they are so heroically fighting to save.

In the UK, seventy-five years after *Carousel's* opening, and fifty-seven years after the record by Gerry and the Pacemakers reached the number one spot, a new recording of the song by British musical theatre star, Michael Ball and the incredible centenarian, Captain Sir Tom Moore who raised over £33million ($45million) for the National Health Service by walking one hundred laps of his garden, saw *You'll Never Walk Alone* reach the top of the singles charts once again. Their choice of song was no coincidence; at a time when the world most needed hope, nothing could possibly better fit the bill.

The song's ability to touch an emotional chord at times of both sadness and joy, is surely unique within the Broadway canon. Today, it is hard to imagine any major public event, be it joyous or sombre, taking place without *You'll Never Walk Alone* as a musical accompaniment. In that respect, it has become a truly international anthem.

Chapter 12

From London to Hollywood

The triumphant Broadway opening proved to be only the beginning of *Carousel's* story. Whilst it would never quite enjoy the popularity of Rodgers and Hammerstein's first show, it nonetheless, was immediately recognised as a classic, one of the shows that define Broadway's 'Golden Age'.[149] Indeed, *Carousel's* reputation as a musical theatre masterpiece has only grown over the years, a consequence of some outstanding revivals in theatres across the world.

The first step in ensuring *Carousel's* longevity was to produce an original cast recording of the score. *Oklahoma!* had been the first show for which such a recording was made, and it proved to be hugely popular; once *Carousel's* success was assured, arrangements were made to record its score too. Like its predecessor, the recordings were issued on old shellac '78' records, and the score was of necessity significantly cut as happened with the 1950 London cast recording. Some of the songs had to be abridged to fit the '78' formats, but it does include a small part of *Soliloquy* found on no other recording, a segment Rodgers subsequently cut from the score.[150]

Whatever acting shortcomings they may have had, hearing John Raitt and Jan Clayton singing *If I Loved You,* makes one realise why Rodgers and Hammerstein ultimately chose them for the

---

[149] The period that began with *Show Boat* in 1927 and ended with *Cabaret* in 1966 This is my personal definition of the 'Golden Age'. Every aficionado has their own opinion as to both its beginning and its end.

[150] *When I have a daughter*
I'll stand around in bar-rooms-
Oh, how I'll boast and blow!
Friends'll see me comin'
And empty all the bar-rooms-
Through ev'ry door they'll go,
Weary of hearin' day after day
The same old things that I always say ...

show. In 1998, the recording was inducted into the Grammy Hall of Fame.

In 1955, *Carousel* became the first Broadway musical for which a "crossover" recording was made, when Victor produced an album featuring opera stars Robert Merrill, Patricia Munsel, and Gloria Lane.[151] Numerous other recordings of the score have been made over the years, some more complete than others. No recording has yet been made of the entire score, an omission which surely must be rectified one day. When it came to making the 1956 film version, some musical sequences were reduced in length and other songs were entirely cut. However, two of those deleted numbers were recorded and ultimately retained on the soundtrack album. An expanded CD version of the soundtrack was issued in 2001, and this contains all the singing recorded for the film, including the cut portions as well as most of the dance music.

The recording of the 1965 Lincoln Center revival featured Raitt reprising the role of Billy. Various studio recordings of the *Carousel* score have been issued, most notably, one produced in 1987 which featured a mix of opera and musical stars, including Samuel Ramey, Barbara Cook (finally recording her role as Julie) and Sarah Brightman, an excellent Carrie.

Both the London (1992) and New York (1994) cast albums of the Royal National Theatre's much acclaimed production contain portions of dialogue that give a sense of the drama director Nicholas Hytner brought to the show. Michael Hayden's portrayal of Billy is on both albums. For the drama, the London cast is probably the better option, whereas musically, the 1994 recording has the edge thanks to Sally Murphy's Julie and the outstanding Audra McDonald as Carrie. Whilst the recording of the recent 2018 production is undoubtedly well sung, too much music has been omitted to make it worthy of consideration for anyone wanting to hear the full score.

Five days after *Carousel's* initial Broadway run ended on the twenty-fourth of May 1947, the show embarked on a nationwide tour, visiting fifty-five cities in two years, opening at the Shubert Theatre in Chicago and ending back home at the Majestic Theatre in New York where it had a final month's outing before *South Pacific* began its own long run at that theatre.

---

[151] Available on Spotify.

On 7 June 1950, *Carousel* followed *Oklahoma!* into London's historic Theatre Royal, Drury Lane, where it began a run of five hundred and sixty-six performances. Getting the show to London was not straightforward. The Theatre Guild had their fingers badly burned with the London production of *Oklahoma!* The high post war level of UK taxation together with restrictions on taking currency out of the country severely limited the profitability of the production. To avoid similar problems with *Carousel,* specific arrangements had to be put in place such as leasing the UK rights to the show to its British producer, Prince Littler.[152] This required certain controls to be put in place, but with the assurance of their trusted lawyer, Howard Reinheimer, Rodgers and Hammerstein were happy to proceed.[153]

Bambi Linn, Eric Mattson and Robert Pagent repeated their original Broadway roles of Louise, Enoch Snow and the carnival boy. Iva Withers, a Rodgers and Hammerstein regular, who had taken over the role from Jan Clayton on Broadway, played Julie whilst Stephen Douglass, the last Billy in the original Broadway run, opened in the role at Drury Lane.

Though the Second World War had ended five years earlier, London in 1950 was a city still deeply scarred by the blitz, grey and littered with the bombsites that would continue to blight the city for another decade. Its people too, continued to suffer from the aftermath of that long, hard struggle with many items, meat, cheese, sugar, and confectionary for instance, still rationed. The euphoria of victory had quickly been replaced by the daily struggle to get by in those austere times. Not until the coronation of Queen Elizabeth II three years later, would life begin to improve. So, when *Carousel* followed *Oklahoma!* into the Theatre Royal Drury Lane on 7 June 1950, if the British press was a little less enthusiastic than their American counterparts, perhaps they, and indeed Londoners in general, were just not ready for a musical quite so dark and different from its predecessor. They, maybe more than their American cousins, were no doubt hoping for a bright and breezy *Oklahoma!* Mark II, and therefore, were left

---

[152] Prince Littler was a British theatrical producer and impresario, and for the avoidance of doubt, Prince was his Christian name, not a royal title.

[153] Memo from Howard Reinheimer, 14 December 1949, Oscar Hammerstein Collection, Library of Congress.

somewhat bemused and perhaps a little disappointed to see something so different. These sentiments were reflected in the critics' reviews.

Drury Lane's traditional programme cover
for *Carousel* in 1950.

J.C.Trewin in the *Illustrated London News* summed up the difficulty the show had always faced. '... Hardly another

Oklahoma! ... If Carousel had come first, I think its qualities would have been more generally honoured'.

Cecil Wilson, in the *London Daily Mail,* noted the change in direction from its predecessor, '... in some respects, it is a better show than *Oklahoma!* ... The music, if less hummable, has more operatic quality. The lyrics are cleverer, but there may be mixed feelings about *Liliom* as a theme'. W.A. Darlington of the *Daily Telegraph* singled out Rodgers' music for special praise. 'It is possible to enjoy a great deal of it without taking the story too profoundly ... The best thing about it is the music ... a real successor to *Oklahoma!'.*

A.V. Cookman, of the *Times,* in his review, caught the general mood with a mixture of praise and concern about the subject matter. '... may slip into excessive sentimentality, but we would be ungrateful to complain of a piece that so liberally adds song and dance to a bizarre story that is not always so dramatic as when Molnár told it ... as a musical play it has very much to recommend it'.

One review that might have particularly hurt Richard Rodgers was that from the *News Chronicle.* 'Many pretty tunes by Richard Rodgers though even these are not the best he can do'. More to his liking would have been the opinion of the critic from the Manchester Guardian. 'The music does not disdain the operatic method of underlining the drama ...'

London would not see *Carousel* again for some forty years, although when it did, it would be a production so special, that it is still spoken of with awe by musical theatre fans on both sides of the Atlantic.

***

Rodgers and Hammerstein remained close to Ferenc Molnár and in 1951, they approached their old alma mater, Columbia University, in the hope that the playwright might be awarded an honour or degree. In a joint letter they wrote:

> Two years ago, we were fortunate enough to be given medals of excellence by Columbia. Perhaps it would not be inappropriate for us to suggest that some similar honour, or

degree, be granted Ferenc Molnár, the well-known dramatist.

... In 1945, we had the honour of making a musical version of Mr. Molnár's 'Liliom'.

And we need hardly point out to you the great contribution made to the venture by Mr. Molnár's play. The printed volume of his other works is a large and valuable one.

Mr. Molnár, now past seventy, is an American citizen and lives at the Hotel Plaza in New York. We hope that you and the Trustees will receive this suggestion favourably.

Yours sincerely[154]

Sadly, the wheels of academe turned too slowly for Molnár, who died on 1 April 1952 before the request could be granted.

Early on in its post first-run life, the show's operatic qualities made it a popular choice for light opera companies. In the 1950s, it was performed by, amongst others, the St. Louis MUNY Opera, the Los Angeles Civic Light Opera, and the New York City Centre Light Opera, twice.

After the first New York City Centre Light Opera performance in 1954, both Lawrence Langner and his wife, Armina Marshall, wrote to Dick Rodgers to say nice things about the show. Rodgers' reply is interesting because it once again emphasises the important role that they and Helburn played in getting it off the ground. 'You were both sweet enough to write to me about CAROUSEL and this is to tell you how deeply I appreciate your enthusiasm and kindness. Very rarely in my life have I had such a deeply emotional experience and in closing this brief note, I have to tell you that I hold you both and Terry responsible for its origin'.[155]

---

[154] Letter, 6 June 1951 to Secretary of Columbia University, New York, Richard Rodgers Collection, New York Public Library, Performing Arts Division.

[155] Letter, 9 June 1954, Richard Rodgers Collection, New York Public Library, Performing Arts Division.

***

Also, in the 1950s came the film version. It took twelve years from its Broadway opening before *Oklahoma!* eventually reached the big screen, the main reason being the continued success of the original production, both in New York and on tour. The producers were not going to risk losing theatre box office takings by having the film released too soon, so although every major studio came knocking on the door, they were all rebuffed. Another reason is that Rodgers and Hammerstein decided, soon after *Allegro* opened in 1947, that they wanted to have complete control of all their own creations. They took on the role of producers for their next show, *South Pacific* and for their following shows. To regain control of their earlier works, they entered into negotiations with the Theatre Guild to purchase the rights of *Oklahoma! Carousel* and *Allegro,* a deal that was finally concluded in 1953.[156] That left them free to negotiate the sale of the film rights to *Oklahoma!* to Magna Theatre Corporation, a company in which they were both directors. Rodgers and Hammerstein were uncredited executive producers and retained artistic control over the film, which was premiered in New York on 11 October 1955.

Obtaining similar control over the film version of *Carousel* turned out to be impossible. 20th Century Fox had produced a screen version of *Liliom* in 1930, with Charles Farrell and Rose Hobart in the lead roles. As owners of the movie rights to *Liliom,* they contributed a significant investment in the original stage production of *Carousel* and although Rodgers and Hammerstein had subsequently acquired one hundred per cent ownership of their musical, when all the labyrinthine negotiations had been completed, Fox still had the right of first refusal to produce the film version, a right which they chose to exercise, (on 30 June 1955) with the result that Rodgers and Hammerstein had far less say in the

---

[156] This was prompted by the Guild's refusal to agree to Rodgers and Hammerstein's request to delay the New York opening of *Allegro* by a week, thereby denying them the extra time in Boston they felt they needed to iron out the remaining problems with the show. They believed with the benefit of that extra week, *Allegro* would have become their third straight smash, rather than the 'nearly' show it turned out to be. After that, they decided they had to have total control over their own shows.

production than they did with *Oklahoma!* It surely is no coincidence that the film over which they had relatively little control is so much less satisfactory than the one in which they had a significant say?

Daryl F. Zanuck executive produced, whilst Henry Ephron was chosen as producer and with his wife, Phoebe, to adapt Oscar Hammerstein's book. They decided to shoot the film in the super wide screen CinemaScope 55 format and a budget of $3,380,000 was set for the film, significantly less than the $6.8m budget for *Oklahoma!*

Veteran Henry King was chosen as director, although his only previous experience of a musical was the 1938 Irving Berlin scored *Alexander's Ragtime Band* starring Alice Faye and Tyrone Power, which delightful though it may be, is a far cry from the altogether more complex book musical that is *Carousel.*

Whilst Agnes de Mille would receive credit as the creator of *The Dream Ballet,* the choreographer for the film would be Rod Alexander, who at the time happened to be married to Bambi Linn, Broadway's original Louise. Hollywood veteran, Charles G. Clarke, was chosen as cinemaphotographer.

Various locations in Maine were selected for exterior shots, including Augusta, Boothbay Harbour and Camden, while *Soliloquy* and parts of Louise's ballet were shot in Paradise Cove, California. Interiors were shot at the 20th Century Fox Studios in Los Angeles.

For the role of Billy, the producers' first choice was Frank Sinatra, who was not only an outstanding singer, but as an actor had just given an Oscar winning performance in *From Here to Eternity*. Sinatra really wanted the part, hounding producer Daryl Zanuck for a firm commitment as he had so many other projects in the pipeline. Rodgers and Hammerstein certainly considered Sinatra an interesting, albeit somewhat offbeat, choice but urged Zanuck to keep Gordon MacRae in mind as well. In spite of this seemingly less than enthusiastic response from *Carousel's* creators, Sinatra, finally was given the part.

There were many rumours at the time about who was going to play the role of Julie in the film. Doris Day's agent called on her behalf, but she had recently filmed a musical with Sinatra, *Four Daughters,* that did nothing at the box office and Zanuck vetoed her. Sid Luft enquired about the role for his wife, Judy Garland but she insisted that *Soliloquy* be rewritten as a duet for her and Sinatra. The Ephrons knew better than to bother Rodgers and Hammerstein with that one.

In any case, Rodgers and Hammerstein always had Shirley Jones in mind for the part. Just a couple of years earlier, Jones had arrived in New York to enrol in veterinary college. Aware of her talent, a friend persuaded her to attend one of the regular open auditions held by Rodgers and Hammerstein at the Broadway Theatre for parts in their various productions. There she sang for John Fearnley, Rodgers and Hammerstein's casting director, who was so impressed that he had her sing three numbers and then asked her to wait while he fetched Richard Rodgers who was conducting an orchestra rehearsal at City Centre. Rodgers, in turn, was equally impressed, and he took her back to City Centre where, singing with an orchestra for the first time in her life, she auditioned for Hammerstein. The upshot was, that Jones was given a part in the chorus of *South Pacific* and a seven-year contract, the only artist ever awarded such a contract by Rodgers and Hammerstein.

Before long, she was singing *No Other Love* in *Me and Juliet* and then she screen-tested for and won the part of Laurey in *Oklahoma!* Now she was an obvious choice to play Julie. She eventually won everyone over because, as Henry Ephron suggested, with her beautiful voice and innocent looks, you would believe that when Shirley fell in love, it would be forever.

Once they were on board, the two leads, Frank Sinatra and Shirley Jones spent eight weeks at the Fox Studios, rehearsing and pre-recording the songs for the soundtrack. Throughout that period, Jones recalled in her memoirs, how hard Sinatra worked and how much he desperately wanted to make this a film to remember.

The unit then moved to the first location, Boothbay Harbour, Maine, the setting for Nettie's Spa, to begin filming. There, they encountered a massive problem. All the cast had been made aware from the very beginning, that shooting in the still new CinemaScope 55 format would require some scenes to be shot twice. The reason for this was that at the time, not all cinemas had screens or projectors able to handle these very wide screen films. This same problem had been encountered on *Oklahoma!* which had been shot in the equally new Todd-AO format.

The first scheduled scene to be filmed was one between Shirley Jones and Frank Sinatra. Jones was on set, waiting for Sinatra when his car drove up. On leaving his car, Sinatra took one look at the set, with its two different cameras in position and is alleged to have exploded. "I signed to do one movie, not two. You do not get two Sinatras for the price of one." Furiously, he returned to his car and ordered his driver to take him straight to the airport. Sinatra had quit the movie on the first day of shooting. For many years, the only explanation ever given for him doing so, was the double shooting.

Shirley Jones, having seen how much the film meant to him whilst they rehearsed together, never quite believed that the double shooting (which he had long known about) was the sole reason for Sinatra walking off the set. She saw him many times over the following years, ironically, even singing *If I Loved You* with him on a 1958 TV show. Every time she saw him, she asked him to explain his sudden departure, but he would just bristle and say, "Drop it, Shirl." Only after Sinatra died in 1998 did she hear of a possible alternative reason for his behaviour. This story came from an old-time journalist she encountered at a press conference.

What he told her was that Ava Gardner, Sinatra's then wife and the love of his life, was on location in Kenya making the film *Mogambo* with Clark Gable at the time Carousel started shooting. Missing Sinatra, she called him and threatened him; if he didn't get on a plane and join her immediately, she would have an affair with her co-star. Sinatra took her threat seriously enough to abandon the film and fly off to join her. The only problem with this story is that the journalist did not check his facts. *Mogambo* had long since finished shooting; it was premiered in October 1953, almost two years before they started filming *Carousel*. In fact, by 1955, Gardner had undergone an abortion of Sinatra's baby in London and had purchased a house in Madrid where she was living with a Spanish actor. The marriage was already over. So, whilst Sinatra certainly had been head-over heels in love with Ava Gardner, the rest of the story just does not stack up.

It may have been the double shooting. It may have been increasing self-doubt about his suitability for the part. It may have been his hating location filming and the fact that on the small plane flying from New York to Portland, he was constantly throwing up. Whatever the reason for his quitting the film, leave it he did, and the Studio issued a $1million lawsuit against him. In a final ironic twist, a way was found to transfer film shot in CinemaScope 55 onto traditional Cinemascope film, so the need to film everything twice disappeared.

Meanwhile, Henry Ephron, whose first picture as producer this was, having watched Sinatra disappear into the proverbial sunset, approached Shirley Jones in tears. He had first thought of replacing Sinatra with Gene Kelly, but Richard Rodgers vetoed that suggestion on the not unreasonable grounds that Kelly's voice was not strong enough for the *Soliloquy* and Kelly refused to be dubbed. Ephron wondered if Jones could get hold of Gordon MacRae her co-star in *Oklahoma!?* Jones knew that MacRae was performing his night club act in Tahoe. Ephron gave her a bunch of quarters and from a payphone on the dock, she managed to get hold of MacRae and asked him if he would like to play Billy Bigelow in *Carousel.* "Give me three days, I gotta lose ten pounds," was the reply. Lose the ten pounds he did, on a diet of grapefruit and eggs; he flew to Boothbay Harbour and signed on to play Billy.

Also in the cast were Barbara Ruick as Carrie Pipperidge, Claramae Turner as Nettie Fowler, Cameron Mitchell as Jigger Craigin and Robert Rounseville as Enoch Snow. Louise was played Susan Luckey and the carnival boy by Jacques d'Amboise.

Don Walker did not get to orchestrate the film as he had hoped. That job went instead to a team presumably put together by Music Supervisor, Alfred Newman that included Robert Russell Bennett, Earl Hagen, Gus Levene, Bernard Myers, Edward Powell, Nelson Riddle, Herbert Spencer and, working on his first film, an uncredited young John Williams, who incidentally, would later marry Barbara Ruick, whom he met on the production.

The film differed from the original stage version in many ways. Some of the changes were made by the producers to take full advantage of the medium; it was a film after all, not a filmed stage show, and had Rodgers and Hammerstein retained control, no doubt, they would have accepted those changes; for example, the moving of the song *When the Children Are Asleep.* Others, especially replacing some of *The Bench Scene's* lyrics into spoken dialogue, they most certainly would not have approved. They might have accepted the cutting of *Geraniums in the Window* and *The Highest Judge of All* - the latter has been omitted from some stage revivals - and maybe *Blow High, Blow Low.* On the other hand, they surely would not have been happy to leave out *You're a Queer One, Julie Jordan* so important in establishing her character. Other changes, such as replacing at the end of *Soliloquy, "I'll try, by God, I'll try"* with *"I'll try, I'll try, I'll try"* were forced upon the producers by the puritanical Hays Code, issued by the Moving Picture Association of America (M.P.A.A.) which was still in place at the time of making the film. A total of twenty-three changes to the script were demanded, the most damaging to the film being Billy dying by accident rather than suicide. 'The suicide by Billy Bigelow violates that portion of the Code which states that suicide 'should never be justified or glorified or used to defeat the due process of law'. We will be unable to approve any indication that Billy took his own life to avoid being captured by the police'.

Yet in the play, that is exactly what Billy does. *"They won't put me in no Prison"* he cries and then stabs himself in the stomach crying, *"Julie."* Suicide was an option for him, offering perhaps the only way he could escape from a life where he was always the outsider, never able to fit in. He knew Julie was strong enough to survive without him, but he knew too that his spirit could not survive years and years in jail. Having him die accidentally as they did in the film just made him look pathetic, not the tormented soul that he was.

Among other lines that the M.P.A.A. found objectionable were:

- Billy's line early on, *"What you think I want with two of you? I meant that* <u>*one*</u> *of you was to wait. The other can go home."*
- *"Damn"* in *Soliloquy. "What the hell"* or *"By God."*
- Carrie complaining, *"If I had more sense, I wouldn't have had nine children."*
- The lines from *Stonecutters "... good man ain't no fun"* and *"Gawd-knows-whattin' all night."*
- In *June Is Bustin Out all Over, "comfort they ken only get in port"* had to go, as did *"All the boys are feeling lusty, And the girls ain't even putting up a fight."*

Individually, these cuts might seem small and insignificant, but taken together, they had a hugely detrimental effect on the film, completely undermining the earthy realism that Molnár, and then Hammerstein had put on stage.

The most noticeable difference from the stage production was at the beginning of the film. Whereas, in the theatre, the curtain rose on a fairground to the opening chords of *The Carousel Waltz* for the scene setting Prologue, the film opened pre-credits, 'Up There', fifteen years after Billy's death. He is occupied polishing stars whilst the heavenly friend tells him that *"Things ain't going so good for your kinfolk down on earth."* and that he still has the chance to go back for a day. After the opening credits, Billy returns to see the Starkeeper who points out that he has already passed up the opportunity to go back for a day but if he can provide a good reason for doing so, an exception might be made. Billy then starts to tell the story of his life and now, as we begin to hear *The Carousel Waltz,* the scene dissolves to the start of the play, fifteen years earlier.

Visually, the film looks very good indeed, and it sounds fine too. What lets it down is that director, Henry King, failed to capture the essence of the show, certainly not in the way that later theatrical revivals did. All the changes, all the omissions (some admittedly forced upon him by the M.P.A.A.), left a sugary Carousel that lacked a soul. The film was too nice, too clean, too Hollywood. Rodgers and Hammerstein's concerns aside, it probably was not helped by Frank Sinatra's abrupt departure. His Billy would have had that hint of menace that MacRae just could not manage, at least not without the preparation and rehearsal time he was denied as a consequence of his last-minute casting. Just like John Raitt before him, Gordon MacRae was to discover that the role of Curly is a much easier one to play than Billy Bigelow.

Carousel was given parallel premieres in New York and Los Angeles on 16 February 1956, and received generally favourable reviews, perhaps more favourable than it deserved, although *Time Magazine* saw it in its true light. '... The melodies have all their clovered freshness still, but if film fans lick their lips over anything else, it will be because they can't tell sweet from saccharine ... in a word: goo'. Bosley Crowther in the *New York Times* on the other hand, said that it was '... a beautifully turned-out film, crisply played and richly sung by a fine cast'. He did, however, take issue with some of the direction. '... The only

Shirley Jones and Gordon MacRae in the 1956 film.

considerable exception is the rather startling confusion of pictorial styles'.

Nearly all the reviews make reference to the score. Typical is Thomas H. Wenning in *Newsweek.* '... A musical play that has become an American classic... At all times, it is good to look at and even better to listen to ... The score, of course, is the loveliest, bar none, of the R&H collection'.

There are conflicting reports as to how well the film did financially - according to Thomas Hischak it made a small profit - but it certainly was no blockbuster. Nor did it feature at the Academy Awards, the only major film version of a Rodgers and Hammerstein musical not to receive a single nomination. That year's (1957) ceremony was dominated by The King and I which was nominated for nine Oscars and won five.

To this day, although there have been numerous theatrical revivals of the show over the years, inevitably, it is this film version of Carousel that is the only version most people will have seen, either in the cinema or on television. It follows, therefore, that this seriously flawed version is all that they have on which to base their opinion of one of Broadway's greatest musicals and that is something to be regretted. If any film version of a Broadway classic is deserving of a remake it is Carousel, which is something actor Hugh Jackman, who was a memorable Billy in a 2002 Carnegie Hall concert version of the show realised in 2009. He announced that a remake of the film was in pre-production, again through 20th Century Fox. He had a completed script, and Anne Hathaway was being suggested as a possible Julie. That, however, seems to be as far as it got and to date the prospects for a remake seem as far away as ever ...

***

In 1967, ABC Television presented a somewhat abridged version of the show starring Robert Goulet, Mary Grover and Patricia Neway. Rather scratchy versions of some scenes can be found on YouTube.

Meanwhile, Carousel's stage life continued. In 1957, the New York City Centre Light Opera Company staged a short run featuring Howard Keel as Billy and Barbara Cook as Julie. The show was featured at the Brussels World Fair, where Jan Clayton once again, played Julie Jordan. Another New York production, this time at the Lincoln Center in 1965, saw John Raitt reprise his role as Billy Bigelow.

Richard Rodgers celebrated his seventy-fifth birthday on 28 June 1977, and that gave rise to a very special Carousel performance. To mark the occasion, Rodgers and his wife Dorothy were invited by President Carter to a White House dinner at which the composer was the guest of honour. It was clearly intended to be a private evening, as apparently there were no reports of it in the newspapers. That we know about it at all is because Rodgers mentioned it in a letter he wrote to his friend, the critic Elliot Norton, thanking him for a birthday tribute Norton had written in the Boston Herald. Rodgers wrote how, after dinner, 'five soloists from the Met. sang a concert version, with a very good orchestra, of the CAROUSEL songs. Then, the President asked Dorothy and me to come up on the stage where he made a rather astonishing speech about me and my work. I will not quote him here, but it was pretty touching and stirring. It all made up, in a way, for the seventy-five-year-old bit'. How the President came to choose the music of *Carousel* for the evening, we shall never know. Was it his favourite Richard Rodgers' score? Was it the First Lady's? Did they perhaps know it was the composer's favourite? Whatever the reason, as we shall see later, this would not be the last time that singers from the Metropolitan Opera would perform *Carousel.*

After the 1965 revival, there were no new major stage productions of Carousel for almost thirty years, until at an unlikely venue on the other side of the Atlantic, there would be the most significant production since the show's Broadway opening; one that would change people's perception of the show for ever.

Chapter 13

The National Theatre and into the New Century

As the twentieth century edged towards its close, the phenomenal success of the film version of *The Sound of Music* together with regular stage revivals and television screenings of their other shows, ensured that Rodgers and Hammerstein's musicals remained as popular as ever. Within the big five,[157] *Carousel* was the one that had become perhaps a little neglected. It was the show with 'the beautiful music, but such a weird story'. It was also the one, as suggested in the previous chapter, the film version of which was least faithful to the original. All of that was about to change, however, because on a stage in London, a new production of *Carousel* was about to restore it to its rightful place as one of the great works of American musical theatre.

The unexpected venue for this turnaround in the show's fortunes was London's Royal National Theatre on the South Bank of the River Thames. Founded in 1963 after years of struggle to secure government funding, the National, as it is popularly known, was established to provide London audiences with the very best that theatre could offer. Under its first artistic director, Sir Laurence (later Lord) Olivier, the National opened with a production of *Hamlet,* at once setting the tone for its future repertoire, a mixture of the classics and high-quality modern drama; Shakespeare, Pinter, Miller, Strindberg, Williams, Beckett, Stoppard, Ibsen.

In 1988, Richard Eyre succeeded Sir Peter Hall to become the National's third artistic director. In 1992, Eyre approached one of the country's most promising young directors, Nicholas Hytner with an intriguing idea. Eyre believed passionately that the great musicals of Broadway's 'Golden Age' should be viewed in the same way as the classic plays that were the National's staple diet. That is, every time they are revived, they should be considered ripe for a new interpretation. Until then, the National had presented only one of Broadway's great musicals; a stunning version of Frank Loesser's *Guys and Dolls*, directed by Eyre himself. That had

---

[157] *Oklahoma!; Carousel; South Pacific; The King and I; The Sound of Music.*

been in 1982. There had also been a production of Sondheim's *Sunday in the Park with George* in 1990. Of course, there followed the inevitable ritual mumblings from the traditionalists who thought it scandalous for the National Theatre to produce anything as low brow as a musical, let alone an American one. That did not deter Eyre, however, and he was ready now to face his critics again. As he went on to explain in the *Carousel* programme, 'There are not many great Broadway musicals, but I believe that as examples of the dramatic art in a singular state of grace, they have as much right to inclusion in a theatre dedicated to excellence as examples from any other dramatic era'.

Hytner was something of a *wunderkind* in British theatre. Born in 1956, he was directing major theatre and opera productions whilst still in his twenties. His first triumph at the National was with Joshua Sobol's *Ghetto* in 1989 and he followed that with Alan Bennett's *The Madness of George III*. His first venture into commercial theatre came in 1989 when Cameron Mackintosh asked him to direct the Claude-Michel Schonberg and Alain Boublil musical, *Miss Saigon*.

With his experience of directing opera, drama and musicals, it was no surprise that Richard Eyre singled Hytner out to direct a 'Golden Age' classic, and when he was approached, Hytner himself had no doubt as to which of the great musicals he would choose.

Whilst growing up in Manchester, his grandmother had taken him to see them all, but his favourites were those of Rodgers and Hammerstein, and his favourite amongst those was *Carousel*. In 1984, there had been a revival of the show at the Manchester Royal Exchange, directed by his close friend, Steven Pimlott. It was a production which Hytner thought, whilst it was completely renewed, it 'didn't quite work'.[158]

Talking to theatrical author John Lahr, Hytner explained his plans for his new production. "I think it's the best of the great romantic musicals. I was surprised at how tough and real it was when I read it: Julie Jordan *picks up* Billy Bigelow. You could not do that on stage in 1945. There's a very interesting tension between the sweetness of the music and the powerful sexual undercurrents of the play. In this *Carousel*, the dark, subterranean sexuality,

---

[158] Daniel Rosenthal, *The National Theatre Story*.

which has traditionally been kept in the background of productions, explodes into the foreground."[159]

He knew it was a show that would "reward any amount of exploration."[160] Years later, Hytner explained to author Daniel Rosenthal in an interview for the latter's award-winning biography, *The National Theatre Story.* "All those Rodgers and Hammerstein shows might sustain the kind of kicking around that we gave things at the National. Since *Guys and Dolls,* there had not been a problem selling sharp, sophisticated musical comedies [at the NT], but the sentimental ones had always been thought to be commercial confections. I had this hunch the sentimental ones would be taken seriously. With *Carousel,* apart from the fact that the score is just fantastic, [the authors] didn't realise how bleak and cynical *Liliom* is; their sensibility was the polar opposite of Molnár's, which is, in the most attractive way, wicked, not sentimental at all. I wanted to explore that odd tension [with] the shadow of the Molnár play."[161]

Having obtained Richard Eyre's agreement on the choice of show, Hytner 'descended on *Carousel* to demonstrate that a masterpiece of American entertainment was in fact, high art'.[162]

That descent began with the job of getting the right choreographer on board. He wanted someone whom he felt could create the wow factor that had been missing from the revivals he had seen. For advice as to who might be a suitable candidate, he turned to Cameron Mackintosh, who immediately suggested he approach Kenneth MacMillan who "adored American Musicals." [163] MacMillan, at that time, was the most important figure in British Ballet and Hytner did not think there was the slightest chance that he would agree to do the show. Nervous and in awe of the great man, Hytner became tongue-tied as he tried to explain the show to him. In despair, he blurted out "Here's the thing about *Carousel.* It's about sex and violence!" MacMillan's response was "Well,

---

159 John Lahr, *Joy Ride,* p390.
160 Nicholas Hytner, *Balancing Acts,* p233.
161 Daniel Rosenthal, *The National Theatre Story.*
162 Nicholas Hytner, *Balancing Acts,* p235.
163 Daniel Rosenthal. *The National Theatre Story.*

that's what I do." The deal was done, and MacMillan was on board.[164]

When MacMillan said he did sex and violence he was being nothing less than truthful. Throughout his career, he had sought to move ballet away from the traditional fairy tale stories and use the medium to tell stories about real people and real emotions. One of his earliest ballets was *The Invitation* (1960) which was about rape, and which created a considerable controversy. Others in which he explored real life were *Mayerling* (1978), *My Brother, My Sisters* about a disturbed family, *Valley of Shadows,* set in a concentration camp and *Different Drummer.* The last three are all about the suffering of the oppressed, just like *Liliom.*

In an interview for the BBC, he said, "The thing about relationships between men and women, it is always sexual, overt, or hidden. There has to be some kind of sexual tension between the man and the woman." Because *Carousel* is full of sexual tension, and this was exactly what Hytner wanted to bring out on stage, getting MacMillan on board was a real coup.

Cameron Mackintosh contributed £250,000 towards the cost of putting on the show through a donation from his foundation,[165] and Hytner and MacMillan began the task of assembling the cast. Hytner was looking for actors who could sing and MacMillan wanted dancers who could sing. Hytner reckoned he had seen just about every actor/singer in Britain when he was casting *Miss Saigon* and experience had taught him that your two very best singers moved around the stage like elephants while your two best dancers couldn't sing at all. MacMillan noted in his diary that after auditions in London's Pineapple Dance Studios on 28-29 April 1992, 'Auditioned one hundred and fifty girls, only three any good. One hundred boys, only two'. In the end, they filled the twenty-four-strong supporting cast with a dozen strong dancers and a dozen strong singers.

For the role of Julie, Hytner chose a young British actress/singer, Joanna Riding, who had just made her West End debut as a replacement Sally in *Me and My Girl.* When she sang *What's the Use of Wond'rin',* she did so with a naked simplicity. As Hytner explained, "The melody is gorgeous, the sentiment

---

[164] Nicholas Hytner, Ibid, p236.

[165] Daniel Rosenthal, *The National Theatre Story.*

apparently uncomplicated. The insidious power of the show is that at the dark heart of an abusive marriage is love and forgiveness no less profound for being misplaced."[166]

Finding a Billy to play opposite her was not easy. There were plenty of good-looking actors with powerful baritones, and Hytner saw a lot of them in London and in New York. He tried to picture them hitting Joanna Riding. "I'd have hated them" he said, "and hated the show for asking me to care about them, and besides, as actors they weren't up to her."[167] In another quote, Hytner said "I was looking for James Dean with a voice." [168]

In New York, Hytner finally saw an actor, fresh out of Juilliard, who came close to matching that description. His name was Michael Hayden. Although vocally, less adept than many of the others he auditioned, when Hayden sang, Hytner saw in him "... the wounded frailty behind the bravado. As Billy, he caused pain because he was in pain." [169] There is a strong echo of Clara Györgyey's description of Billy in these comments, reinforcing how strongly Hytner believed in the necessity of re-examining Molnár's *Liliom* as he prepared his production of *Carousel.*

To play Nettie Fowler, Hytner recruited award winning actress Patricia Routledge who had achieved huge popularity in the UK, playing the outrageously snobbish Cynthia Bucket, (which she insisted be pronounced Bouquet) in the TV sitcom *Keeping up Appearances.* Carrie Pipperidge was played by the then, relatively unknown, Janie Dee. It was the casting of Enoch Snow, however, that would raise more than a few eyebrows; to play the role, Hytner chose black actor Clive Rowe. This was at a time when colour-blind casting was still a relatively new concept. The eyebrows raised the highest belonged to Dorothy Rodgers, widow of Richard who considered that casting a black man would be 'inappropriate' and that because of the character's name would seem a very poor joke.

Hytner flew to meet Mrs. Rodgers in her apartment overlooking Central Park. She was, by then, eighty-three-years old and suffering from the emphysema from which she would die just

---

[166] Nicholas Hytner, *Balancing Acts,* p236.
[167] Nicholas Hytner, Ibid, p237.
[168] John Lahr, *Joy Ride,* p391.
[169] Nicholas Hytner, Ibid, p237.

a few months later. Breathing with the aid of an oxygen cylinder, she was accompanied by her daughter Mary, a successful composer in her own right.[170] Also, there were Jamie and Bill Hammerstein, the sons of Oscar. After a while, Hytner realised that the opposition to Clive Rowe was coming solely from Dorothy Rodgers. In fact, Mary Rodgers and the Hammerstein brothers were smiling their approval. They understood how important it was for their fathers' shows' survival, that they should be re-imagined by succeeding generations.

On the first day of rehearsals, Rowe introduced himself to the rest of the cast by saying, "I'm Clive Rowe. I play Mr. Snow, and that's the first and last time you'll laugh at that gag." [171]

MacMillan had no problem in obtaining two fine dancers for the roles of Louise and the carnival boy. He went back to the Royal Ballet and asked their principal soloist, American ballerina, Bonnie Moore to take a leave of absence to perform in the role of Louise. To dance opposite her, he selected from the London City ballet, Bolshoi-trained Stanislav Tchassov.

To design the show, Hytner called on an old colleague and regular National Theatre designer, Bob Crowley. Though vastly experienced, this would be Crowley's first musical. Together, they travelled to Maine, where they spent a week driving down the coast, a Carousel CD playing on the car stereo. What struck the pair particularly on their journey was the abundance of blue: most notably in an old shaker meeting house in Sabbathday Lake. There, the ceiling was painted a gorgeous shade of indigo that they were told represented Heaven. Crowley used this blue as the basis of his set, in Hytner's words, "a vast empty box. Big enough to make Billy feel tiny ... It accommodated visions of loneliness that recalled the paintings of Edward Hopper and Andrew Wyeth." Crowley believed that unlike English musicals which up to then, mostly lacked substance and therefore, were "design-oriented," Carousel was such a dramatic masterpiece, it could withstand a more minimalist approach. His design incorporated a pair of clapboard houses with their external rear walls hung with dozens

---

[170] Mary Rodgers' most successful show was *Once Upon a Mattress.* She was also the mother of Adam Guettel, composer of several successful shows, most notably *Light in the Piazza.*

[171] John Lahr, *Joy Ride*, p392.

Clive Rowe and Janie Dee at the National Theatre, 1992
©Clive Barda / ArenaPAL

of fishing marker buoys. The houses revolved to reveal the split-level interior of the Whaler's Inn, as well as the kitchen and upstairs bedroom of Nettie's house and the canopied terrace of Julie's cottage. For the scenes in Heaven, once again, the bare blue box served the story well.

The costumes too, played an important part in Hytner's vision of the show. Molnár's play is about people at the lowest level of society, scraping out a most meagre existence. Whereas in the film, Gordon MacRae looked like he was stepping out for a Sunday afternoon stroll in the park, Michael Hayden had the appearance of someone who has not seen a bath in weeks. Hytner grew to dislike the use of the word 'dark' which had become the adjective most used to describe the production. What he gave us was the realism of the original play, the sweat and the grime and the oppressive poverty, and he saw no reason why those qualities should not be shown in the musical version.

This was a Real Nice Clambake.
National Theatre, 1992
©Clive Barda / ArenaPAL

Don Walker's original orchestrations were adapted by William D. Brohn, whose previous experience included working with Hytner on *Miss Saigon*, and orchestrating a ballet, *The*

Informer, for Agnes de Mille. A skilful adaptor, Brohn ensured that the overall sound of this revival remained Don Walker's.

Rehearsals began on 12 October 1992. Hytner's first task was to make sure each of the cast members read *Liliom* so that they would better understand the characters they were portraying. In all probability, few of the leads in earlier productions of the show, cast primarily for their singing rather than their acting ability, could successfully have played their counterparts in *Liliom.* Michael Hayden and Joanna Riding could. They might not have been quite as strong vocally as their predecessors, but for Hytner, their voices were still good enough, and their acting skills would ensure his vision for *Carousel* would be realised.

In his desire to present *Carousel* as though it was a brand-new work, Hytner decided to start at the very beginning. To him, the sombre, almost menacing opening chords of *The Carousel Waltz* did not belong in an amusement park; it took him a while, but eventually, he realised that what those chords portrayed to him was the daily grind faced by Julie and Carrie in the mill.

He discussed these thoughts with MacMillan who then devised a new sequence with which to open the Prologue: it showed eight young girls hard at work at their looms in the oppressive gloom of Bascombe's Cotton Mill, under the watchful eye of a strict foreman. Overhead, dominating the entire set, is a giant clock, slowly ticking their lives away. When at last, the clock strikes six, the girls leap from their looms and, having cast off their drab working clothes and replaced them with colourful dresses, joyfully dance through the forbidding mill gates to meet up with waiting boys and hurry to the fair. The cast is seen assembling and enjoying the usual fairground attractions, including a bearded lady and, in anticipation of the violence to come, an animal trainer cruelly beating a bear. Whilst *The Carousel Waltz* swells towards its climax, almost without the audience realising it, a carousel has appeared as if by magic on the stage. One by one, everyone except Julie finds a horse on which to ride until Billy, the carousel barker spots her and helps her onto the one remaining horse; on seeing this, Mrs. Mullin, the carousel owner, shows her displeasure, acting remarkably like the foreman at the mill as she does so. Nicholas Hytner sought and was granted permission, to change the Prologue as described above; also, to make some slight changes to the book and to drop the song, *The Highest Judge of All.*

As well as working on the revised Prologue, MacMillan was devising and rehearsing the Act 2 ballet which he knew to be key and to which he devoted considerable energy. According to his biographer, Jann Parry, 'Exhausted and insomniac, he drove himself hard. He needed to inspire the *Carousel* cast to reach the rampant level of energy the ensemble numbers required'.[172] Nicholas Hytner thought that MacMillan was working to his own deadline, one that was well ahead of the actual production schedule. If that was not stressful enough, he was simultaneously overseeing a revival of his ballet *Mayerling* at the Royal Opera House to which he was no doubt devoting just as much energy.

The first night of *Mayerling* was 29 October and during the opening act, MacMillan suffered a panic attack. He went to rest in the green room but sometime during the second act he collapsed and died. He was just sixty-two.

Hytner and all the cast were devastated, but the next day, he asked the *Carousel* ensemble to run through the dance sequences to demonstrate what MacMillan had achieved. Jane Elliott, the ballet mistress filled in the missing sections that MacMillan had already outlined.

A few days later, MacMillan's wife and teenage daughter attended a run through of the show, "one of the bravest and most generous things I have ever witnessed" Hytner said. "They helped a stunned company realise what we had. Kenneth had choreographed nearly everything and in the magical Act 2 ballet, he never stopped speaking to us."[173]

One macabre consequence of MacMillan's tragic death was that *Carousel* received far more publicity than is usual for a subsidised theatre production where the promotions budget is inevitably much smaller than for the commercial theatre. The newspapers were full of stories about MacMillan and the new show for weeks: so much so that one journalist, Paul Taylor of The Independent joked about opening a copy of Angler's Weekly expecting to find a clam being interviewed about the clambake scene.

The new production opened on 10 December 1992 to rave reviews. Any reservations that London might have had about

---

[172] Daniel Rosenthal, *The National Theatre Story.*

[173] Nicholas Hytner, *Balancing Acts,* p237.

Carousel in 1950 were completely dispelled. The London Evening Standard's drama critic reported, 'Never before have I been so emotionally overwhelmed by a musical. 'Triumphant ... confirms Mr. Hytner as one of the finest directors of modern times', said the Daily Mail. Frank Rich came to London to report for the *New York Times* and confirmed that the raves were not unjustified. 'This is without question the most revelatory, not to mention, the most moving revival I've ever seen of any Rodgers and Hammerstein musical. The National has recently found startling new ways of looking at the dramas of Tennessee Williams and Arthur Miller ... and now it proves just as imaginative in sweeping away decades of clichés from an American musical classic of the same period'.

The reviews were quickly followed by a host of awards, led by four Oliviers: Best Revival of a Musical; Best Director of a Musical; Best Actress in a Musical, for Joanna Riding and Best Supporting Actress in a Musical for Janie Dee.

The limited run was completely sold out and in September 1993, it transferred to the newly refurbished Shaftesbury Theatre where it ran for a year. Cameron Mackintosh took his investment in the show to more than $1million when the production transferred to the Vivian Beaumont Thrust Stage Theatre at New York's Lincoln Center.

Michael Hayden was the only member of the NT cast to reprise his role in New York. Audra McDonald launched her stellar career playing the role of Carrie. Sally Murphy was Julie and Shirley Verrett was Nettie. The production opened on 24 March 1994 and ran for three hundred and twenty-two performances. This time it triumphed at the Tonys, winning five awards: Best Musical Revival; Best Performance by a Featured Actress - Audra McDonald; Best Direction of a Musical - Nicholas Hytner; Best Choreography - Kenneth MacMillan; Best Scenic design of a Musical - Bob Crowley.

I have devoted a lot of space to this revival because it is impossible to overstate just how important it was in the continuing life of *Carousel* and indeed, in the lives of the other great shows from the 'Golden Age'. Hytner showed that like any other dramatic work they were open to re-interpretation and his radical, yet sensitive reimagining of *Carousel* must surely have been a significant factor in Time Magazine declaring it to be the greatest musical of the 20th Century.

Sir Kenneth MacMillan: *Carousel* Rehearsals
©Clive Barda / ArenaPAL

Notwithstanding the awards and the plaudits, Nicholas Hytner still had one major regret about the production. Whilst he considers *Carousel* an 'infallibly moving show', he remains very cross with himself for not fighting to change the ending. 'In both Liliom and Carousel, when Billy comes down to earth and attempts to give Louise a star, she refuses to take it and he slaps her. It does not hurt of course, because he is a ghost. When Louise tells her mother Julie about it, she asks that awkward question, "Is it possible, mother, for someone to hit you, hit you hard like that - real loud and hard and it not hurt you at all?" Julie replies, "It is possible, dear, for someone to hit you, hit you hard, and it not hurt at all."

'It's presented as a climactic act of grace, but it's bullshit. Why didn't I tell old Mrs. Rodgers, while I was on her case, that I wasn't going to be responsible for putting it in front of an audience? I suppose because I told myself that, like too many victims of domestic violence, Julie Jordan has no alternative but to lie to herself. But it's not just Julie saying that violence doesn't matter; it's the show. I should have cut it'. [174]

"How I loved you, How I loved you."
Joanna Riding: Michael Hayden
©Clive Barda / ArenaPAL

What Hytner did do, was to have Billy, who was watching the conversation between Julie and Louise, shake his head, "no, no," whilst Julie was saying her line, but Louise could not see him at that point, although the audience did. Clearly though, Hytner does not think that was anywhere near enough.

---

[174] Nicholas Hytner, *Balancing Acts,* p238.

***

The year 2002 was Richard Rodgers' centenary and numerous events were held around the world throughout the year in celebration. One such event was a concert version of *Carousel* held at Carnegie Hall. Led by the Orchestra of St. Luke's under the baton of Leonard Slatkin, the cast included Hugh Jackman as Billy and Audra McDonald as Julie. John Raitt made a special guest appearance. A similar concert version of the show (with a different cast) was performed for two nights at London's Royal Festival Hall.

"Listen to him. Believe Him"
©Clive Barda / ArenaPAL

Another centenary tribute was a special gala given by the New York City Ballet which featured a piece entitled *Carousel (a Dance)*. The choreographer was Christopher Wheeldon, an English-born former protegee of Kenneth MacMillan. Primarily set to *The Carousel Waltz* and *If I Loved You,* in some eighteen minutes, it gives a sense of the story of *Carousel.* It was only intended to be performed at the gala, but so well received was it by critics and public alike that it has been revived on numerous occasions since and appropriately, has also been added to the repertoire of London's Royal Ballet Company.

In the years since those centenary concerts, there have been several revivals, interestingly many of them being by opera companies rather than traditional theatre. In the UK, there was a well-received revival at London's Savoy Theatre in 2008 followed by a notable production by Opera North in 2012 that opened in Leeds before transferring to London and Paris, whilst in 2017, it ran for a season at the English National Opera. 2015 saw what the *Tribune* described as a 'profoundly moving' production by the Chicago Lyric Opera and Houston Grand Opera and there have been productions by opera companies in many other cities around the US.

It seems that Richard Rodgers' fear back in 1944, that audiences might be scared off if they thought the show was too operatic, was completely misguided. Were he alive today, he probably would be delighted to see opera companies around the world staging *Carousel* alongside their regular diet of Puccini, Verdi and Mozart.

Another major *Carousel* event took place in 2013. This took the form of a concert version of the show, featuring the New York Philharmonic under the baton of Rob Fisher, and a combination of stars from the Metropolitan Opera and Broadway. It was presented at Lincoln Center for a week, with one of the performances aired live on PBS. Billy was sung by the Met's Nathan Gunn whilst Julie was played by Kelli O'Hara, herself now a Met star too. Nettie was portrayed by the Met's legendary mezzo-soprano Stephanie Blythe and Carrie was played by Jessie Mueller, (who would later play Julie in the 2018 Broadway revival).[175]

Twenty-four years after Nick Hytner's National Theatre production, *Carousel* was back on Broadway, this time at the Imperial Theatre in what promised to be a lavish new production directed by Jack O'Brien and produced by Scott Rudin. Presenting a seventy-three-year-old musical, a central theme of which is domestic abuse, at a time when the #Me Too and #Time's Up

---

[175] A DVD is available of this beautifully staged version.

movements were dominating the news cycle on an almost daily basis, must have given them both plenty to think about. That dark theme, which whilst it may not have been a problem in 1945, was certainly considered one in 1992, and one as stated earlier, Nicholas Hytner has always regretted not confronting more directly. By 2018, that problem had grown significantly. In fact, the word problematic was overworked in a season which saw not only a new *Carousel,* but also the Lincoln Center revival of *My Fair Lady* and the London revival of *The King and I.*

A daunting challenge, maybe, but both Rudin and O'Brien brought a wealth of experience to the task. Rudin is a highly successful producer, having won Tony awards for plays such as – *Copenhagen, The History Boys, Death of a Salesman, The Book of Mormon* with many more wins and nominations. He has won Oscars as producer of films such as *No Country for Old Men* and *There Will be Blood* and has won Emmys and a Grammy, one of the few people to have on all four major awards.

Jack O'Brien also had a distinguished career as a director, having won Tony awards for *Hairspray, Henry IV* and *The Coast of Utopia.* He was also familiar with the works of Rodgers and Hammerstein having directed a highly successful tour of *The Sound of Music.*

It was not only the built-in plot problem that was on their minds when they decided to mount this revival. There is the fact that today, Broadway is in thrall to new types of musicals. There are the Disney musicals, *The Lion King, Frozen, Beauty and the Beast* and *Aladdin,* spectacular stage adaptations of the company's cartoon films. There are also the 'Juke Box' musicals such as *Beautiful, Mamma Mia* and *Summer,* shows where the audience really does go into the theatre, humming the tunes. Finally, there are the new original shows such as *Hamilton* and *Dear Evan Hansen* and *Waitress,* but these shows are written in a contemporary style, far removed from that of Rodgers and Hammerstein. Would audiences still come to see a musical that might seem old fashioned and dated to a new generation of theatregoers?

To help meet the challenges they faced, they made an important early appointment. Rising young choreographer Justin Peck was signed for the important task of staging all the show's dance numbers. Although making his Broadway debut, the thirty-year old Peck is the youngest ever resident choreographer at the

New York City Ballet. Such was the importance that the producers attached to the choreography that Peck was given equal billing with director Jack O'Brien. Peck brought along very firm ideas about what he wanted to do with the show. He told *Playbill* he had looked at what Agnes de Mille had created for the original and at what Sir Kenneth MacMillan had created for the National Theatre production and dismissed them both. He said, "*Carousel* is a really important show in the musical theatre canon", and added, "There is an opportunity to interject a new voice into this show in regard to the choreography ... I think it's great we're able to update and create *Carousel* for the twenty-first century. And I'm proud to say that I feel like the version we're developing is a more integrated version than the versions that have existed in the past."[176] One can understand that when staging a revival of a classic show today, directors and choreographers want to make use of the additional versatility of the cast that was not available to their predecessors. Today, actors sing and dance, singers act and dance and specialised dancers are fitter, stronger and more athletic than ever before. Why not take advantage of all that?

Clearly, the producers thought carefully about casting the leading parts, choosing actors who had established considerable reputations performing in the new style musicals that have dominated Broadway in recent years and would, therefore, appeal to a younger audience. To play Billy, they chose Joshua Henry, Tony-nominated for *In The Heights* and *The Scottsborough Boys,* and fresh out of touring in *Hamilton.* For Julie, they chose Jessie Mueller, another Tony-nominated actor for her performance in *Waitress* and Tony winner for her role as Carole King in *Beautiful.* As mentioned above, she had also played Carrie in the Lincoln Center special in 2013. The role of Carrie went to Lindsay Mendez whose Broadway experience included *Godspell, Wicked* and *Grease* and Alexander Gemignani (*Les Miserables, Chicago* and *Sweeny Todd)* was chosen to play Enoch Snow.

Then, having learned that the Metropolitan Opera's beloved soprano, Renée Fleming was retiring from the opera stage, they persuaded her to accept the role of Nettie Fowler giving her the chance to sing in its original setting, *You'll Never Walk Alone,* the song she had sung on so many state occasions.

---

176 *Playbill Magazine*, 3 April 2018.

A stellar backstage cast was hired as well. Tony award winners, Santo Loquasto and Ann Roth were hired to design sets and costumes that were perhaps rather too bright and colourful for a poor New England coastal community in Maine in the 1870s.

Another EGOT (Emmy, Grammy, Oscar and Tony) winner, Jonathan Tunick, was hired to re-orchestrate the score. There would be twenty-four musicians in the orchestra, which although big by 2018 standards, was still much smaller than the original, and there was, perhaps, a desire to have a less operatic, more twenty-first century musical sound.

A number of major cuts were made both to the score and to the book. The songs *Geraniums in the Winder* and *Stonecutters Cut it on Stone* and the introduction to *June is Bustin' Out all Over* were all omitted. The entire final scene in Act 1 was deleted. There were many other dialogue cuts as well, including part of the opening scene of Act 2 and the scene between Billy and Jigger just before the robbery. The Prologue which Hammerstein had insisted should not be a ballet, is now performed, as a ballet, and there is no carousel, just one horse and a canopy floating down as the Prologue nears its climax.

Justin Peck was determined to put his own stamp on the choreography and that he certainly did. The dances after both *June is Bustin' Out All Over* and *Blow High, Blow Low,* are energetic and unquestionably entertaining, (somewhat reminiscent of Michael Kidd's choreography for the film, *Seven Brides for Seven Brothers*), but did they, and Louise's Act 2 ballet achieves the narrative quality that was so important to both Agnes de Mille and Oscar Hammerstein?

After six weeks of previews, the production opened at the Imperial Theatre on 12 April 2018 to mixed reviews. Ben Brantley in the *New York Times* reported '… For its first two-thirds, though, this Carousel tingles with the rapture of life in all its contradictions. And the chemistry between this show's leading, mismatched couple is so charged, that when tree blossoms fall mysteriously over their first meeting on a windless night, it makes perfect sense'. He went on to say that he 'missed Agnes de Mille's more lucid story ballets'.

Back on Broadway, 2018

Michael Feingold, writing in the *Village Voice* found the production uneven as though Jack O'Brien was trying to shirk away from the darker side of the story. He also queried the wisdom of some of the cuts and again commented on the lack of narrative detail in the ballet.

Other reviews, whilst praising the quality of the voices, found a lack of chemistry between the leads. 'A spark-free match', said one. Other critics regretted that O'Brien did not look at the material through contemporary eyes, relying on the strength of the score to save the evening.

Nonetheless, Peck's choreography won him a Tony and a second Tony went to Lindsay Mendez for her spirited performance as Carrie.

The revival ran for what must have been to all those connected with the production, a disappointing one hundred and eighty-one performances, closing on 16 September.

If you are a fan of *Carousel,* that disappointing run might make you wonder if in this age of rap, pop and juke box musicals, the great classics of Broadway's 'Golden Age' can survive. The evidence suggests that they can. A Lincoln Center revival of *My Fair Lady,* which opened a week after *Carousel,* ran for five hundred and nine performances. Also, in the summer of 2018, *The King and I* enjoyed a sell-out run at the vast London Palladium. These successes indicate that when the production is right, the audiences will continue to come. Then too, there is a new generation of directors, such as Tim Sheader, prepared, indeed eager, to take on the never-ending challenge of making this unique body of work relevant to the present day. Nor do they have to be full scale West End or Broadway productions. In 2014, there was a delightful re-imagining of *Carousel* at the Arcola, a small, fringe theatre in London's East End. Director Luke Fredericks advanced the setting to the 1930s depression era, a clever device which brought Billy's behaviour and motivation into even sharper relief. The five-piece orchestra performed wonders with the score and the choreography was both joyous and moving, notwithstanding the relatively tiny space available. Reimagined it may have been, but it remained entirely true to the spirit of the original. With an excellent cast, the production earned unanimous five-star reviews.

Revivals such as these provide an encouraging indication that *Carousel*, problematic or not, will continue to be presented in theatres and opera houses around the world. It does not matter how *Carousel* is defined today, for as Richard Rodgers said, the labels don't matter at all. What does matter is that it should survive, and with its glorious score, be seen and heard by theatre lovers for generations to come. It may be controversial. It may pose awkward questions. It might leave one feeling a little bit uncomfortable. But then, isn't that what art is supposed to do?

Appendix 1

Hammerstein's Original Outline

Note: In transcribing this outline, and the documents in Appendix II and III, I have retained Oscar Hammerstein's spellings and tried to reproduce his layouts as they appear in the original typed documents, all of which are to be found in the Library of Congress

LILIOM OUTLINE

(Song Titles Tentative, merely indicative idea for memorandum. Ditto names of scenes and characters.)

ACT ONE

Scene 1: Merry-Go-Round.

"Waltz Suite" - Ensemble Pantomime, introducing characters.

Scene 2: Park - or A Path Near The Shore

> Muskat threatens Julie. Marie on too.
> Liliom enters, opposes Muskat and she fires him. She exits. Later Liliom exits.
> Marie now confides her problem, now that she knows that Julie has one. Should Marie choose Solid and Sensible Wolf, or Romantic and Unreliable Dwight?

"What's on Your Mind?" - Duet: Marie & Julie, and "occasionals."

(When you work at the loom or spindle? When you lie awake at night? When you rise at six? etc.)

> Marie confesses frankly. Julie reveals her feelings by implications. Occasional girls insert line for laugh or punctuation.

Liliom comes back, Marie exits. Liliom & Julie start scene, interrupted by Mill Owner crossing and firing Julie. Now they are both fired.

Their scene drifts from dialogue into singing, eventually developing into a major refrain.

"The Wind Blows the Blossoms" - Duet: Liliom & Julie.
(And they fly before they fall.)

SCENE 3: Pier Restaurant

"Bustin' Out All Over!" - Mill Owner & Ensemble.
(The sap is runnin', the buds are poppin', I'm full o' ginger and my gal's full o' beans, cows're jumpin' fences and the bees're busier'n I ever see 'em before ...)

"Sand Dance"

Julie, Hollunder, maybe Marie & Dwight.

Dwight exits. Two girls discuss Julie's problem with her husband, Liliom, and Marie's problem. If Dwight passes through, take him off so that only girls are on to lead into Holl's number.

"Just As If It Happened to Me" - Hollunder.
(When a sparrow falls, I'm hurt, when a child laughs, I'm happy.)
The character who lives her whole life vicariously.

Liliom and Fiscur.
Liliom rejects hold up scheme, here described by Fiscur in some detail, hooking it up with clambake & treasure hunt.

"Sea Chanty" - Fiscur, Liliom and Men.

Wolf and Marie.

"Put Your Faith in Sardines and Me" - Wolf & Marie

Marie, Julie, Muskat, Hollunder.

"That's My Idea of a Man" - Quartet. Form of Desert Song Number. Each soloist getting a chance, probably augment with girls cho[rus].

Muskat & Liliom.

She tries to lure him back. Julie insists on talking to him alone. Muskat exits. Julie tells him she's going to have a baby.
Leaves him alone.

"I'm Going to Have a Baby!" - Liliom.

After Number crowd comes on, ready to get into boats and go out to islands. Mill Owner with them. Loud and lusty reprise:

Finale: Bustin' Out All Over" - Entire Company.

Julie happy, not realising what Liliom is saying to Fiscur
in corner. Obviously, he has changed his mind.
He will go ahead with Fiscur's scheme. He must get money for his wife and baby and take them to New York! If this cannot be made clear in pantomime - and it probably can't - there is no reason why Fiscur can't come on before crowd for a scene with Liliom before the finale gets under way.

ACT TWO

SCENE 1: Island.

"A Song Drifts Over the Bay" - Ensemble& Principals.
(Quiet, beautifully harmonised "Just a song at Twilight" type.)

All exit, to get clues for treasure hunt. Marie is detained by Dwight and his guitar. Wolf enters and demands a showdown. Lead into "Marchbanks Song." "Here's What I Can Give You" - Marie, Wolf & Dwight.

(Each Makes his bid, as in Candida.) Finally, Marie, thrilled by Dwight's music, succumbs to Wolf! (Cyrano) [de Bergerac]

They exit on number. Liliom & Fiscur come on. Rehearsal. Problem of knife. They take bread knife used by Julie for sandwiches. Julie on. Tries to dissuade Liliom for going without her on the hunt. Distrusts Fiscur, scents something wrong. Liliom resists. Crowd on, celebrating Marie's announcement she is to marry Wolf.
All ready to start on hunt. Julie joins gay wishes to Marie, but in midst of all, after Liliom & Fiscur gone, discovers breadknife missing!

"Finaletto"
(Containing substance described above.)

SCENE 2: Culvert

Action as is. Possibly "mystic" number based on reflections in early Part of scene. Card game to be scored with dialogue and each gesture Synchronised to music.

SCENE 3: Pier Restaurant. Possibly, even probably Interior.

"Reprise: "Bustin' Out All Over"

Crowd back. When noise at height, Liliom brought in by police! Scene. Consolation. Everyone wants to be "right" as Liliom used to say. All off but Julie who stands over his body. Hollunder in b.g. [NB background] comes forward slowly.

"Female Duet" - Holl & Julie.

a. Holl – "lullaby" quality. Holds Julie on her lap.

b. Contents of Molnár's speech & memories of little inconsequential and "funny" things about Liliom.

Meanwhile the Heavenly Policemen come in and take him.

He stops on the way out, listens to Julie & smiles.
He is off before curtain. Both women singin(g) at curtain.

SCENE 4: In Transit.

Liliom & Two Policemen on three merry - go - round - horse(s), Pointing upward. Horses have wings. He sees the next 17 years. Reprises and new music, singing, dialogue, pantomime and dancing are all used throughout this sequence. The baby is born, Fiscur is hanged. The baby grows to a child. Wolf & Marie get richer and increase their family steadily. Dwight keeps strumming along. Julie keeps turning carpenter down. The child is a young woman. Bambi! Dance! Liliom wants to go Back. Can't. Organ! Pearly Gate.

SCENE 5: Front Parlour.

The Organ diminishes to a more reedy quality.
Lights come up on a woman playing a harmonium. She is an old and very wise looking woman. Liliom is ushered in and they have a nice talk and then her husband comes in. It develops that God is a married couple. They talk over all problems together. A woman's viewpoint is needed as well as a man's. They decide that Liliom should be allowed to go back and see his daughter and prove that he has changed - tho he is no more repentant than in the Molnár version. A simple little song may be sung to harmonium accompaniment in this scene.

"Life Is As Simple As You Make It" - Mr. & Mrs. G & Liliom.

Whether or not we shall have other characters in this scene will be determined later. Liliom steals a cookie shaped like a star before he goes - or is it a star that looks like a cookie?

SCENE 6: Louise's bedroom

Julie is helping her dress for her graduation exercises. Liliom

Comes on with the cookie - star. Same content as now - whatever musical reprises that may be appropriate.

"Reprises" - Julie? Liliom?

SCENE 7: Outside Schoolhouse - On the Lawn.

The local minister is finishing his address. Julie looks On. So do Marie & Woolf, with their progeny. So does Holl vicariously enjoying it.

"Graduation Song: Finale"

The girl, all in white organdie, holding bouquets, start to sing. Liliom looks on. The organ plays, and their voices sound not unlike angels. The heavenly policeman who came down accompanying Liliom nods to him. The voices swell loud and gay. There is hope for all these young girls, and for Louise too, even though Liliom was her father. Julie looks tearfully happy and probably wishes Liliom could be there to see it. The sun is shining and the singing continues, sweet and celestial as the curtain falls.

Second curtain, the group breaks and all join their respective families and there are shouts and congratulations and laughter and kisses. Liliom leaves for good now. The curtain falls on the gay picture.

Appendix II

Hammerstein's Concept for Act 2 Ballet
(As included in the script of 9 January 1945)

INTERLUDE

There now occurs on the stage a narrative of the ensuing fifteen years on earth, revolving about the two people closest to Billy's heart, Julie and their daughter Louise. Tom [later renamed Jigger], Mrs. Mullin, Nettie, Carrie and Snow pass through the various episodes, influencing their lives for good or ill.

BILLY's reactions, from his flying horse, point up the story. He will have spoken lines and lyrics to sing, while on the stage the story will be told by a union of ballet, opera drama and pantomime. The characters will be portrayed by the same artists who have played them up to now. There will be no ballet substitutions. The details of the narrative are to be worked out later, but the general theme is the growth and development of Billy's child against a background of evil that constantly threatens her. He is tortured by the dangers that result from his retreat from earth and his responsibilities. The child is his in a deep and real way. When she is tempted, he knows why. He knows she has his weakness as well as his strength and revolutionary defiance to society.

The narrative reaches a theatrical climax, but there can be no dramatic conclusion. The fate and future of Louise are, of course, in abeyance. She is fifteen when the interlude comes to a close.

Now a giant celestial organ peals out awesome notes. The characters fade from the stage. The pearly gates of heaven come in view and the stage is drenched in golden light. BILLY'S companions dismount. He follows suit. Slowly they lead him towards the gates. The lights fade.

End of interlude

Appendix III

The 'HE and SHE' Scene

(In first draft script, dated 9 January 1945)

Act Two

Scene 4

MUSIC: The heroic organ music that ushers BILLY to the gates of Heaven fades, in the darkness, to the reedy tones of a parlour harmonium.

SCENE: The lights come up on a small New England sitting room circa 1885. The harmonium is on the extreme Left, its back to the audience so that the player faces us. In the Center is a small round table with a Victorian globe lamp on it. A chair is placed on the Right of the table. Down Right is another chair, facing Center. Above this, the door.

AT RISE: "SHE" is playing the harmonium. "SHE" is a plump spic and span, comfortable looking little woman with unusually keen eyes. "HE" sits next to the table, Center. Definitely not a "Little old man". HE looks rugged yet gentle. HE and SHE might be in their fifties, if they could be judged by the standards of earthly age.

As the lights come up, while SHE is playing, HE is doing nothing. HE sits, perfectly relaxed, one hand on each knee, waiting for something to happen. A few seconds after the lights are up, HE turns and looks towards the door, up R. although there has been neither knock nor ring. Soon after HE looks, however, the door opens. The 1st HEAVENLY FRIEND enters, looks off and nods his head to BILLY who follows him in. BILLY looks around and is immediately disappointed and suspicious.

Billy

(Swinging around to the Heavenly Friend, indignantly)

Hey! What is this? You said you were taking me straight up to the head man!
(The Heavenly Friend does not answer. BILLY turns to HIM)

What are you? A justice of the peace?

("He and SHE" study Billy silently and calmly)

Is it going to be like it was down there? Don't I ever get a chance to talk to anybody important?

(They still watch him, without answering. He becomes a little ill at ease under their gaze)

I got nothin' against you personally, understand? But I made my mind up that this time I'm goin' to be judged by the highest judge - I don't care what he does to me, but this time - just fer once - by God -!

(He breaks off on the word as if someone had grabbed him by the throat. "HE" nods to the Heavenly Friend who immediately slips out the door. The "HE" addresses BILLY)

Sit down, Billy,

Billy
No I won't. I ain't goin' to stay here. I -

("HE" and "SHE" look steadily and sternly at him. To his amazement, and sudden awe, he finds himself backing up and sitting in the chair down R)

Say! Are you - ?

HE

You must lose your anxiety about who is high and who is low. There is no such thing here. What you are seeking is in no particular throne room - nor is it in the person of a huge man with a long white beard wearing a golden nightgown.

SHE

What you are looking for is hidden deep in your own heart. We want to help you find it.

Billy

(Leaning over towards HIM and whispering out of the side of his mouth)

Sir … Who's the lady?

HE

I suppose you are like all the others. You thought, when you arrived here, you'd have to deal only with a man.

Billy

Yes, sir.

HE

Strange that the world doesn't realise it needs a mother as well as a father.

(Billy looks across at HER with new respect)

Billy

Nobody ever told me, ma'am

SHE

Don't worry about it now, Billy. It takes time for people to get used to it.

Billy

(Turning to HIM)

Can I ask another question?

(HE nods)
Does everybody come to this little room - first?

HE

No, Billy. It depends on what we think people would like.

SHE

Is this room anything like the one you imagined you'd live in after you got to San Francisco?

(He averts his eyes defensively)
With Julie and the baby?

Billy

I don't remember thinkin' anythin' like that.

(THEY exchange a wise smile. HE turns to Billy, with the air of one "getting down to business.")

HE

Billy, suppose you were allowed to return to earth for one day. What would you do with it?

(Billy considers)

SHE

Is there anything you would like to do - for anyone?

Billy

You mean <u>really</u> - <u>honestly?</u>

SHE

Yes.

Billy

I'd like to go down and bust Tom Trainor's *[Jigger Craigin's]* head for him!

HE (smiling)

Better leave that to us.

SHE

(Shooting the question at him suddenly)
Why did you beat Julie?

Billy

I didn't beat her. I wouldn't beat a little thing like that. I - hit her -

HE

Why?

Billy

Well - I - I couldn't stand seein' her -

SHE

Cry! Why are you so ashamed to say it?

(Speaking incisively)

You couldn't stand seeing your wife cry! Why are you afraid of words?

HE

Why are you ashamed to say you loved her? And that you loved the child she was bearing under her heart?

SHE

Don't try to deceive us. We see through you as through a pane of glass.

Billy

(Becoming agitated under their sudden pressure)
If you see so much, why do you ask me all these questions? Why don't you let me "rest in peace"- like it says on that wreath?

HE

First you must earn that rest.

(Leaning forward and speaking slowly)

Are you sorry you hit her?

(Pause)

Billy

(Sorry is a word he hates to say)

She wasn't always right, you know.

HE

Are you sorry?

(Pause)

Billy (Averting his eyes)

I ain't sorry for anythin'!

HE

(Rising, his voice betraying a loss of heavenly patience.)

You make it difficult for us to help you.

Billy

I didn't ask for any help. Never did and never will.

("HE" walks upstage and looks out through the door.)

Why don't you yell me what you're goin' to do with me and have it over with?

SHE

We're not going to do anything with you. You must do something with yourself. Then you'll feel better.

Billy

I feel all right.

SHE (Firmly)

No, you don't. You don't feel "all right.) You're a very unhappy boy.

HE

(Coming down again)

Why did you kill yourself?

Billy

I was headed fer jail and I'd lost all the money anyway and – oh, the whole thing was no good.

SHE

What was no good?

Billy

My life. It never was any good. I always knew it and I always said so.

HE

Did you ever do anything about it?

Billy

I even told Julie.

HE

But did you ever do anything about what seemed wrong to you – except talk – or strike out blindly – and hit those you loved?

Billy

Do? What could I do? Two little people like Julie and me – who cared what happened to us?

(his voice lowering. He addresses the next line to HER as if feeling SHE is more sympathetic.)

That's an awful feelin, you know – feelin' you don't count.

SHE

Yes, Billy.

Billy

You feel alone. You got nothin' to live up to.

SHE (Quietly)

That's how Louise feels.

(Billy looks at her quickly, questioningly)
Your daughter. She needs help.

HE

The kind of help you needed when <u>you</u> were young.

SHE

And didn't get.

HE

When I asked you if you would like one day on earth, I was thinking of her.

Billy

What could I do fer her in one day?

HE

That would be up to you.

Billy

It's the same old talk they give you down there! "It's up to you, young man". That's what the perlice magistrate tells you. "Go out and make an honest livin', son!" Only they never tell you where you can find it.

(He looks at THEM to see the effect of his words, but they stand still, silently watching him)

Easy enough to talk. Give advice. "Go down to earth and fix up yer daughter's life in one day" ... Quite a trick. And I got to figger out how to do it all by myself. You give me advice – but no help.

HE

You said you didn't want help.

Billy

I don't. I never asked fer help and I never will.

(Pause. Then "HE" turns from Billy as if he doesn't want to waste any more time on him.)

HE (To Her)

I'm going out to clear up the sky a little.

SHE

Don't clear it up too much. I took these stars in to polish them and I haven't finished.

(She points to a wicker basket on the table piled with silver stars)

Don't unveil the part of the sky where they belong.

HE (Smiling)

Wouldn't be very fair to the astronomers, would it?

(He starts to go)

Billy

Ain't you goin' to give me any sentence? Any punishment?

HE

If we were concerned with the foolish business of punishment, we couldn't improve on what you are doing to yourself.

(HE exits)

SHE

(Polishing stars with her apron)

You've made him angry. He always loses His heavenly patience with people who complain and don't do anything.

(Billy sits in his chair and sulks)

Did you ever hear of the two dogs who were tied up? Prince and Rover. Prince barked his head off and pulled and choked himself pulling, and then barked some more. Rover didn't make a sound. He just chewed and chewed at the rope till he bit it clear through, then trotted away....

(SHE goes to the harmonium and starts to play "My Little Girl")

Louise is graduating from High School this year.

Billy

How could she? She's only fifteen.

SHE

She's seventeen. You've been talking to us fir two years ...

Billy

I forgot about that...So if I did go back, the trip would take fifteen years again, and she'd be thirty-two!

SHE (Laughing softly)

No, Billy. You can be back there in an instant – if we will it so.

(Continues to play)

She will look sweet in her graduation dress. Julie's making it for her. All the girls in the class will be dressed alike – white organdy – I wish Louise could be as happy as the other girls – she has no faith – thinks she "doesn't count" – "nothing to live up to" –
(Billy rises)
She feels alone.

(Billy tiptoes to the door – stops – looks over at HER then stealthily steals a star, puts it under his coat and glides out. SHE keeps playing all the while, obviously knowing what is going on behind her.)

HE (Entering)

Went down, did he?

(SHE stops playing and turns to him)

He stole a star - to give to her.

HE (Smiling)

He's a wild one, isn't he?

SHE

Yes. He's wild and he's bad – and he's not very bright … still –

HE

Still – you're hoping very hard for him. Aren't you?

SHE

Yes.

HE

(Looking out through the door)

So am I ... So am I.

(SHE starts to play "My Boy, Bill" softly. The lights fade. The orchestra picks up the melody and plays it loudly and buoyantly through the change.)

Permissions

Grateful acknowledgement is made for the use of the following materials.

"Carousel (show)" By Rodgers & Hammerstein II
©1945, Renewed 1981 Williamson Music Company,
c/o Concord Music Publishing.
All Rights Reserved. Renewed by Permission.

"Hello Young Lovers" By Rodgers & Hammerstein II
©1951, Renewed 1979 Williamson Music Company,
c/o Concord Music Publishing.
All Rights Reserved. Renewed by Permission.

"A Wonderful Guy" By Rodgers & Hammerstein II
©1949, Renewed 1981 Williamson Music Company,
c/o Concord Music Publishing.
All Rights Reserved. Renewed by Permission.

All materials created by Oscar Hammerstein II are used by permission of the Trust Under the Will of Oscar Hammerstein II.

Excerpts from the letters and writings of Richard Rodgers are used by permission of the Estate of Richard Rodgers.

Extracts from Balancing Acts by Nicholas Hytner published by Jonathan Cape. Copyright © Nicholas Hytner 2017. Reprinted by permission of The Random House Group Limited.

The Complete Lyrics of Oscar Hammerstein II Edited by Amy Asch. ©2008. Extract reprinted by permission of Penguin Random House LLC.

"Opera and Broadway", by Richard Rodgers; OPERA NEWS, Volume XXV, No. 16, pp.9-11; ©1961 by The Metropolitan Opera Guild.

"Richard Rodgers" by William Hyland. ©1998. Reproduced with the permission of The Licensor through PLSclear.

"You've Got To Have A Dream" by Ian Bradley. ©2004. Reproduced with permission from SCM Press.

Illustrated London News article reproduced with permission.

Daily Telegraph article reproduced with permission from Telegraph Media Group.

Extracts from "Joy Ride" by John Lahr. ©2015 Reproduced with permission from Bloomsbury Publishing Plc.

Extracts from "The National Theatre Story" by Daniel Rosenthal. ©2013 Oberon Press. Reproduced with permission from Bloomsbury Publishing Plc.

Extracts from Ferenc Molnár by Clara Györgyey. Cengage Learning Inc. Reproduced by permission.
www.cengage.com/permissions

Selected Bibliography

Asch, Amy (2008). *The Complete Lyrics of Oscar Hammerstein II.* New York, NY: Alfred A. Knopf.

Bennett, Robert Russell (2002). *The Broadway Sound.* Rochester, NY: University of Rochester Press.

Block, Geoffrey (1997). *Enchanted Evenings: The Broadway Musical from Show Boat to Sondheim.* Oxford, UK: Oxford University Press.

Block, Geoffrey (2015). *Richard Rodgers.* New Haven, CT: Yale University Press.

Block, Geoffrey (2002). *The Richard Rodgers Reader.* Oxford, UK: Oxford University Press.

Bradley, Ian (2004). *You've Got to Have a Dream: The Message of the Musical.* London, UK: SCM Press.

Brahms, Caryl & Sherrin, Ned (1984). *Song by Song*. Bolton, Greater Manchester: Ross Anderson Publications.

Carter, Tim (2007). *Oklahoma! The Making of an American Musical.* New Haven, CT: Yale University Press.

Carter, Tim (2017). *Rodgers and Hammerstein's Carousel.* Oxford, UK: Oxford University Press.

Citron, Stephen (2014). *The Wordsmiths: Oscar Hammerstein II and Alan Jay Lerner.* Montclair, NJ: Applause Theatre & Cinema Books.

D'Andre, David Mark (2001). *The Theatre Guild, Carousel and the Cultural Field of American Musical Theatre.* PhD: Yale University.

De Mille, Agnes (1959). *And Promenade Home.* London, UK: Hamish Hamilton.

Easton, Carol (2000). *No Intermissions: The Life of Agnes de Mille.* Boston, MA: Da Capo Press.

Ephron, Henry (1977). *We Thought We Could Do Anything.* New York, NY: W. W. Norton.

Engel, Lehman (1967). *The American Musical Theatre: A Consideration.* New York, NY: Macmillan.

Ewen, David (1972). *Great Men of American Popular Song.* Hoboken, NJ: Prentice Hall.

Ewen, David (1957). *Richard Rodgers.* New York, NY: Henry Holt.

Flinn, Denny Martin (1997). *Musical! A Grand Tour.* New York, NY: Schirmer Books.

Fordin, Hugh (1958). *Getting to Know Him.* New York, NY: Random House.

Frankl Viktor E. (2004). *Man's Search for Meaning.* New York, NY: Rider - Random House.

Gardner, Kara Anne (2016). *Agnes de Mille.* Oxford, UK: Oxford University Press.

Green, Stanley (1980). *Encyclopaedia of the Musical Theatre.* Boston, MA: De Capo Press.

Green, Stanley (1963). *The Rodgers and Hammerstein Story* London, UK: W.H. Allen.

Györgyey, Clara (1980). *Ferenc Molnár.* Woodbridge, CT: Twayne Publishers.

Hammerstein, Oscar (1985). *Lyrics.* Milwaukee, WI: Hal Leonard Books.

Helburn, Theresa (1960). *A Wayward Quest: The Autobiography of Theresa Helburn.* New York, NY: Little Brown.

Hyland, William G. (2003). *Richard Rodgers.* New Haven, CT: Yale University Press.

Hytner, Nicholas (2017). *Balancing Acts.* London, UK: Jonathan Cape.

Jones, Shirley (2013). *A Memoir.* New York, NY: Gallery Books.

Langner, Lawrence (1951). *The Magic Curtain.* New York, NY: E.P. Dutton.

Lahr, John (2016). *Joy Ride: Lives of the Theatricals.* London, UK: Bloomsbury.

Lerner, Alan Jay (1978). *On the Street Where I Live.* New York, NY: W.H. Norton.

Logan, Josh (1976). *Josh: My Up and Down, In and Out of Life*. New York, NY: Delacorte Press.

Marmorstein, Gary (2013). *A Ship Without a Sail.* New York, NY: Simon & Schuster.

Marx, Samuel & Jan Clayton (1977). *Bewitched, Bothered and Bedevilled.* London, UK: W. H. Allen.

McHugh, Dominic (Editor) (2019). *The Oxford Handbook of Musical Theatre Screen Adaptations.* Oxford, UK: Oxford University Press.

McMillin, Scott (2006). *The Musical as Drama.* Princeton, NJ: Princeton University Press.

Mielziner, Jo (1965). *Designing for the Theatre.* Seaton, Devon: Bramhall House.

Molnár, Ferenc (2010). *Liliom.* New York, NY: Samuel French.

Molnár, Ferenc (1948). *Companions in Exile.* London, UK: W. H. Allen.

Mordden, Ethan (2015). *Anything Goes - A History of American Musical Theatre.* Oxford, UK: Oxford University Press

Mordden, Ethan (1999). *Beautiful Mornin': The Broadway Musical in the 1940s.* Oxford, UK: Oxford University Press.

Mordden, Ethan (1992). *Rodgers and Hammerstein.* New York, NY: Harry N. Abrams.

Meiltziner, Jo (1965). *Designing for the Theatre.* Seaton, Devon: Bramhall House.

Nolan, Frederick (2002). *The Sound of Their Music: The Story of Rodgers and Hammerstein*. Montclair, NJ: Applause

Nolan, Frederick (1994). *Lorenz Hart: A Poet on Broadway.* Oxford, UK: Oxford University Press.

Purdum, Todd S. (2019). *Something Wonderful: Rodgers and Hammerstein's Broadway Revolution.* New York, NY: Henry Holt.

Rodgers, Dorothy (1977). *A Personal Book.* New York, NY: Harper and Row.

Rodgers, Richard (1975). *Musical Stages; An Autobiography.* New York, NY: Random House.

Rodgers, Richard & Hammerstein, Oscar (2017). *Rodgers and Hammerstein's Carousel: The Complete Book and Lyrics of the Broadway Musical.* Montclair, NJ: Applause Theatre & Cinema Books.

Rosenthal, Daniel (2013). *The National Theatre Story.* London, UK: Oberon Books.

Secrest, Meryle (2001). *Somewhere For Me: A Biography of Richard Rodgers.* New York, NY: Alfred A. Knopf.

Spergel, Mark (1993). *Reinventing Reality-The Life and Art of Rouben Mamoulian.* Lanham, MD: The Scarecrow Press.

Steyn, Mark (2000). *Broadway Babies Say Goodnight.* London, UK: Faber and Faber.

Suskin, Steven (2011). *The Sound of Broadway Music.* Oxford, UK: Oxford University Press.

Swain, Joseph (2002). *The Broadway Musical.* Lanham, MD: The Scarecrow Press.

Viertel, Jack (2017). *The Secret Life of an American Musical.* London, UK: Sarah Chrichton Books

Walker, Don (2013). *Men of Notes.* Pittsburgh, PA: Dorrance Publishing.

Index

Page numbers for illustrations are in *italics*.